New York, behind the Public Library, memorial to Gertrude Stein, October 1998. "Everybody's Autobiography, *yours which tells* you *so well that there is no thinking* that *one was never born until you hear accidentally that . . .*" ("Circumfession"). (Jacques Derrida Archives)

Catherine Malabou and Jacques Derrida, working session for *Counterpath* at the Lutétia, Paris, 6 November 1998. (Eric Jacolliot)

Eric Jacolliot acted as much more than a witness to, or cartographer of, the comings and goings that constitute this book. Solicitous host and vigilant advisor, present at every stage of its progress, he took an active part in the composition of the work, for which we thank him sincerely.

J.D., C.M.

Translator's acknowledgment: I sincerely thank Louis Stelling for his generous and assiduous assistance in the preparation of this translation.

D.W.

COUNTERPATH

Cultural Memory
in
the
Present

Mieke Bal and Hent de Vries, Editors

COUNTERPATH

Traveling with Jacques Derrida

*Catherine Malabou
and Jacques Derrida*

Translated by David Wills

STANFORD UNIVERSITY PRESS

STANFORD, CALIFORNIA 2004

Stanford University Press
Stanford, California

This book has been published with the assistance of the
French Ministry of Culture—National Center for the Book.

La Contre-allée by Catherine Malabou and Jacques Derrida, including
L'Ecartement des voies: Dérive, arrivée, catastrophe by Catherine Malabou, and
Correspondance, lettres et cartes postales (extraits) by Jacques Derrida © 1999, La
Quinzaine Littéraire–Louis Vuitton, Paris.

Selection from "Letter to a Japanese Friend," in *Derrida and Différance*, translated by
David Wood and Andrew Benjamin, edited by David Wood and Robert Bernasconi,
1988. © Northwestern University Press. Reprinted with permission of the publisher.

Printed in the United States of America on acid-free, archival-quality paper

Library of Congress Cataloging-in-Publication Data

Malabou, Catherine.
   [Contre-allée. English]
   Counterpath : traveling with Jacques Derrida / Catherine Malabou and Jacques
   Derrida ; translated by David Wills.
      p.   cm. — (Cultural memory in the present)
   Includes bibliographical references and index.
   ISBN 0-8047-4040-2 (cloth : alk. paper)
   ISBN 0-8047-4041-0 (pbk. : alk. paper)
      1. Derrida, Jacques.   2. Derrida, Jacques—Travel.   3. Philosophers—
   France—Biography.   4. Critics—France—Biography.   I. Derrida, Jacques.
   II. Title.   III. Series.
   B2430.D484M34513   2004
   194—DC22

                                                                    2004008720

Original Printing 2004

Last figure below indicates year of this printing:
13   12   11   10   09   08   07   06   05   04

Designed by Eleanor Mennick
Typeset by Tim Roberts in Adobe Garamond and Optima

Translator's Note

This book was published in French as *La Contre-allée*, in a series entitled *Voyager avec . . .* [Traveling with . . .]. Previously published titles included Ernst Jünger, Blaise Cendrars, Virginia Woolf, Marcel Proust, Rainer Maria Rilke, Mário de Andrade, Natsume Sōseki, and Vladimir Mayakovski. *Counterpath* is my neologism for *contre-allée*, which refers to a sideroad, service or access road, or "alley" that runs alongside a main thoroughfare, such as one finds providing access to the buildings lining the boulevards of French cities. In this sense it is a tributary to the main road. However, as the word suggests, *la contre-allée* here conveys also the sense of going [*aller*] *counter* to that grain, main current, traffic, circulation, fare, way, or path.

D.W.

" . . . the margin within which, save certain (drifting)
(*à quelque dérive près*), I shall remain . . . "
—SPURS: NIETZSCHE'S STYLES

Contents (Random Order)

THE PARTING OF WAYS

Drift, Arrival, Catastrophe

Presentation and Choice of Texts
by Catherine Malabou

CORRESPONDENCE

Letters and Postcards (Extracts)

Jacques Derrida writes to Catherine Malabou
during his travels from May 1997 to May 1998,
as he waits for, then reads her essay
"The Parting of Ways"

Note to the Reader

The chapters comprising Catherine Malabou's essay, *The Parting of Ways: Drift, Arrival, Catastrophe*, have been randomly arranged. Their numerical sequence (1 to 25) does not therefore respect their logical order. As explained at the end of the Preface, this is designed to enable several different reading trajectories. The reader who wishes to establish the original order of the text, that is, to explore successively Pathways 1, 2, and 3, should begin with chapter 1 and proceed as directed by the numbers given in brackets at the end of each chapter, following this sequence: 1, 4, 17, 16, 19, 9, 10, 12, 25, 14, 2, 5, 13, 7, 15, 20, 21, 18, 23, 8, 3, 6, 11, 22, 24. A logical table of contents, reproduced as an appendix to this volume, will serve as a reminder and resolve any uncertainty.

Against a gray background and in a smaller font, mimicking or whispering unguarded confidences, are selections from letters or postcards that Jacques Derrida addresses, as if *sotto voce*, to Catherine Malabou between May 1997 and May 1998, while awaiting, then reading *The Parting of Ways*.

The extracts selected from that correspondence, a sort of *outwork* or bookend [*hors livre*], may be read continuously or randomly, for example, by testing them according to this or that code or decipher proposed by Catherine Malabou.

Arriving and *deriving* [dériver] have separated. *Catastrophe* is the name for the parting [*écart*] that henceforth keeps each out of range of the other. "Henceforth" means since Derrida has passed by since he has situated the very possibility of the *voyage* within that space or parting.

I invite the reader to follow the path of this demobilization of what is derived [*la dérive*] so that what arrives, under emergency conditions, as a catastrophe, will be the chance that starts the voyage.

* * *

Dériver, from the Latin *rivus* (stream) or *ripa* (bank), literally means "to leave the bank or shore," in two contrary senses. In the first instance, deriving can characterize a continuous and ordered trajectory from an origin to an end. One thus speaks of the etymological *derivations* of a word—the slow and regular movement of variation within language—or of the leeway within which a sailboat is able to maintain its course against opposing winds. In the second instance, however, deriving as drifting refers to a loss of control, to deviation or skidding. A boat that is *à la dérive* is drifting off course, losing its way. Necessity and chance thus cohabit, in a paradoxically complicitous way, within the same verb.

The same double game is again found in *arrival. To arrive*, from the same Latin root, refers to the fact of approaching or reaching the bank, shore, or port. To arrive is first and foremost to reach a destination and attain one's goal, reach the end of one's voyage, succeed. But *arriver* is also the term for what happens, what comes to, surprises, or falls from the event in general, what is anticipated as well as what is not expected. What "arrives"—or befalls—can thus sometimes contradict, upset, or prevent arrival in the sense of the accomplishment or completion of a process.

Traveling with Jacques Derrida means first of all discovering that everything that the West calls a "voyage," in all its forms and modalities, has always presupposed or had as its condition of possibility an unshakeable solidarity, even a synonymy between the two terms. For a long time, deriving and arriving have been traveling together. The logic of that solidarity presupposes that *everything that arrives derives;* such is the axiom governing the essential relation that traditionally obtains between voyage or traveling on the one hand, and *destination, event,* and *truth* on the other.

A voyage ordinarily implies that one leaves a familiar shore to confront the unknown. The traveler derives or even drifts from a fixed and assignable origin in order to arrive somewhere, always maintaining the possibility of returning home, of again reaching the shore of departure. Travelers drift as far as their arrival, thus completing the circle of *destination.* Within that circle there can and must be produced what confers on the voyage its sense and allows it to be distinguished from a simple movement or displacement, namely *the event of the foreigner.* In fact, the very thing one always expects of a voyage is that it will deliver "the other"—the unexpected, a type of defamiliarization if not adventure or exoticism. One can always travel afar, but if there is not this sudden emergence of otherness, whatever form it may take, the voyage isn't accomplished, it doesn't really take place, it doesn't happen or *arrive.*

The event that abducts the traveler's identity and allows an opening to alterity to become experience of the world in general must occur by surprise and remain incalculable. But since this event is the condition of possibility of any authentic voyage, it obeys a type of programmed chance. There is no true voyage without an event, no arrival without arrival. What must happen or arrive is the drift or deviation that allows the other to ap-

Istanbul, 10 May 1997

"Traveling with [*Voyager avec*]!" With me? With me, really? You're joking! What a title.

I'm having fun, Catherine, I'm smiling at your expense: what will she really be able to do with that "with"? How is she going to get past it, once she gets down to it and sets out, she who can no more see me traveling than I can see her coming or know what to expect? I'm trusting but expecting the worst, I can't predict a thing. Isn't that what traveling is all about? In fact, yes. What does *voyager* mean in good French after all? Agreed, it is already difficult to think the *concept* of the voyage, and risqué as well, especially if one wants to steer clear of all its neighboring senses with the rigor that is called for. What is traveling correctly speaking, once it no longer reduces to leaving arriving moving around moving on going coming budging crossing (yes, yes, there's something there perhaps, "crossing [*traverser*]"), or visiting exploring changing places? But if "voyage" is already hard to get a hold on, then isn't "traveling with," isn't it . . . what? Isn't it precisely more obscure yet, quite impossible to grasp? Is it *viable, pathworthy*? Isn't it im-possible?

I'm not sure that I have ever traveled, myself, with "me," in fact. With a "me" who was living or vigilant. Other than as a sleepwalker. It isn't enough to open one's eyes in order to be awake. Moreover, somnambulism is something I find attractive this morning—like a figure of seduction—as something or someone to refer to my experience of the trance or transition called the "voyage." I see the silhouette of the sleepwalker pass by, very quickly, commanded by a single dream: to finally wake up, which would perhaps be, perhaps not—that is why my voyages vacillate—a nightmare. How to explain otherwise—other than by means of this apprehension regarding the "perhaps"—the anxiety of a double, simultaneous, and contradictory desire, the desire to return home, to *my* place, as quickly as possible, but also to adjourn the return indefinitely? This is the unique obsession that I transport while traveling: alas, let it soon be over! So, and this is what I wanted to arrive at, the question will never have been about the voyage or travel, but about "traveling-with."

But with whom? The adventure finds its point of departure, one that will displace the old question of the voyage, and keep it moving, in and on the doubly abyssal ground of this "with [*avec*]," *apud hoc* (*apud* means "next to, in the company of, at the home of," but also *cum*, "with, company, community, sharing"). The "with" gives a figure for it and assigns limits to it. As for the other, he or she or it who accompanies me—or never accompanies me—the experience of the voyage (but the experience *is* the voyage, isn't it, as the word suggests?), it is in that, as you would say, that I can *see coming* the beginning or the end of

pear in the flesh. Every surprise, every digression, every *errance* comes thus to be inscribed, *in truth*, on the horizon.

According to the traditional conception of the voyage, everything comes to pass as if one of the senses of deriving and arrival (provenance, accomplishment) in fact had priority over the other (drift, sidetracking, fortune, accident). Derrida shows that *this systematic locking-out of chance constitutes the metaphysics of the voyage and perhaps governs metaphysics as a whole.* For him, the way in which the relation between voyage and destination, voyage and event, voyage and truth, is currently determined corresponds to a certain *treatment of catastrophe.* In fact, the Greek word *katastrophē* signifies first the *end* (the end of a life, or the dénouement of a dramatic plot and the end of the play), and second, a *reversal* or upset, the tragic and unforeseeable event that brings about the ruin of the established order. As a result, catastrophe refers as much to the *truth*, the accomplishment of a play or a life, as to the *accident* whose surprise interrupts the teleological trajectory.

The metaphysics of the voyage installs a hierarchy among the plural senses of catastrophe: dénouement exercises control over event, thus implicitly but surely determining the meaning of the voyage. It should be remembered that the verb *strephein*, that gives *strophe* (as in apostrophe, catastrophe, etc.), means "to come and go," "to turn toward," again in two contradictory senses: on the one hand turning toward in order to remain or sojourn, on the other hand turning toward in the sense of swirling, failing to remain still, wandering. In *principle*, however, what stays always carries the day over whatever detours or disconcerts.

The solidarity between deriving and arriving, marked by a disciplined catastrophe, is what justifies the paradigmatic value accorded, in the West, to a certain form of voyage: the Odyssey. In one way or another the Western traveler always follows in the steps of Ulysses. For Derrida, the Odyssey is the very form of an economy, literally the "law of the house" (*oikonomia*, from *oikos*, "house," "residence," and *nomos*, "law"). It is as if, according to what is a paradox in appearance only, the voyage that is the Odyssey signified in the first instance the possibility of returning home: "*Oikonomia* would always follow the path of Ulysses. The latter returns to the side of his loved ones or to himself; he goes away only in view of *repatriating* himself, in order to return to the home from which [*à partir duquel*] the signal for depar-

every "being-with." Therefore I call "traveling" the experience of all experiences, the greatest ordeal, my ultimate question-of-the-other, a question of life and death: whom to travel with? Travel, yes, but first of all, with whom? The question seems lodged in the "with," but it doesn't stay around anywhere; it remains anxious also, it tosses and turns like an insomniac, it obsesses me in a permanent, concrete, explicit, and literal way: let's see, could I travel *with* this or that man or woman? Not "live with" or "be with," which are secondary accommodations, but "travel with"?

Now I must tell you, Catherine, that my answer is *almost always* "no." The decision is serious, dangerous in any case, more threatening than marriage or sedentary cohabitation—with a woman, a family, compatriots, or even enemies. Whom would you consent to travel with? It is like being asked whether you would consent to being born or to die with this or that one, at the *same* moment, in the *same* place. To die, especially. For, and this is something I'll come back to, I never go away on a trip, I don't *go*, I never put any distance whatsoever between me and my "house" without thinking—with images, films, drama, and full orchestral soundtrack—that I am going to die before I return.

"Traveling with": it is as if I were to accept in advance to share the instant of my death, or even my grave. Whom am I going to be buried with? or burned with?[1] You can laugh, Catherine, but it is as serious as that unknown quantity. There is nothing less abstract or less virtual than these scenarios I construct. Those who don't realize that know nothing of my *cross-truths* [transvérités], but what the hell. I shall verify this when I get back, but I think it is in connection

[1] Reading over what I have written I am tempted to add the following here, and it perhaps goes for everything I write or at least publish: "for whom" means "with whom?" "whom to share with?" "with which addressee?" "in view of which destination?" The question of travel traversed by the letter, is it not? I am really not sure that what I want to do here is share with just any addressee, the first one who comes along, confidences concerning what, under the heading of travel, remains for me the most sacred and secret, the most protected part of my life. How to play this game? Within what is called autobiography travel is for me the most reserved movement, another way of protecting, hiding, keeping watch over a secret. Even if I am seen out far too much, I don't travel in order to expose myself, rather in order to hide myself. Less in order to arrive than to leave. In truth, in order to come back and to go against [contre aller]: when I am at home but just as much in new places that I never see the first time. Even if I didn't shy away so much from the word "pilgrimage" and its history (we would have to reconstitute that), I would divulge to you the fact that the only thing I like about travel is the moment when, *for the first time*, I am able to find a place of sanctuary, and how, from the time of this first welcome, a type of melancholy sacredness emerges there. Reserved for me alone. With no beyond. Only an atheist pilgrim, only a believer in death can be that much in love with places—with a ritualistic love obsessed by the finite future of returns. By the finite future of a *counterpath* from whose perspective I keep watch over my memory in advance, as if I were skirting its path at a dreamer's pace, outside of time, not in the *contrary* direction, in the adversity of death, but according to the anachrony of an absolute *contretemps*, in order to celebrate silently the symbol, marriage, and hope of a mysterious "counterpart." This old word, *contrepartie*, belongs first of all to the code of writing: I love it as much as *contre-allée* and the feminine silhouette that could be nicknamed *counterpart* or *counterpath*. The counterpath would be a counterpart that never leaves me; it would be the same.

ture is given and the part assigned, the side chosen [*le parti pris*], the lot divided, destiny commanded (*moira*)."[1]

Ulysses' path would therefore be a *derived drift*, apart from yet toward a founding point. Deriving understood as indicator of provenance wins out over the drift that disorients, inasmuch, precisely, as the origin itself remains immune from the drift that it renders possible: *the origin does not travel.* When drift as deviation happens [*arrive*], like some unforeseen catastrophe, it always occurs as an accident befalling an essence, and far from causing structural damage, reaffirms it rather. The border between same and other is always distinct and indivisible, restricting any wandering between the two. The horizon of the "allotted share" always survives the tempest of misadventures, and, to the extent that it ever opened them, the Odyssey closes up whatever accidents gape along the length of its path. "Fate," "case," and "destiny" are always circumscribed. Because expatriation only occurs for a time, the surprise of whatever can occur is softened in advance. Ulysses cannot not return; and Penelope does everything, or pretends to do everything, in order not to "lose the thread."[2]

To arrive, by drifting, in a foreign place: such is the order that renders possible *the unveiling of the other*. An "apocalyptic (Gk. *apokaluptō*, "I uncover") tone" tops off the Odyssean paradigm by doubling it with what Derrida calls a "phenomenological motif,"[3] that is to say, an essential dimension of manifestation. Every unveiling is in fact an unveiling of some presence. The voyage would be given the phenomenological mission of permitting access to the presence of the other in general, of revealing the secret or authenticity of countries visited and places explored, of causing the dominant traits of a civilization to appear, in a word, of lifting, as if miraculously, the veil of foreignness.

One thus sees that Ulysses' path characterizes both "real" (if one wants to call them that) and "symbolic" voyages. For Derrida, there is no "lived" voyage, no "experience" of travel that does not involve a venture of *sense*. It is precisely this conjuncture of experience and of sense that determines the voyage as economy, or, which amounts to the same thing, as metaphysic. The Odyssean paradigm presumes that in being transported to places of vacation—by means of metaphor for example—sense keeps close to itself, thereby anticipating a return to itself. And this is so even if

with traveling that Montaigne writes that superb word (more than anyone, he said everything there was to say about "peregrinations," about "dwelling [*demeure*]," and about "distancing," often associated with death in his case also, and with various other things). His word, and I'm very envious of it, is *commourans*.[2] Now there you have a subtitle for the series "Traveling with": the *commourans*—those one dies with, or eats and lives with [*convives* (who are also *commourans*)]. It sounds like a word for a sea bird, the dying bodies [*corps mourants*] that can hunt underwater. To death.

Okay, I have gotten started already. I promised you a postcard from Turkey, Catherine. This will no doubt be a letter, but I am keeping to the tone and rhythm of the postcard.

In truth, as always, I only ever think of that, really, and you can read that as a symptom: my way of *traveling with*.

---

[2] "Since each man has some choice between forms of dying, *let us try* a little further to find one that is free from all unpleasantness. Might we not even make it voluptuous, as did the 'partners in death [*commourans*]' Anthony and Cleopatra? I leave aside the harsh and exemplary achievements of philosophy and religion" (Montaigne, *Essays* III: 9 [in *The Complete Works of Montaigne*, trans. Donald Frame (Stanford, Calif.: Stanford University Press, 1958), 752, translation modified]. I underline "let us try" [*essayons*] as if "essay" and "to essay" meant first of all "let's try to die together [*commourir*] or pass, or "pass the very time" together, to leave, at the arrival, at the same instant. For me, *Romeo and Juliet* is a travel romance: absolute inopportunity [*contretemps*] in death. They each die, and they both die before *and* after the other, before *as* after the other.) Travel and divisibility. The voyage divides as it is multiplied. In that respect it is life itself, that is to say, death. Montaigne's whole chapter is an immense treatise on travel, in short a *Traveling with Montaigne*, an "art of traveling with," and especially, no less important, of "traveling without," and alone. Before signifying experience and bringing to presence, the voyage would recall a delight in inexperience and bringing to absence, that of the other. Dissymmetry, irreversibility, no return. For my part, as one who no doubt loves distancing himself from those he loves more than I would admit, as if to protect them from me, and to protect myself from that self, I accept such a thinking of "distancing" (it goes for everything that could be called the "distancing" [*esloingnement*] of the letter, the *Purloined Letter*, but read from the perspective of my postcard): "In true friendship, in which I am expert, I give myself to my friend more than I draw him to me. I not only like doing him good better than having him do me good, but also would rather have him do good to himself than to me; he does me most good when he does himself good. And if absence is pleasant or useful to him, it is much sweeter to me than his presence; and it is not really absence when we have means of communication. In other days I made use and advantage of our separation [*esloingnement*]. . . . Separation in space made the conjunction of our wills richer. This insatiable hunger for bodily presence betrays a certain weakness in the enjoyment of souls. . . . My plan [*dessein*] is everywhere *divisible* [my italics, J.D.]; it is not based on great hopes; each day's journey [*chaque journée*] forms an end. And the journey [*voyage*] of my life is conducted in the same way. However, I have seen enough of distant places [*lieux esloignez*] where I should have liked to be detained. . . . If I were afraid to die in any other place than that of my birth, if I thought I would die less comfortably away [*esloigné*] from my family, I should scarcely go out of France; I should not go out of my parish without terror. I feel death continually clutching me by the throat or the loins. But I am made differently: death is the same to me anywhere. However, if I had the choice, it would be, I think, rather on horseback than in a bed, and out of my house, away [*esloigné*] from my people. There is more heartbreak than consolation in taking leave of our friends" (ibid., 746–47).

it is a matter of a "voyage of no return." Home and hearth may be at the end of the world; what is essential is the fact of their being a *place to abide* [*l'essentiel est qu'il* demeure]. At bottom, the catastrophic truth of the voyage comes from its never being conceived of other than as a *derived phenomenon* . . . of the truth.

* * *

Derrida's whole work produces the *catastrophe*, that is to say, the *reversal*, of this catastrophe.

In fact, *Derrida does not drift*. He even claims not to like the word *dérive*, promising (himself) to take steps not to overuse it, or not anymore: In "To Speculate—on 'Freud'," he declares:

I have abused this word, it hardly satisfies me. (*Drifting*) designates too continuous a movement: or rather too undifferentiated, too homogeneous a movement that appears to distance itself without fits or starts from a supposed origin, from a shore, a border, an edge with an indivisible outline. Now the shore is divided in its very outline, and there are effects of anchoring, collapsing at the edge, strategies of approaching and overflow, strictures of attachment or of mooring, places of reversion, strangulation, or *double bind*.[4]

"The shore is divided in its very outline . . . " This division is precisely the place of a radical dissociation between deriving and arriving. All of Derrida's work consists in disturbing the derivative schema that governs metaphysics and at the same time prescribes for the voyage the sense of a forward march. Whether it is a matter of deriving conceived of as regulated movement of distancing from an origin, or on the contrary as an uncontrolled process, in both cases the word signifies too continuous a trajectory away from the shore, one that is always assured of indivisible borders, always capable of being remedied or compensated by a return. Deriving does not permit the coming of the other without immediately leading it back to the frontier of the same; it is powerless to offer the possibility of an "awaiting without horizon of the wait, awaiting what one does not expect yet or any longer, hospitality without reserve, welcoming salutation accorded in ad-

Manuscript of letter of 10 May 1997.
(Jacques Derrida Archives)

I only think of that, I mean of her, of it, of the letter. In this case, of that of the Turks, of the transliteration that befell them, striking them full in their history, of their lost letters, of the alphabet they were forced so brutally to change, a short time ago, from one day to the next, on the orders of an extravagant, lucid, but cruel emancipator of "modern times," as you know, the brilliant military hero

vance to the absolute surprise of the *arrivant* from whom or from which one will not ask anything in return."[5]

Traveling with Derrida thus implies taking the Odyssey by surprise, exploring a jagged landscape, full of "effects" and "collapsing," finally following the thread of a strange and perilous adventure that consists in *arriving without deriving.*

* * *

The reader will forgive this somewhat abrupt entry into the thick of things. But how can one proceed otherwise? Certainly, Derrida is always traveling; he is without a doubt the most world-traveled of all philosophers. But how, without some other procedure, can one fix the point of departure of voyages outside of deriving? How to determine their destination? How to speak of their event or truth?

The reversing of a logic of destination, the failure of the origin or of the point of departure imposes itself the moment one approaches his texts. It is in fact impossible to isolate something like the "theme" or "thesis" of travel in a body of work that presents itself as a series of steps, a displacement, "an ongoing process."[6] One can accept that certain books by Derrida appear more immediately or more obviously than others as "travel writings": *The Post Card,* "Circumfession," "Back from Moscow" for example. In those works the writing is woven with the thread of itinerant contexts. But it very quickly becomes clear that any number of other texts are also dated or signed from the place in which they were written and name each time the host they are addressed to, that they are all found, in one way or another, in an "almost epistolary situation."[7] Countries, cities, universities, friends who invite him, are inevitably brought into the discussion. And the names of places, every name in general is overloaded with meaning like the encrypted columns of *Glas.* Although it is possible, here and there, to see how the outlines of a city emerge from the tight weave of the discourse—by means of the shell from Amsterdam in "Tympan" in *Margins of Philosophy,* the phantom from Prague in "Back from Moscow," the Tokyo basements of "Ulysses Gramophone"—these phenomena are so closely intertwined with the philosophical thematics that it would be absurd to try to detach them.

Jerusalem, overlooking the cemetery, 1998.
(Jacques Derrida Archives)

K.A., who brought his subjects into step with modernity. *En route*, onward, on with the grand voyage! Forward march! How traumatic. Imagine such a thing happening to us: the President decides that starting tomorrow we will have to use a new writing system. Without changing the language! And any return to yesterday's letters is forbidden! But perhaps this *coup de la lettre*, this chance or blow is struck against us every time something happens: one has not only to undress but to leave, to set out again naked, change bodies, convert the flesh of the words, of signs, of every manifestation, while pretending to stay the same and to remain master of one's own language. The violence of this transliteration lays siege to all my Istanbul streets, it superimposes its scars on everything I decipher, on displays of merchandise, faces, architecture, everywhere I take a walk or where, by means of so many signs, my memory of Algiers is revived, my Moroccan, Greek, Palestinian, and Israeli memory also. Turkey is different again, but I had a certain "memory" of it even before arriving here. I "recognize" everything, fatally, for one can recognize without being cognizant, whence the principle of ruin at the heart of travel.

That would also have the capacity to destroy in advance the appearance of the new, but events are tricky, something leaves, arrives, and has always just happened through that very ruin, by means of the movement wherein, in "recognizing," or "identifying," I always tend to appropriate for myself and to replace the memory of the other. Such a powerful phantasm. It goes so far as to

The impossibility of leaving, or starting, in his work, from a precise *topos* of travel, of isolating or situating a locality, definitively prevents us from considering travel as an accident of thinking, something that befalls conceptual rigor as a type of distraction, coming to rend the philosophically deductive fabric with a few biographical pulls or tears. For Derrida the motif of travel is not "empirical" to the extent, precisely, that it is not "derived."

Differance, we read in *Margins*, cannot be submitted to the question "What is it?": "If we accept the form of the question, in its meaning and its syntax ("What is?" . . .), we would have to conclude that *differance* has been (derived), has happened, has been mastered and governed on the basis of the point of a present being, which itself could be some thing, a form, a state, a power in the world."[8] It is therefore no more legitimate to ask what a voyage is. On the one hand because travel is differance itself—temporalization, spacing, incessant displacement of the letter and of sense—and on the other hand because no originary sedentariness pre-exists it. No more than writing is derived from speech is travel derived from a localizable and localized identity. Every identity has, always, from its origin, to arrive at itself, to travel as far as itself. *Travel takes the origin away with it.*

A new meaning for catastrophe is born from this vacating of the origin by means of the voyage, one that is close to that proposed by the mathematician René Thom. Developed from topology, the mathematical concept of catastrophe describes what one can call, in general terms, an "edge- or shoreline-effect." Catastrophes designate the deformations and perturbations that occur when a given space submits to a particular constraint: "For me, any discontinuity at all occurring within phenomena is a catastrophe. The edge of this table, where the wood becomes lighter, is a surface of separation, a place of catastrophe. . . . There is catastrophe as soon as there is phenomenological discontinuity."[9] One can therefore consider every border as a catastrophe, one that constitutes, in its own way, an *end* and a *drama*: the drama of the absence of a regular passage from one form or one shore to the other, the end of continuity. The end of the possibility of deriving, Derrida would say.

The porousness of edges and limits is continually experienced in his work, beginning with that affecting the dividing line traditionally held to

evoke in me a nostalgia for moments that I haven't lived through abroad; as if
the homesickness, the sickness of missed chances that were nevertheless due to
me, that had befallen me, were things that I encountered at home, at *my place.*
It is as if I have been deprived of these virtual chances in the history of another
nation: for example the French Resistance, the Indian or Irish struggle for independence, swimming and risking drowning with Byron or Shelley near Lerici (I
could write books on such examples). Here, and everywhere I speak, especially
in public buildings, K.A. the "modernizer" rises tall; he is represented standing,
as you know, but I am not so sure that the Turks love him, even those who organize the cult of him. Don't they still hate him for this story of writing (the
deepest cut as I see it, in any case, the figure of evil, in terms of every fate it has
sealed)? My feeling is that the Turks celebrate, respect, cultivate him—while
cursing him. And not only the Muslims! Unless I am making it all up once again,
inventing stories without even managing to leave, to really *go out,* even when I
wander the streets, to leave behind *both* my "phantasms" *and* this sort of sump-
tuous, unused French Embassy they have lodged me in, as the single guest in a
hundred or so rooms. I am all alone, as in France. It is immense, a castle full of
"Orientalist" artwork; I can get lost here. I am all the time about getting lost [*je
suis tout le temps à me perdre*].

As is often the case, I go looking for exiles, and have discovered a very old
Sephardic community near here. There are various hypotheses about them (I
met a Muslim francophone woman whose name, I think, is "Ammour" and who
is doing research on these survivors) and I feel, a little like them perhaps, like a
survivor, more Marrano than ever. Most often I watch myself traveling without
changing places, an immobile voyeur who would analyze what befalls his body
in movement in the world. Movie camera without a camera, kinetoscope for a
sort of *errance* that is forever encrypted: the always incognito displacement of a
secret that I transport without knowing. Even when I speak in front of large
crowds. I feel that I transport this secret (I can hear its heartbeat like a child in
the womb) but don't understand anything about it. Perhaps it will be told to me
while abroad: revelation, bedazzlement, conversion, I fall down backwards, I
am born, I die at the moment when, at the end of an unknown alley, I meet the
Messiah who will come out of me where he has been hiding for so long. You are
giving birth, no? Think also of a spy charged with a mission. They have confided
to this secret agent a message that he can't read, perhaps his own death sentence, the story I often recount to whomever wants to listen to what I have to tell
them: Bellerophon, Hamlet, etc. That is why I call myself a "Marrano": not because of the peregrinations of a wandering Jew, not because of successive exiles,
but because of the clandestine search for a secret that is greater and older than

obtain between the "theoretical" and the "biographical." In traveling with him, it is impossible to start out from the "lived experience" of the voyage in order to subsequently derive a "theoretical" or "philosophical" sense from it. He warns: "As Montaigne said, 'I constantly disavow myself,' it is impossible to follow my trace";[10] or again, the "borderline" separating work and life "is most especially not a thin line, an invisible or *indivisible* trait lying between the enclosure of philosophemes, on the one hand, and the 'life' of an author already identifiable behind the name, on the other. This divisible borderline traverses two 'bodies,' the corpus and the body, in accordance with the laws that we are only beginning to catch sight of."[11]

Conversely, neither can one start out from "philosophemes" in order to prop up, articulate, or circumscribe private experience. The same catastrophic destiny—porousness and divisibility of the edges—has life and thinking traveling together without there being any possibility of *naturally* distinguishing the domain of each. This destiny is the same one that links, originarily, geography to discursivity. From the time of his commentary on Husserl's *Origin of Geometry*, Derrida shows that what happens to the earth at the same time happens to thinking, and vice versa, whence the impossibility of clearly distinguishing the "proper" and "figurative" senses of each of the terms of the toponymy that writing puts into operation. Thus, for example, the now famous "concepts" such as *differance, destinerrance, dissemination, trace, trait, retreat/withdrawal, limitrophy,* and *tropic,* are neither properly philosophical nor properly geographical. From a rhetoric developed as a theory of tours or turns, tropes or vehicles, to a *metaphorology* that exceeds rhetoric, from center to margin, from the presence-to-itself of the spoken word to writing conceived of as a loss of the proper, Derrida never stops demonstrating that the problem of *territorialization* in general requires precisely that one renounce territorializing *in any simple manner.* Between the register of space—world or earth—and that of the concept, there cannot but pass, however improbably, the line of a series of catastrophes.

From that perspective, one must also renounce determining a "proper" and a "metaphorical" sense of travel in Derrida's work, noting as he does that words of language in general already raise in and of themselves the question of displacement. When he announces his intention, in *The Post*

me, eschatological, fatal for me, *as me*. That is why I *hunt* it—there is no other word—I am in pursuit of it while making it flee. I don't travel like a hunter, but I run as if I were chasing someone by pretending to track them down all over the world, while knowing all along that they are buried within my body and that, in a word, I want to help them save themselves by running from me. It is I who is hunting and I who is pursued. There is someone I would like to save from me by keeping them in me. Me save me, perhaps that is the most economic formula for my "traveling with"; there you have it, follow that guide, the *vademecum* or *viaticum*, lower your head when entering the pyramid. Like certain Marranos I would have begun by forgetting, by believing that I have simply forgotten my own filiation. I have the feeling that the people I meet while traveling, or who flock to hear me speak, can sense that. They expect one day to see the Thing or the Cause revealed. Like those who get buried in the old cemetery in Jerusalem, facing the Gate. They want to be *being-there*, on *that day*, standing (as one says for a "standing ovation"). They wait so as to reserve their place in the cemetery or lecture hall, like in Jerusalem. I am exaggerating, as I always do, with these Messianic scenarios, but they terrify me at the same time, for I am also pleading—contradictory as that might seem—for each voyage to pass in the most insignificant way possible, without accident, without surprise: please don't let anything happen! As if I had already had my share of catastrophes. I give the impression of being *for* the event, of elaborating, as they say, a thinking of the event, of *arrivance*, of the *singular* exposure to what comes. You know the refrain. You've got to be joking [*tu parles*]! For I will tell you in all confidence, Catherine, just for this one book, and you only: I am *also* pleading (someone in me is pleading) all the time for *nothing to happen*, as if nothing could happen without being something bad. Leave the event to others! For that, isn't it better to stay at home or, on the contrary, to rush and hide outside so that nothing will happen [*arrive*], since the most *arriving* [arrivantes] things, and often the worst, come to pass in the bosom of one's own home?

I am therefore trying to take upon myself, and with me, as it were in me, to comprehend or relive what, I imagine, here in Turkey, to have been an extermination of the letter, a voyage one never comes back from. I am trying here, as always, without getting there of course, to identify with the "people" (the word is as good as it is), but also with the "individual" who premeditated the metempsychosis of this transliteration, one who could make such a decision and manage to implement it. I think of them all the time, but as though I were dreaming. A propos of that, have I told you how I dream quite differently when traveling, in fact as soon as I am in a different bed? That is perhaps what I am looking for. You know, everyone asks me why I travel around like a maniac although I say I don't like it, not at all, really. One possible response among others: I am trying

Card, to write a "history of the postal," he comes up against a difficulty that resembles our own point by point:

I must not let anything pass, not a clue, not the slightest lapse, the slightest betrayal. But where is one to pass this blade, or apply the tip, even, of this *grattoir*? For example do I have to yield all the words which, directly or not, and this is the whole torture, refer to the *envoi*, to the mission, to *tranche-mission*, to emission (of stamps, or of tele-programs), to "remission" . . . to commission, to the *commis-voyageur* [traveling salesman], without forgetting omission? This on the pretext that the book and its preface treat the *envoi* in all its forms? Should I also cauterize around the "destinal" prepositions, "to," "toward," "for," around the adverbs of place "here," "there," "far," "near," etc.? around the verbs "to arrive" in all its senses, and "to pass," "to call," "to come," "to get to," "to expedite," around all the composites of *voie*, voyage, *voiture*, viability? It's endless, and I will never get there, the contamination is everywhere and we will never light the fire. Language poisons for us the most secret of our secrets, one can no longer even burn at home, in peace, trace the circle of a hearth, one must even sacrifice one's own sacrifice to it.[12]

If the question of travel is already at work in the least preposition, the least being of language, how then is one to start out? From where and toward what could one derive in order to arrive? "Language poisons us," or rather it contaminates everything it touches, that is to say everything. The virus of the limits (the contagion between regions of the world and regions of discourse, linguistic and conceptual borders, literal and figurative senses) eats away at and ruins the hierarchization of current meanings of catastrophe: unforeseeable accident and programmed outcome. The first sense can no longer be subordinated to the second. Because "contamination is everywhere," it may well be that no spectacular ending, no dénouement ever takes place ("We will never light the fire").

The "geocatastrophe," that contradicts teleology, involves a veritable *tragedy of destination*. Inasmuch as it does not derive from an assignable origin, every address made to the other, and consequently every correspondence, every apostrophe *can always not arrive*, or miss its addressee. From voyage to voyage the text of *The Post Card* as a whole inscribes *upon inscription itself* this "*destinerrance*," the being-destined-to-wander of the

to change the order and work of my nightly dreams. I am keeping vigil in order to be able to transliterate the world in the middle of the night, only in the dark, or in order to find my sleep again, the truth of a certain type of sleep, as if in sum I traveled only at night, under a false identity, which is the condition of truth. I thus let come to me, literally travel *with me*, a new population of dream figures and characters who would not otherwise dare to enter "my home." My ethics of hospitality. That is how, in another bed, in a quite different organization of images, the themes seem strangely unrecognizable, the oldest and most familiar ones suddenly liberated; they were waiting for that alone, they were waiting for me to leave in order to return. It is as if I catch a plane in order to go and liberate my dreams! The very intensity, the *emotional* color of my dream landscape gets changed. As well as the daylight wake that follows my nights. If I were to keep a travel diary it would resemble in the first place an oneirograph, even an oneirocritique. I am sometimes tempted to consider my travels as untrained self-psychoanalytical experiments: whether good or bad, one hell of a dream work [*travail*] gets into gear once *je "travelle"* and change countries or beds. And this "travail"—which is also an English word for childbirth—resembles something like the labor of giving birth. Whence, perhaps, the feeling of being regenerated in spite of the extreme fatigue. Whence the survival, for now, of someone who loves traveling as if condemned to it. And who asks himself every second, "But why don't I just stay home? With my kith and kin? It really lends itself to deeper 'thinking,' is more conducive to 'writing'!" For I travel in shame, blushing at the idea of appearing naked in front of all these "thinkers," not to mention my friends, those who condemn my "flight." My alibi, my confidant, is Montaigne. I play him off against Heidegger, the non-traveler par excellence. Heidegger (Blanchot also, but in a completely different way)[3] plays the part of the implacable prosecutor and of the counter-model. What would he have thought of me? The "Heideggerian" indictment never leaves me for a second. I imagine Heidegger, he always travels with me without knowing it—if only he had known, the poor guy!—I hear him pull me aside ("Aren't you ashamed to travel all the time?"). He teaches me a lesson in every airport all over the world,

[3] Upon rereading this, just before publishing this letter, I need to add this detail—and to differentiate. I never met Heidegger or spoke to him, but one day Blanchot expressed his anxieties in front of me, spoken in friendship. He worried less about the traveling than about how writing was thereby exposed to the oratorical scene of the "lecture." Genet was more suspicious still, and as though I were consenting to exhibit myself or what I wrote in an undignified way, more or less said, "But how could you?" Both were aiming less at traveling itself, then, at leaving or inscribing a distance (Genet was hardly the one to talk), than at the thing travel is often associated with in my case, namely speaking in public and being heard more abroad than in France. I could try to justify myself in the eyes of those who share their concern, but I'll refrain from doing so. My defense would in that case call upon what I *do* with these addresses given abroad, what I *say*, in this or that way and not another, to those addresses.

message and of destining itself. No longer assigned to residence, the event of encountering or *accosting* the other [*l'abord de l'autre*] owes its chance, paradoxically, to the possibility that it won't reach its goal. The gamble that governs, without governing, the destiny of the letter, card, telegram, the immense "postal" apparatus, prevents us from considering Ulysses, the archetype of every traveler, as anything other than a "gramo-phone," other than by means of the trace of death and absence in his voice. Joyce knew this, for in *Ulysses* "the motif of postal difference, of remote control and telecommunication, is already powerfully at work."[13]

Destinerrance is in fact accentuated further by "the new structure of spatio-temporal *différance* constructed by new techniques of telecommunication."[14] This "new structure" is also one of "*deracination, delocalization, disincarnation, formalization,*"[15] rendering more undecidable still the frontier between here and elsewhere. The world is henceforth a spectral space in which everything is reproducible "from anywhere to anywhere," and "the event itself, like the concept of experience and of the testimony that claims to refer to it, finds itself affected, *in its inside*, beyond the public/private opposition, by the possibility of the camera shot and of reproduction from practically anywhere to anywhere."[16]

What does *the event of the other* become, therefore, in the course of the voyage? What place can the other come from once the difference between nomad and sedentary loses its sense?

In the history of architecture and the reflection on space, whether implicit or explicit, the discourse and the subject of discourse have always tended to be localized. Even when they moved toward the themes of nomadism, instability, delocalization, dislocation, they claimed to proceed from a site, from a fixed place, and always to maintain a mooring. They wanted to know where they came from and where they went; they insisted on reining in the indefiniteness of an "anywhere." The subject of discourse signed from a birthplace, a habitat, a language, an ethnic belonging, etc. Its compass moved around an irremovable point. Its point plunged into an invariable place. Nomadization itself, whether discourse or experience, operated from a center or a capital, or at least from their mirage, from a place that was not just anywhere. Can we indeed speak of nomadization today? Is the opposition between nomadic and sedentary still current? Is there place to refer to a place, to a

Istanbul.
(Erik Bullot)

and for example (this is what happened to me some years ago, in 1992, but I could recount any number of other similar escapades, worse than this one, enough to fill more than one book), for example, then, like the time I left a small island in the south of Japan at three o'clock in the morning after a lecture on the politics of architecture and habitat ("Faxitexture," no longer poetically dwelling), driving for hours through the night (black car, chauffeur with white gloves, his ear glued to the telephone) before taking a plane from Fukuoka to Tokyo, where I had to change airports with not a minute to spare (black car, chauffeur with white gloves, his ear glued to the telephone) so as not to miss the change of planes for Paris, then leaving Charles-de-Gaulle for London and Cambridge, the year of the honorary doctorate affair(!), after a 24 hour stopover in Ris-Orangis. How *uneigentlich*! How can you *denken* at that speed? There you have it! Is that what it is really about? Yes, indeed.

Oh well, so where was I? Yes, everything will have begun with you. Thanks to you. You were the first to talk to me about this first visit to Istanbul, Catherine, to plan it, to warm me to it in advance. Well, of course, I am sorry that you didn't come, but I am delighted that the happy arrival of Félix had something to do with that. But you precede me here. Therefore, I follow you: Önay, Gabriella, Zeynep, and Freda have told me practically everything about your last passage through here. "Passage," moreover, has been the password here since my arrival. Our friends have told you that besides the public lecture I have to "respond," as is often the case, during a conference they have organized on my

"Wandering circumnavigation" ("Ulysses Gramophone"). Iceland, 1993.
(Jacques Derrida Archives)

unity of place, be it even this earth, from which to measure a determination or in-determination?[17]

Another question echoes the previous one:

"What happens to or arrives at the earth?" "what does 'happen to or arrive at the earth' mean?. . . what can be the architectural or urban consequences, that is to say, the political consequences of that which 'happens to or arrives at' the earth in this way, of what happens when, on the eve of the year 2000, the body of man can leave the earth or observe it from a satellite?"[18]

In a space where mooring points are lacking, *what happens or arrives never reaches its ends.*

The traveler-intellectual endlessly experiences this strange "*adestinerrant*" condition, and his destiny is henceforth sealed by a "wandering circumnavigation"[19] rendered possible by the new structure of spatio-temporal differance, pre-empting deriving or any continual departure from the shore. That destiny requires that in order to speak, write, and teach, he perpetually ex-work, relating precisely to the "border crossing [*passage des frontières*]"—"*Pera Peras Poros*, Spacing and Temporalization of the Foreign(er)," it could work as the title of your book. You know why I pass for a philosopher specializing in the "question of borders." Önay must have sent you the outline for the conference, but I'll enclose it with my letter with some scribbling in the margins.[4]

Therefore, I follow you—and I am grateful to you for agreeing to the risk of "traveling with" me through this book in this series where, for the moment, if I am not mistaken, at least within the series of titles already published, I am the only "living" subject, thus the first one alive.[5] Now, as happens to me every time I publish a book or leave on a trip (this bizarre connection must indeed signify something befalling [*échéance*]), other than the anxiety I have at every moment for "my" loved ones (but I need only go from Ris-Orangis to Paris for this anxiety to manifest itself), a single question dominates all the others: will I get out of this? Translated: will I come back alive? And if I die while traveling, what will "my" loved ones do with my body? There, perhaps, you have my first concern (theirs, that is to say, having to take care of a dead body), the moment that I leave my home. No, I am exaggerating a little, as usual, I don't *only* think about this return of the body, of this form of my return home. But the thought of this traverse made by my remains [*restes*] traverses the rest. It does so at a lively pace, stepping out hale and hearty [*au pas d'un bon vivant*] like one who spends his time showing himself the color film—a talkie also—of his death while abroad, even going so far as to pretend, for example, dangerously and

---

[4] In particular one can read the following, which I underline since Istanbul and all my trips still to come won't feature in your book: "The name for what is now the center of Istanbul used to be *Pera* . . . intensely cosmopolitan. . . . As its Greek name indicates, Pera referred to the other side, beyond the Galata quarter, where merchants and sailors, as well as foreign ambassadors lived. Like Pera, Galata had also been in its time the other side, beyond the quarter of the mosque-church of Haghia Sophia and the Topkapi Palace . . . neighborhoods delimited by border walls broken by gates that were closed at night but allowing passage by day [I'm the opposite, closed by day I open at night: password, dream, and pass]. Such a structure, the other side, the beyond the limit/frontier/passage (*pera-peras-poros*), certainly constituted the life of the city, and this was so from the perspective not only of urban history, but also of symbolic genesis. The Byzantium of old that Mehmet the Conqueror had intended to transform into the new Islamic center of Istanbul was also itself, originally, the other side, the beyond. . . . From then on the foreigner was no longer simply one who lived outside of the city but within it. Istanbul thus appears as a city whose foundations, constantly shifting [*différés*], were constructed and deconstructed . . . living figure of the aporia (. . . impasse, the impossible *poros*), where there is an indissoluble admixture of same and other, where different peoples and cultures live side by side in the porosity of the at home and the foreign. The myth of the Bosphorus—more originary than any logos—is already an illustration of this structure in itself: Io, loved by Zeus and transformed into a cow thanks to Hera's jealousy, had to *traverse* the ford, which as a result took on the name Bos-phoros, passage of cows—contrast between alienation and identity." To be compared with the history of Europa, abducted by Zeus transformed into a bull. What to do with this *raptus*, and with this Eurocentrism, once I leave Europe, for example in order to come to Istanbul?

[5] There was indeed Jünger already, but he died very soon after, and even though I am much younger than him, this "traveling with" makes me afraid (note added after the event, following Jünger's death). [See translator's note at beginning of volume. (D.W.)]

patriate himself and respond to the new demands of the power of the media. A permanent displacement is what motivates each book or lecture, bearing witness also to the reality of an involvement in thinking that uproots the researcher and writer, implicating him in a constant timelag, between one continent and another, one country and another, one language and another: "The time difference [*décalage horaire*] is in me, it is me."[20] In another context, between his return from Moscow and departure for Irvine, he admits: "I ask myself what I am doing with my life today when I travel between Jerusalem, Moscow, and Los Angeles with my lectures and strange writings in my suitcase."[21] The catastrophe of this pace or race comes from its never allowing one to settle down, from the constant hesitation—that prevents any clear distinction once again—between two meanings of *strophe*, staying and going on tour [*tourner autour*].[22]

The imperative of the voyage, now indissociable from the fate of thinking, forces one who submits to it to run in circles, to allow himself to be preceded, tired and harassed by his own words, as if thinking advanced faster than he did and remained something of a secret, even to himself: "I resemble a messenger from antiquity, a bellboy, a runner, the courier of what we have given one another, barely an inheritor, a lame inheritor, incapable even of receiving, of measuring himself against whatever is his to maintain, and I run, I run to bring them news which must remain secret, and I fall all the time."[23] Elsewhere, he writes of "being 'exported' now from Moscow to Los Angeles, with a brief landing in Paris, just time enough to remind my loved ones of my existence, I am sighing to know until when I will be going round myself in this way, phantom or prophet charged with a mission, heavily charged with a secret unknown to him."[24]

In a text that was written to celebrate the fiftieth anniversary of the journal *Les Temps modernes*, Derrida reassumes the figure of the antique messenger, referring to a statement by Sartre that compares the writer to the Marathon runner who, according to the legend, kept running although he was dead:

"It was said that the courier of Marathon had died an hour before reaching Athens. He had died and was still running; he was running dead, announced the Greek victory dead. This is a fine myth; it shows that the dead still act for

more than once, that he was having a heart attack in a cinema in New York or Newport Beach. I told you, I think, that I go to the cinema a lot, I am at the cinema when I travel, much more than in Paris. Travel, of course, means "politics" in the end, politics first of all, politics and little else, the fascinated observation and tireless analysis of the geopolitical backdrop, for one can only measure the political dimension by crossing a frontier; but before all else travel signifies cryptography + politics of the dream + cinema + television (I am more worried by the prospect of a hotel room without a television than one without running water) + political history, hence the politics of "politicians" in the strict sense. Yes, even going so far as to pretend dying, dangerously, as I was saying, just to see what would happen, from the perspective of the one who is dying, with the whole parade of images, hypotheses, narratives, and virtual orations. What are they going to do upon my death? What are they going to say? Especially if my body is never found? They will carry on, of course, as always, as if nothing had happened, but all the same. Since my childhood this has been the source of an indefatigable surprise before the fact of what I will never really understand or accept: being adult for me, for the child that I still am, means continuing or beginning once more to live after the death of someone close. I remember the day that I saw my father in the garden, in 1940, lighting a cigarette a week after the death of my brother Norbert: "But how can he do that again? Eight days ago he was sobbing!" I never got over it.

Concerning the "traveling with" that you are taking a chance on, I don't know who will follow whom, you me or vice versa. I am preparing myself for all sorts of surprises. No idea how you are going to take it on, but it's good that way. For my part, I wonder what I would do if I didn't have only to "think" travel, the "concept" of the voyage, but recall it, and *recount* it, something I have never been able to do. I would be completely incapable of recounting this first trip to Turkey, overwhelmed by the certainty that it would take hundreds of volumes and the invention of another language. So, out of sheer perversity, in order to confirm my illiterate prejudices, I will limit myself to one remark, to a political "metonymy": as I told you to begin with, since my arrival I have been obsessed by what must have been going on in the head of the handsome Kemal Ataturk when he decided to impose a new form of writing on his "subjects": "Okay, to work, it's done, there is a new alphabet! Let's set out on the road to new letters!" On the pretext of entering modern culture a disciplined people thereby becomes as it were illiterate, no longer capable, from one day to the next, of reading centuries of memory. There you have it, a terrifying way of leaving one's country in search of who knows what adventure, the most monstrous but perhaps the only way of doing so, by means of amnesia! Learning to write differently, to write an unpublished letter (this one and not that one, totally

a little while as if they were living. For a while, a year, ten years, perhaps fifty years; at any rate, a *finite* period; and then they are buried a second time. This is the measure we propose to the writer."[25]

Derrida comments:

I can also remember the chickens sacrificed in the garden of my childhood, several days before Yom Kippur, how they set about running still, after they had been decapitated, not knowing where they were heading [*sans cap*], in short, as if to save themselves covered with blood from the misfortune that had just befallen them; and it is perhaps thus that I imagine for myself the time of writing, but I only see myself *running after my death in this way, after it truly*; and there where I already *see myself* thus, I try to understand, without ever getting there, for what and for whom, after what and after whom I am running in this way, in the experience of an anticipation that has lost its heading and without capitulation; I try in vain to know who and what comes back to me or falls back on me from this strange time of the dead courier, *coming back to me* meaning at the same time, *at once*, identifying with me, constituting my ipseity there where *I find myself*—or else, then, the ipseity of my time (for this ipseity does not find itself before this strange possibility)—and *coming back to me* like the returning specter of me *after* which I run out of breath: the specter goes so much faster than I do![26]

What comes back to the traveler-intellectual, the benefit he draws from his travels, what returns to him as his share in it, can only be his death. This is the shadow that stalks a life lived running, a life that runs after its own death, that is to say, at once behind it and some time after it, in the spectral space of a finite survival assured perhaps by the importance of a secret that it will not have had time to know. Derrida always writes in the imminence of this catastrophe, as if each of his voyages were going to be the last.[27] This is the imminence of a "verdict without unveiling," apocalyptic in the absence of apocalypse, the imminence of an unanticipatable event which is at the same time already upon us and yet still to occur, which doesn't finish arriving because it is precisely underiveable. The catastrophe comes from the other, from every wholly other. One doesn't know where death comes from; nor, moreover, chance or fortune.

On board the *Liberté*, leaving New York, June 1957.
(Jacques Derrida Archives)

unique but a borrowed letter, one that seems borrowed in the brand new novelty of its address). Under the threat of the whip, of the dictatorship of time, under the constraint of an apparently arbitrary discipline, but one which, as always, provides the best reasons in the world for what it does. Isn't this the necessary and malevolent condition, this machination, for something to happen? for a leaving [*sortie*] to take place, that is to say *without return*? Who knows?

With me it's the contrary, a counter-example. I risk the "no return" as far along as possible but only in order to intensify the coming back [*revenance*], the *countercoming* [*contrevenue*], the contravention, another counterpath or *countergoing* if you like, in order to try to make of it an unheard of event that will in fact provide me with the revelation of the departure. Memory, if you like. I love only memory, another name for the future I am running after, and I run, and run. And I chase . . .

To begin with, therefore, I would try to awaken the memory of what is nick-

How is this catastrophe to be spoken of? How can one recount it when it isn't *present?* The ruin of the "phenomenological motif" simultaneously brings about the ruin of the "travel narrative."[28] In "Back from Moscow" Derrida justifies his refusal to add his contribution to such a genre by writing, for example, his own "Back from the USSR": "I could, if I were ready, here attach my own 'travel narrative' and say in turn, 'As soon as I arrived at the Moscow airfield . . . ,' from Paris, after having explained, as I will do later, why I accepted an invitation that I had refused for a long time. But I am not ready to begin such a narrative nor even to decide if and how I would do it."[29] He prefers rather to "avoid the risks of every well-argued [*raisonné*] travelogue," the "selectivity" and therefore the "censorship," the "after the fact *rationalization*."[30] Authors of "Back from the USSR," such as Gide, Benjamin, and Etiemble, cannot avoid these traps to the extent that they believe themselves able to translate "impressions of their trip" into "political diagnoses." The premise of every travel narrative—and a "Back from the USSR" is only one case of this—is that the

operation of a political and social apparatus, first, phenomenalizes itself for the most part (this does not go without saying, far from it); second, its supposed phenomenality remains accessible to the traveler (which goes even less without saying); even when, third, this traveler does not speak the language, languages, or subdialects of the country within the state visited (which seems to me to be completely out of the question, yet it is the case with most of these travelers, in particular with Gide and Benjamin).[31]

In other words, the travel narrative always presumes to accord a privilege to the *present*—presentation of the country, phenomena of a culture, manifestation of a political apparatus—and the possibility of recounting would be *derived* precisely from that, with writing becoming transparent to the actual "object" of the narrative. The "mode of *presentation* (and hence of the form of writing)" would adjust itself to "the 'present' of the thing itself (Moscow) as it presents itself."[32] All types of travel narratives, journals, stories of conquest, diaries, ethnological observations, "pilgrimage narratives, . . . every poem in the direction of a 'paradise lost' or a 'promised land,' . . . utopias, . . . old or new Jerusalems, Athenses, Romes (Moscow was also the other Rome of Christianity), . . . accounts of the French Revolution, all named "traveling" in my life. The temptation is to proceed, at the outset, in the most naive way possible, as near as possible to an innocent sensitivity, naked, without drifting toward philosophical meditation, which is no doubt where you will head, where it is better to let you write, on your own, a solid, thoughtful, well equipped, subtle, analytical book . . .

Soon after setting out I would disarm myself in two ways, I am going to tell you which. As if in order to return home unexpectedly, I would like to be able to return to the first time, to the "natural" ingenuousness of my birth, to my child-hood, during which, before the thing itself, the word alone, the word "voyage" must have climbed aboard my life. You know that I didn't travel, at all, before the age of nineteen (1949: first departure by boat and train, Algiers, Marseilles, Paris). Since then, recounting the history of my travels would also necessarily imply, not only but also, reconstituting their very condition, a history of travel in general, modes of travel, technical, economic, linguistic means of conveyance, etc. They underwent more radical transformation in my generation and in the last half century than during previous millennia. Travel, the concept of the voy-age has traveled faster than ever, and that is my first critical experiment, my first curiosity. Within this history of travel (aviation, telephone, hotels, credit cards, the so-called "computer revolution" in general, which has meant more than one revolution in the politics of the border), one would have to find a place for the history of academic travel, of university or cultural diplomacy, etc. I have trav-eled, more and more quickly, through travel—and I am not only thinking of ve-hicles of transport but of the speeds of telephoniconic exchange (from 1949 to 1975 I hardly ever made telephone calls while traveling, now I do it at every moment, all over the world). . . . Apart from the occasions when it came to me through literature, often at school—I could quote randomly *Gulliver's Travels*, *Paul et Virginie*, *The Indian Cottage*, *René*, and especially *The Reveries of a Soli-tary Walker*—as best as I can remember the word "travel" revealed *two worlds*. The word itself navigated between two worlds. And between two heteroge-neous, even incompatible senses. In other words, this homonym belonged to two families of phrases. It also had two "poles," if I can name them thus, the Fa-ther and the Mainland [*Métropole*]. This took place in Algeria, as you know, be-fore, during, and after the War. In the middle, there was the Allied landing in November 1942, the surprise of what was probably the first encounter with for-eigners who came from afar. Another culture. Discovery of America. Before I ever went to America, America took over my "home." I don't know whether, or how, you plan to take on my "American question," by the way. There is more than one of them, of course (first serious voyage, first stay of any duration abroad, 1956–57, the number of universities I have taught in, of translations, friends, and enemies, etc., and I have written about that a lot myself, although

of which are so many reflective, historical, philosophical narrations signed by foreign travelers,"[33] obey a law that decrees that the truth of travel amounts to unveiling a sense of the foreign that remains accessible to the traveler and conforms to criteria drawn from their own culture.

Against such assurances, Derrida stakes a claim for a voyage *without truth*, one that "would never again reach the thing itself, . . . would above all never touch it. Wouldn't even touch the veil behind which a thing is supposed to be standing."[34] Such a voyage would stand rather in the imminence of a catastrophe that "tears no veil."[35] Derrida travels in the twilight of that imminence, perpetually missing his appointment with Ulysses, whispering "No apocalypse, not now": "I would also like, in my own way, to name . . . the voyage, but a voyage without return, without a circle or journey round the world in any case, or, if you prefer, a return to life that's not a resurrection . . . neither an Odyssey nor a Testament."[36]

* * *

"How, then, are we to interpret this impossibility of founding, of deducing or (deriving)? Does this impossibility signal a failing?"[37] In a sense, it is true; such an impossibility is indeed the mark of a failing, the failure of certainties concerning the actual sense of the voyage. But Derrida's insistence on the motif of catastrophe, though it "sometimes appears infinitely hopeless,"[38] should not be read as the symptom of any "catastrophism." The failing is in fact another name for a promise, promise of a voyage that, because it does not derive, is always in the process of arriving. Deconstruction gets going from the vantage of this failing; it is from that perspective that it invents its *via*bility, the chance of a voyage that reverts, in an unheard of manner, to a sense that, if one still believed in literality, one could literally call the cutting [*frayage*] of a path(way) [*voie*]. Writing must indeed "open itself to a thinking of the earth as of the cutting of a path."[39]

Faithful to the possibility of such an opening, I have organized the trajectory of my reading in a network of three pathways. The first explores the deconstruction of the derivative schema that traditionally upholds the Odyssey of sense. The second sketches a biographical traversal. The third interrogates the *accosting* of the other and the imminence of the absolute

rather inadequately). But if I were you, and had to deal with the so-called "American question," I would first of all be tempted to adopt a satirical tone. I have always found the way in which the "American connection" is spoken of, in France especially, to be more comical than anything else. A great deal of incompetence, ignorance, or naivety comes into play, of course, which isn't funny in itself, but its tone and pose make one laugh. Even when it is of a provincial kind ("He is very well known abroad, you know, you wouldn't think it, this little guy from our place, especially there, in America"), it is no less dismissive, arrogant, and anti-American, even xenophobic, pouting ("That's all right for the Americans especially, but we don't go for it," implying, accompanied by a sigh or grimace, "Well, if only he were to stay there!"). The same people who react that way pretend not to know—since in order to speak as they do they cannot not know—that if I spend some few weeks each year in the United States, while teaching regularly and fulltime in Paris, I am anything but indulgent with respect to a whole "American culture." Not to mention the fact that for decades I have been traveling much more, and been much more and better "received" in many other countries around the world, inside and outside of Europe, notably in what is called Eastern Europe. . . . You can hear the noises they make, malicious, orchestrated. Between the press and the university which, as always, echo each other on cue.

Where was I now? Oh yes, two poles, Father and Mainland.

My father, first of all. There were what we called my father's "voyages." The noun "voyage" never meant anything to me before hearing what could be said in the house on this subject, on the subject of these forced expeditions of which my father was, in short, the first and only subject. The poor victim, in fact, thrown onto the road, *geworfen*, my first, and painful image of abandonment. To begin with, my father was the only one who left, and it was on the basis of his leaving alone that the term "voyage" took on a sense for those of us who never went far from the El Biar house. Until the age of nineteen I had never slept anywhere but at home, never changed beds. My father often said: "I am traveling [*en voyage*] on that day." "Traveling salesman," as he was also called, he "traveled" four days per week. If someone asked him his profession, he would say "traveler." Not "commercial traveler" [*voyageur de commerce*] or "traveling salesman" [*commis voyageur*], but "traveler," period. (I love the term *voyageur commis*: *commis d'office*, commissioned, appointed, mandated, sent on a mission [*en mission*], a little like me, in short, but sent by whom and commissioned to do what?)[6] "Voyage" had a synonym, "tour [*tournée*]." The days he went on

---

[6] [The noun *commis* means "a clerk or shop assistant," but can refer to a variety of professions (e.g., *commis aux vivres*: "ship's steward," or *commis voyageur*: "commercial traveler"), including, in the past, advanced bureaucratic positions such as First Secretary to a government Minister. As past participle of the verb *commettre*, the word is used in the expression *avocat commis d'office* to mean a court-appointed lawyer, with the sense of someone commissioned, charged with a mission or mandate. *En mission* is used, especially for functionaries (including academics) for someone traveling on official business, on assignment. (D.W.)]

arrivant. Each pathway proceeds by means of a signposted itinerary, indicated first by a foreword that prepares an arrival by organizing a controlled confrontation between the motifs of deriving and catastrophe. No pathway has either logical or chronological priority over the others, which is why I have not presented their elements in linear succession.[40] They cut across and fold back on each other while remaining irreducibly separate, *parting* one from the other.

The reader is free either to undertake a continuous reading of the whole in the order in which it appears, or to follow the thread of one pathway at a time, or else to follow no particular thread but rather to saunter here and there, carried along by their desires or by their ~~driftings~~ drives.[41]

[1]

"My father really spent his whole life on the job in the Tachet's sweatshop under the arcades of the port of Algiers." (Collection Viollet)

tour he would leave the house by car at five o'clock in the morning and return late in the evening, for he never slept away from home either. He would come back exhausted, stooped over, a heavy briefcase in his hand, full of money and orders for goods. The kilos of change and bills were cash payments for the factory or trade in "Wines and Spirits," the Tachet (sic!)[7] company, an old paternalist Catholic family for which he was the "(sales) representative." They had their own brand of Anisette (*Araki*), and my father, who wore the smell of distilled aniseed like a perfume, really spent his whole life on the job in the Tachets' sweatshop [*à la tâche pour les Tachet*], under the arcades of the port of Algiers, facing the ships. He was a docile employee, from the age of twelve to sixty, like his father before him who gave him at birth, for one of his forenames, that of Grandfather Tachet, Charles. My father therefore "traveled" for nearly forty years on account of and in the pay of Charles, Louis, and then the young Charlie Tachet, three generations of "bosses." Very early in the morning, before leaving, he had to do the cash accounts with the money spread out on the dining room table. I often helped him, and when the accounts didn't balance, it was a catastrophe, all was not

[7] ["Tachet" suggests *taché*: "stained," or *tâchez*: "keep trying," "get on the job/task." To work *à la tâche* is to do piecework. (D.W.)]

well with the world. Sometimes I would accompany him on his "tours," in Kabylie or to Vialar, south of Algiers, from the age of eighteen on, once I had learned to drive. These were literally my first explorations, perhaps the only ones, always in Algeria and never more than two hundred kilometers from El Biar, so that we returned the same evening. There will never be any triumph for me in the multiple long trips I have made around the world in the years since then, from Tokyo to Moscow, from Stockholm to Calcutta, from Ramallah to Santiago, Reykjavik, or Cotonou, etc. They remain pale imitations, after-effects or repercussions, nothing but flea-jumps that I could in no way compare, not ever, with my first breathtaking discoveries of Algeria, in Kabylie especially. No name can ever be inscribed for me in the same series as these Berber names. I love to pronounce them with no other desire than—today I should say with no other hope but—to hear them sing for me once more. As if, in order to preserve them, I was keeping some power of invocation that might yet indemnify them against the current tragedy:[8] Tizi Ouzou, Tigzirt, Djidjelli, Port Gueydon—that was the itinerary our tour took—and then the Yakouren Forest. But I am afraid of losing them rather than saving them, of forgetting them by publishing them, by thus consigning them to the outside, to the impoverished archive of a few letters. I enjoyed so much driving on those winding roads, but I was especially determined to help my father, to demonstrate a sort of "political solidarity" with him, to show my concern for this "wretched of the earth." Like him, I found his work exhausting, humiliating especially. . . . In my childhood I looked upon him as a sacrificial victim of modern times, and his "voyages" as an intolerable ordeal. My first political experience linked the unjust suffering of two unfortunates [*misérables*]: the "Arab," and my father, the "traveler." Before coming to designate the colonizer, the word "boss" was the name for the cruel and paternal chief under whose orders my poor father had to set out on his voyages ("my poor father" always spoke of his own by calling him "my poor father," both "poor fathers" having worked their whole lives for the same bosses, Tachet father and sons). . . .

Why am I recounting that to you? Perhaps, among other reasons, because I sometimes also have a "bad image" of my own travels, or more precisely, of my lecture "tours": fatigue, heavy suitcases, nervousness in front of immigration officers, especially since the Prague prison affair,[9] the speeches by means of which

---

[8] By recalling in this way the period before I left Algeria, an Algeria that I always knew as both wounded and murderous, I ask myself again today whether the taste of death that has never left me didn't in fact come from there; I don't hold very much to that hypothesis, but sometimes that country seems to me to bear, without deserving it, the death in its soul that has persecuted its body throughout time. For centuries.

[9] All things considered, my arrest in Prague in 1981 constituted the voyage that, in my whole life, was most worthy of the name. Not that everything in it was unforeseeable, granted, nor was it foreign, however obscurely, to a type of repetition. But the commotion, irruption, I would even say the "forced entry" of what was most "new" took place within that narrow cell, within what was most cramped about being locked up

"My arrest in Prague in 1981 in the end constituted the voyage that, in my whole life, was most worthy of the name." Prague Prison. (Jacques Derrida Archives)

one has to convince or seduce, the whole "market of academic culture" that I have always had a bad run of. In saying that I am giving in somewhat to a code, I don't totally believe what I am saying, nor that it is as simple as that; and I certainly don't want to make erudite pronouncements here about what I have done or wanted to do in traversing this "market"—for "deconstruction" would, in a word, be a certain experience of the voyage, wouldn't it, of letters and of language *en voyage*. If it were that true or that simple, if the bad image dominated everything else, I would no doubt stop traveling, but there remains the shadow

(Footnote 9 continued)
in prison. One would therefore have to remove the figure of the *homo viator* from that old poetics of escape, of open spaces, of the headlong flight, of adventure even. If time and place permitted, I would add here a long note concerning Ruzyne, the Prague prison, concerning what I planned to write during the time I didn't know when I would get out, and concerning my rereading of Chateaubriand's *Mémoires d'Outre-Tombe* in the French Embassy building the night I was liberated, on New Year's Day 1982. I tip my hat here, in passing, to Xavier de Maistre, who wrote in his *Voyage autour de ma chambre*, while in prison: "The new manner of traveling that I am introducing to the world." Perhaps you remember his last words, a motto for the counter-history of tourism that should serve as the background for our correspondence: "How many times have I not been duped by my confidence in these gentlemen! I was even saying something about that here in a note that I deleted, because it turned out to be longer than the whole text, which would have altered the just proportions of my voyage, whose small volume is its greatest merit."

and a smattering of truth in it, to the extent that a voyage doesn't just consist in passing from one language to another: it passes language, and beyond.

This "bad image" thus reminds me of the "tours" undertaken by my father. Would I be doing the same as he, perhaps, after protesting my whole life against his enslavement? Would my lecture tours be the theatrical, respectable, sublimated version of a humiliated father? My father's suffering when traveling, my impotent compassion in the face of what thus threw him onto the road and put him at the mercy of "bosses" and "clients," is an inexhaustible well for all my commiserations, for every "sacrifice" itself. I first knew the word "sacrifice"— which he himself used in order to complain with a sigh, he sighed all the time— with this sense alone, and something of it stays with me. In my primitive French, "voyage" equals work, servitude, slavery [*traite*]. And a certain shame even, the origin of social shame. The consequence of that, and what governs travel, is this: never associate it with leisure, with idleness, nor even with active tourism, with visiting, with curiosity (journey, travel, trip, *Reise, Fahrt*). In spite of or because of the attention paid to those whose language, and much else, I don't share, I do everything I can to avoid indulging in an ethno-sociological gaze (which, moreover, never teaches me anything, naturally, nothing that is not already familiar to me, in any case). And everything I can to make the enjoyment, discovery, the exposure to the foreign signify only the furtive contraband and protection of what is secret. In broad daylight, of course, that is the best. The effectiveness of a speech, the public gratification that comes from the performance, is promoted only in order to divert the gaze of the curious, to give oneself time for a satisfaction [*jouissance*] that they will never know about. A convincing alibi, all things considered, the legitimization of the unavowable. That doesn't prevent the fervent desire to bear witness, to call to witness and to confess. But before whom? And where is the evil? . . .

While waiting, one has indeed to encrypt the truth of the experience. Even if only to put it in a safe place. Which is the surest way of losing it, the other will reply. Well, yes . . .

So, of course, what one most likes about traveling is the chance to become invisible. *Travail*, travel, isn't therefore for earning a living but for paying for one's disappearance (I have talked about that, *jouissance* and the dreamwork, traveling by night, flirting with death).

I always hoped that my father would realize that, and exonerate himself in that way, secretly. . . .

The other pole of the word "voyage," like a miniature X-ray of Algeria, is not the Father but the Mainland: the "rich" families traveling to France, for vacations or to take a cure (Vichy, Evian, Vittel, Contrexéville are no doubt the first names of French towns that I heard, and associated with "traveling"). To cross the sea,

Algiers, aged about 17.
(Jacques Derrida Archives)

go over to the other side, meant to leave for a spa town. Once it was no longer a question of my father's "tours," to leave on a voyage thus meant to board the *Ville d'Alger*, the *Ville d'Oran*, or the *Kairouan* in order to "go to France" for a cure. Something that was for "bosses." My father, the "traveler" by trade, never took a vacation. My parents only left on a voyage to take a cure two or three times, late in life, a short time before the last convoy, the exodus to the Mainland in 1962. Since they never came back, never went back to Algeria, I imagine them to have died while traveling. They are seen to have died, and especially to have been buried abroad.

As for me, I never left El Biar before I was nineteen. Not even a train or a boat, let alone an airplane, of course, before embarking for Marseilles, then for Paris by train, in 1949. No voyage will ever displace the memory, the unmovable *here itself* of this perpetual immobility. Everything that has happened to me, since then, by dint of travel, has the virtual violent form of a revolution or trauma, of a wounding or a conversion. Everything comes down to the history of a deadening [*amortissement*], to an economy that allows me to protect myself from this aggression by "virtualizing" it. But that long history has its limits, which is why death shadows me everywhere I travel, and as you can see, everywhere I speak of it. Besides, to the extent that, in the narrowest sense of the term, "to travel" does not reduce to anything like what it nevertheless implies, neither movement, a path taken by walking, or vehicular displacement, nor returning, walking or running, distancing, absence or separation, I am tempted to call my states of travel *commotions*—"with," "without," or not, *cum et sine*, *sans*. To travel is to give oneself over to commotion: to the unsettling that, as a result, affects one's being down to the bone, puts everything up for grabs, turns one's head and leaves no anticipation intact. After each commotion one has to be reborn and come back to consciousness. Nothing is more frightening, nothing more desirable. Whatever the pretext, place, moment, vehicle, so many mediations, I would nickname them means of *locommotion*. That is why I "visit" very little when I travel, no tourism, except by pretence and by dying of boredom when I am forced into it. A single "curiosity" cultivates me more than I cultivate it, carrying me first toward the expectation, the frightened memory, the lodestone of this commotion, its unconscious and mortal center. . . . I'll stop there, Catherine. . . . Later, as I begin to read what you are writing *en voyage*, I will send you some "real" postcards. . . . Have I told you that my mother's maiden name, Safar, when spoken with a certain accent, means "voyage" or "departure" in Arabic? I am told by a young poet who is herself named Safaa (Fathy), that when pronounced with a different accent the word designates the second month of the Muslim "lunar" year of Hegira (*hijrah*, Mohammed's "flight" from Mecca): exile, emigration, exodus.

REVERSAL

1. i . Tropics

"This is why deconstruction includes
an indispensable phase of *reversal*."[1]

Pathway I is in fact double: two directions that
proceed from a single fork or crossing are sketched
out here. I will therefore separate I. i ("Tropics")
from I. ii ("*Envoyage*" and "Setting Out").

1

Foreword

Map

I would wish rather to suggest that the alleged (derivativeness) of writing, however real and massive, was possible only on one condition: that the "original," "natural," etc. language had never existed, never been intact and untouched by writing, that it had itself always been a writing.[2]

I have always known that we are lost and that from this very initial disaster an infinite distance has opened up

this catastrophe, right near the beginning, this reversal that I still cannot succeed in thinking was the condition for everything, not so?, ours, our very condition, the condition for everything that was given us or that we destined to each other, promised, gave, loaned, I no longer know what . . .[3]

31 August 1977. No, the stamp is not a metaphor, on the contrary, metaphor is a stamp: the tax, the duty to be paid on natural language and the voice. And so on for the metaphoric catastrophe. No more is the post a metaphor.[4]

This (derivative) opposition (of *physis* to *tekhne*, or of *physis* to *nomos*) is at work everywhere.[5]

Itinerary

In the Western tradition an entire conceptualization of the sign is upheld by the Odyssean paradigm of the voyage. According to that thinking the sign is organized, in both concept and function, as *the adventure of representation*. Its destiny condemns it to travel, like a representative or missionary, in the place and stead of the instance—the presence of the referent—that it is charged with designating.

> *The adventure of representation* is confused with that of sense in general. Sense gets exported, removed from itself, is sent anywhere at all, only to the extent that it remains capable of returning to itself, that is to say of recalling its delegates to itself. This adventure, which constitutes the history of metaphysics as a whole, is structured by a series of   oppositions— presence/representation, cause/effect, essence/accident, transcendental/
> empirical—which are governed in their very principle by the overarching opposition between "originary" and "derivative." Derrida gives a number of synonyms for the adjective "derivative": dependent, secondary, representative, induced, whatever operates on the basis of something presumed to be already constituted.[6] He emphasizes in particular two exemplary cases of this schema of derivation: that of the relation between spoken and written, and that between literal, or proper, and figurative sense. Traditionally, writing is conceived of as a phenomenon derived from speech, and metaphorical sense as derived from, or a drift away from, the literal. Writing and figures of speech would therefore act as the zealous ambassadors of a sedentary origin that would resist any expatriation, just as the virgin, natural, and local resist the violence of the technology, abstraction, and corruption which nevertheless constitute them.

This symbolic economy of the voyage structures at the same time the concept of travel itself. The voyage is an exportation, a provisional drift or diversion between the two fixed terms of departure and return. On the other hand, it is presented most often as breaking and entering, a violation or catastrophe with respect to the intimacy of the places to which it has access. This is shown in *Of Grammatology*, in Derrida's reading of the chapters from *Tristes Tropiques* that Lévi-Strauss devotes to his voyage among

Cerisy-la-Salle, 15 July 1997

. . . once again in this chateau, Catherine, for my seventh ten-day conference. In 1959 I spoke in public for the first time in my life here. Came back for *Nietzsche* (1972), *Ponge* (1974), *"Les Fins de l'homme"* (1980), *Lyotard* (1982). For this conference I proposed the title "L'Animal autobiographique." You remember that of 1992 on "Le passage des frontières," you were there, it could have been nicknamed "traveling with," the same subject when it comes down to it.[10]

. . . I am beginning to read you. Since we have planned to publish a part of this correspondence in our book, I will be careful what I say. Watching that the words of praise are neither indulgent nor unseemly, I express my thanks to you once and for all. The road you are taking is unique, you marry the grand art of forging a path (unusual world atlas, unalterable perspective, and unprecedented itinerary) and the force of a deciphering. You can see and understand everything. The privilege that you have decided to accord the word *dérive* is really a stroke of genius. Insanely economical. The plastic art of an unexpectedly subversive plastician.[11]

As if you were inventing what was to be thought. What I could have known concerning drifting derivation and the word *dérive*, what I could have foreseen or calculated about it belongs to a night of the unconscious or of forgetting that, without you, I would myself now find very difficult to analyze or formalize in such an accurate way. Why does the word insist to such an extent? You say everything there is to say about it, about *dérive*, the only thing missing is my name, the fragments of my father's name. In order to sign from *dérive* to *héritage* and hedgehog [*hérisson*]. But it would be quite overdoing it [*de l'outrance*] to sign anything at all here. *Outrance*, yet another word that I don't think I have ever used, but it has fallen across my path now, and I wonder why I associate it in a vague way with travel. . . . Last night in the Cerisy "stables," dreamed of the burial of my Uncle Robert, the last survivor, my father's youngest brother. The coffin had already been lowered into the bottom of the earth, but why were they waiting for a subterranean stream to come and cover it, as if that were expected, like some ritual moment that was at the same time hoped for yet terrifying? At the instant when the water burst forth, I woke up all anxious. Tell me Catherine,

---

[10] [The Cerisy-la-Salle ten-day conferences *"Les Fins de l'homme,"* *"Le Passage des frontières,"* and *"L'Animal autobiographique"* all concerned the work of Derrida, as did the recent *"La démocratie à venir"* (July 2002). This "postcard" to Malabou is written on Derrida's birthday. (D.W.)]

[11] [*"L'Art plastique d'une imprévisible plastiqueuse." Un plastiqueur*, used here in the feminine form, is someone who plants bombs. Malabou's work on Hegel, begun under Derrida's direction, elaborates a concept of "plasticity" (cf. Catherine Malabou, *L'Avenir de Hegel: Plasticité, Temporalité, Dialectique* [Paris: Vrin, 1996] (D.W.)].

the Nambikwara natives of the Amazon. The traveler-ethnographer depicts himself as an intruder who brings to the tribe the technology of writing from the outside, and so sows the seeds of corruption within a community that was previously "innocent."

Starting out from this primal scene, Pathway 1.i will explore the way in which Derrida travels in a counterdrift [*à contre-dérive*] by effecting a reversal—a catastrophe that is not, as we shall see, a simple inversion—of the order of priority, and consequently of the regime of causality that structures traditional oppositions. This trajectory will follow three main stages.

First, between the Amazon and France, Derrida's analysis of Lévi-Strauss and the calling into question of the ethnocentrism that grounds the distinction between "savage" and Western societies in an opposition between societies without writing and industrialized societies. This ethnocentrism is the vehicle for an *epigenetist* conception of the transmission of writing, based on an epigenesis that involves the precise sense of derivation that is being analyzed here.

Second, a certain "Oxford scene" will reverse the order of the filiation and lineage that is immanent to that epigenetism.

The third stage will be devoted to the "metaphoric catastrophe" that overturns the relation between literality and figuration, liberating the turning of the sun from its signifying function.

Envois of all sorts—letters, telephone calls, telepathy calls—will accompany the undertaking in order to confound its apparent deductive intention.

[4]

Cerisy-la-Salle, with Jean-François Lyotard, Sarah Kofman, and Jacques Trilling, 1980. (Jacques Derrida Archives)

why is the "I" of my "I dream" someone else when I am abroad? With my eyes barely open, as if I were coming to, coming back to myself, as if I were reappropriating myself by interpreting it as quickly as possible, here I find myself thrown immediately back onto the old ambiguous fear, the terror-stricken desire to die by drowning, the interminable deliberations on the incineration of my "remains" brought back (water or fire? yes or no? ashes in the garden? let them decide without imposing on them anything to do with my body? without imposing, even on their unconscious, some radioactive waste that cannot manage to be buried deeply enough?). These hesitations belong to the time of travel. As long as my body remains in the hands of the other, without defense, without even being able to answer for itself, fighting tooth and nail [*à son corps défendant*], a thousand deaths can befall it, it is up to "my" loved ones to dispose (of it). Is disappearing while traveling a good solution? That question puts me in a state of agony [*est une transe*], and before being the transposition of a metaphor, metonymy, a trope for pathways, displacements, passages, transports, and translations, travel is the speed of a fearful trance, and the excess of "passing over," overdoing it altogether [*l'outrance*] . . .

TRAVERSAL

"*Experience* . . . : the word also means passage, traversal, endurance, and rite of passage, but can be a traversal without line and without indivisible border."[1]

2

Foreword

Map

The language called maternal is never purely natural, nor proper, nor inhabitable. *To inhabit*: this is a value that is quite *disconcerting* and equivocal; one never inhabits what one is in the habit of calling inhabiting. There is no possible habitat without the difference of this exile and this nostalgia. Most certainly. That is all too well known. But it does not follow that all exiles are equivalent. From this shore, yes, *from this* shore or this common drift [*(dérivation)*], all expatriations remain singular.[2]

I therefore admit to a purity which is not very pure. Anything but purism. It is, at least, the only impure "purity" for which I dare confess a taste. It is a pronounced taste for a certain pronunciation. I have never ceased learning, especially when teaching, to speak softly, a difficult task for a *pied noir*, and especially from within my family, but to ensure that this soft-spokenness reveal the reserve of what is thus held in reserve, with difficulty, and with great difficulty, contained by the floodgate, a precarious floodgate that allows me to apprehend the catastrophe. The worst can happen at every turn.[3]

But being already strangers to the roots of French culture, even if that was their only acquired culture, their only educational instruction, and, especially, their only language, being strangers, still more radically, for the most part, to Arab or Berber cultures, the greater majority of these young "indigenous Jews" remained, in addition, strangers to Jewish culture: a strangely bottomless alienation of the soul: a catastrophe; others will also say a paradoxical opportunity. Such, in any event, would have been the radical lack of culture [*inculture*] from which I undoubtedly never completely emerged. From which I emerge without emerging from it, by emerging from it completely without my having ever emerged from it.[4]

There is then a state within the state in the two senses of the word "state": both in the sense of the political organization (and these theoretical jetties are also institutional fortifications—and we are paid and we pay to know this, even if it is clearer to some than to others—fortifications which are increasingly flexible, mobile, and the state of California is once more exemplary in that respect: we are used to theoretical earthquakes here, and institutional architectures are erected to respond to the seisms or seismisms of all the new *isms* which might shake the structures, both post and new structures); and in the sense of state as report, assessment, account = *statement*. Each theoretical jetty is the institution of a new statement about the whole state and of a new *establishment* aiming at state hegemony. Each jetty has a hegemonic aim, which isn't meant to subjugate or control the other jetties from the outside, but which is meant to incorporate them in order to be incorporated into them.[5]

Itinerary

How does Derrida traverse various countries, frontiers, cities, and languages? How does he set about his *experience* of traveling?

It is possible to claim in the first place that Derrida has three countries: his native Algeria, France, and the United States. He divides his life, his teaching, his work, and his home(s) between the last two. We should say more precisely that his way of life in France owes its stability only to the turbulence of a tension, that of the thread tying, by means a complex network, his country of birth (Algeria) to his chosen country (United States).

Derrida often presents this tension as a love story, a type of magnetism or, indeed, a transference. The young French-Jewish-Maghrebian felt enamored of France, as for a country that appeared to him, before he ever went there, as a "place of fantasy [*rêves*]," an "invisible but radiant hearth."[6] There was the inconsolable love of a Frenchman for Algeria (his "*nostalgeria*,"[7] as he coins it); but there was also a Franco-American romance: "Deconstruction, as we know it, will have been first of all a translation or a transference between French and American (which is to say also, as Freud has reminded us about transference, a love story, which never excludes hatred, as we know)."[8]

Derrida therefore has roots in each of these three countries, as is shown by the erotic radius that encompasses them. But should we consider that these roots, peregrine as they already are, constitute a home ground, a pedestal in relation to which the other countries he visits, on all his other travels, would be merely accidental, occasional, or *derivative* phenomena? Can we or should we try to inscribe these three countries of "origin" within the weave of a *Bildungsroman,* yet another Odyssey?

Derrida shows the impossibility of such an undertaking. In *Monolingualism of the Other,* having just spoken of his own "(hi)story," he declares:

> What I am sketching here is, above all, not the beginning of some autobiographical or anamnestic outline, nor even a timid essay toward an intellectual bildungsroman. Rather than an exposition of myself, it is an account of what will have placed an obstacle in the way of this auto-exposition for me. An account, therefore, of what will have exposed me to that obstacle and thrown me against it. Of a serious traffic accident about which I never cease thinking.[9]

What "serious accident" is he referring to? Has it ever occurred or does it owe its force to some phantasm? It is impossible to know, since from the origin there is an apparatus put in place to prevent it. *Monolingualism of the Other* presents this apparatus as a "floodgate," "Some Statements and Truisms," a "jetty." The floodgate is a piece of hydraulic equipment comprising doors in the form of sluices, designed to release or retain water as necessary. The locks of a canal, for example, allow a boat to move from a mill race to a tail race or vice versa, producing a level water surface to make such a passage possible. A jetty is a wooden, stone, or concrete construction creating a causeway, that juts into the water in order to protect a harbor or define the limits of a channel, also permitting safe passage for vessels.

Both these constructions, destined as they are to avoid catastrophes, are inscribed by Derrida in his language and his memory. They protect him while at the same time keeping accidents or a rupture of the dyke in a type of imminence. They both save and threaten the amorous commerce among these three countries and his love story with the world in general.

The floodgate apparatus, which contradicts yet at the same time calls forth the catastrophic drive, prevents us from deriving Derrida's travels from sure and stable roots. However, what is also striking is the fact that what prohibits that derivational drift in this way is, paradoxically, *a certain logic of derivation, a non-derivative logic of derivation.*

In order to understand this logic, one has to show what Derrida calls its "transcendental condition," that of an *originary exile,* undermining every habitat, habit, (assignment to) residence. Originary exile is what tears the speaking subject away from its mother tongue even as it remains attached to it. In *Monolingualism of the Other,* Derrida poses the following "antinomy":

1. *We only ever speak one language.*
2. *We never speak only one language.*[10]

He first formulates it as: "I have only one language; it is not mine," and later makes clear that "when I said that the only language I speak is *not mine,* I did not say it was foreign to me. There is a difference. It is not entirely the same thing."[11]

That means that one never possesses a language—not even one's mother tongue—as an object or chattel:

There is no given language, or rather there is some language, a gift of language (*es gibt die Sprache*), but there is not a language. Not a given one. It does not exist. Like the hospitality of the host even before any invitation, it summons when summoned. Like a charge [*enjoignante*], it remains to be given, it remains only on this condition: by still remaining to be given.[12]

There is my language, but in order, precisely, that it be *mine,* I must invent it my whole life through, enter it in my own way, delineate my style within it (my "*prior-to-the-first* language")[13]; conquer a space in it that is no longer just language, but my language within the language without which I wouldn't be able to speak. In a sense I am therefore required to *colonize* my own language. At the same time, this idiom that I invent is not absolutely peculiar to me, for it bears the scars of another colonization: every integral style takes on, interiorizes rules that don't belong to it but which issue from the law of the mother tongue, its history, the political genealogy of its institutions. I am therefore always at once master and hostage of my language, only inhabiting it from the position of speech's originary exile.

Derrida analyzes this condition on the basis of his own experience, that of a French Jew in Algeria who lost his citizenship during the Occupation, then found it again; who worked at speaking and writing the purest French by repressing his accent, forcing it back, holding it in check. That accent always threatens to return, it remains imminent, like the inevitable catastrophe of the difference with respect to oneself that structures all identity. Audible but illegible (but is it really illegible all the same?), the accent is a trait of belonging, the witness to a first linguistic exile (it is the trace of the place from which an idiom emerges within idiom), a trait that Derrida maintains he has to efface, neutralize, in the name of a purity, that is to say, nevertheless, in the name of yet another trait of belonging: belonging to the community of those who know how to speak French, the community of the "educated," of "intellectuals." A derivation, or originary exile, is caused by the impossibility of mooring this double trait to the same shore. When the accent returns, when Derrida "forgets himself," his "pure French" is put on hold; when his "pure French" dominates, the accent jolts his memory like a phantom limb. The sluice that allows him to pass from one closes off the other, and his repressed language—either pure or accented—painfully insists like what Lacan calls "the core" [*trognon*] of language. The wound remains open, threatening the circulation of blood and of sense: "The worst can happen at every turn."

In speaking of the destiny of deconstruction in "Some Statements and Truisms," making his remarks in that convulsive state of the United States that is Southern California, subject as it is to seismic catastrophes, and in invoking for that reason the figure of the jetty, Derrida imports this experience of language into the scene of "theory." Every "theory" is a language, that is to say, more than one language and no more a language, and it must forge its path or project its style within the landscape of thinking. "More than a language and no more of a language [*plus d'une langue*],"[14] he says, is the only definition he would ever risk giving for deconstruction. Every theory seeks to swallow up or introject all others, to speak all their languages, and so carries within it a multiplicity of idioms; at the same time, unable to master them, it will most often stabilize itself and congeal in its own language, become its own stereotype, accent, "-ism." A given theory is always in exile from theory in general, failing to erect its own watertight system. The jetty refers to both the launching and scrutiny of thinking, regulating, by means of a controlled play of openings and closings, the passage and alternating circulation of a theory and its multiplicity, of the group of theories that it delineates itself from while seeking to comprehend them.

Between the floodgate controlling the speech of a young French Algerian Jew and the jetty that structures the thought of a great and world-renowned intellectual there opens the very particular space of "the experience of travel in the work of Jacques Derrida." At the origin, therefore, there is drift, inscription of the outside within the intimate space of a language or native soil. A drift that seems, according to Derrida, to be the common shore for every exile and for every individual voyage.

However, doesn't presenting it in these terms mean reintroducing the distinction between the transcendental ("common drift or shore") and the empirical ("every exile and every individual voyage") that constitutes yet again the traditional schema of derivation? Indeed, it is on the condition of this transcendental edge (one does not possess one's own language), and by starting out from it, deriving from it, that every phenomenal, empirical, or individual exile opens up. Every particular *destinerrance* would be no more than a case of or testimony to that universal uprooting.

Derrida is perfectly conscious of the risk he runs by reverting to such formulations. In *Monolingualism of the Other* he speaks of "the philosophical tradition that supplies us with the reservoir of concepts I definitely have to use, and that I have indeed had to serve for a short while now in order to describe this situation, even in the distinction between transcendental or ontological universality and phenomenal empiricity," immediately adding, "I would now like to show that this empirico-transcendental or ontico-ontological re-mark, this folding which imprints itself upon the enigmatic articulation between a universal structure and its idiomatic testimony, reverses all the signs without any hesitation."[15]

There is certainly a universal condition; it reflects "a type of originary 'alienation' that institutes every language as a language of the other,"[16] but since, at the same time, this prior-to-the-first language does not exist, it re-

mains always to be invented ("Since the prior-to-the-first time of pre-origi-
nary language does not exist, it must be invented").[17] Far from being pre-
constituted, far from preceding what it sets the conditions for, the transcendental here depends precisely, in order to be what it is, on the
particular occurrences of the voyage that give rise to it. In this sense, it "is"
not transcendental; it only becomes so by means of the voyage. "How one
becomes transcendental," would that not be a beautiful possibility, a beautiful voyage or invention?

Every one of Derrida's trips in fact invents each time the conditions of
its possibility. It is in this sense that they are singular and "underiveable"
events. It is also because of this that the traces of them within his work are
so difficult to follow. One has to extract the autobiographical evidences,
the snippets of a narrative, the references to such and such a place within
the body of a text that encrypts them by perpetually doubling as the travel
diary of their logical genesis. Derrida makes clear:

The splitting of the ego, in me at least, is no transcendental claptrap . . . , I am,
like he who, returning, from a long voyage, out of everything, the earth, the
world, men and their languages, tries to keep after the event a logbook, with
the forgotten fragmentary rudimentary instruments of a prehistoric language
and writing, tries to understand what happened, to explain it with pebbles bits
of wood deaf and dumb gestures from before the institution of the deaf and
dumb, a blind man groping before Braille and they are going to try to recon-
stitute all that, but if they knew they would be scared and wouldn't even try.[18]

Without attempting even the slightest "reconstitution," Pathway 2 will
respect the particularity of each place that is traversed (Italy, Greece,
Czechoslovakia, Japan, . . .), while still insisting on the radiating hearths
that are Algeria and the United States. Here and there, from country to
country and from city to city, the threat or imminence of catastrophe will
emerge or show its outline, that is to say as much the possibility of accident
as the chance of the event.

[5]

Villefranche-sur-Mer, Meina (Lago Maggiore), 4 September 1997

. . . Family vacations, without commotion, without any apparent trance, between Nice (brother and sister, visiting the Château cemetery, Matisse), Ville-
franche (where I am reborn every day—read "I swim"), Saint-Paul-de-Vence (after the paintings and sculptures of the Fondation Maeght, the timeless dinner we
have every year, with the Delormes, Jean-Louis Prat, André Verdet, the Lyotards
also this year—Jean-François happily in good form). Each time, as always at
every moment, I am asking myself, although no one notices, "Will this be the
last time?" We also went up to Eze, from where I send a postcard to Blanchot
every year. You know that he lived there, and according to my habit, I ask myself each time, "Will this be the last time, the last card?" Two days ago we arrived at Adami's place above Lago Maggiore. Same as in previous years, but
now a summer seminar has been added to the program: two or three days in the
sun in an amphitheatre overlooking the lake, speaking about something like the
origin of the work of art in front of Italian artists and students. Perhaps I will understand why I do all that by the end of your book. And whether I escape my
paternal destiny (did you see *Death of a Salesman*? the film, I mean, "Death of a
commis voyageur?"). I am continuing my reading of what you have written, it's
great, you are right about everything, I won't add a word to what you say. But
there would need to be interminable narratives, and endless descriptions,
worlds on grains of rice! The readers will orient themselves all alone, on one
side or the other, left or right, Orient or Occident. Here's a laugh: would Kant
call that "orientation in thinking?" Do you recall that great little text that begins
with an elementary cartography, a theory of sides and coasts, and as in my first
letter, by recalling the *poles*, the polar star and cardinal points. It is addressed to
traveling philosophers, but he himself knocked around as infrequently as my
counter-supervisor [*contremaître*] Heidegger. In *Sein und Zeit*, however, the latter asks Kant some good questions about the meaning of "orienting oneself." He
thus splits this concept of *Ent-fernung*, dividing gathering in the way in which
the distant undoes itself, but really by itself, that is to say, without leaving itself
(that's me right there? No way!): *going away, distancing* [éloignement] = *de-
awaying* [dé-loignement]= *the opposite of distancing* [déséloignement], the
double movement that, by undoing or unmaking it, creates the distant, close to
Montaigne's *esloingnement* and to the "purloined letter." The existence of the
Dasein could basically be said to tend to approximate closely what is close [*se
rapprocher du proche*], it tends toward *rapprochement*, proximity (*auf Nähe*). Its
first, and therefore last, movement would develop—even when it moves away—
in view of an approaching, one could perhaps say, "in view of seeing *itself*
come." For that very reason, it would depend on an experience of *é-loignement*,

on the distancing of distancing. *Ent-fernung/Näherung.* But doesn't distancing *from* and *in* distancing, distancing as *rapprochement,* approximation, reappropriation, still remain within Ulysses' circle? Not that every traverse is *necessarily* an Odyssey, but the phantasmatic logic of the Odyssey remains all powerful. Unless it hits the snag, fatally, of *Ananke* or *Tukhe,* the necessity of fate. Unless it champs at the bit in order to *come back from leaving.* (Me, I don't know if I champ at the bit when I think of the return, or the bit.)[12] That is no doubt where Heidegger's thinking concerning one's country comes into play, concerning the return and the at-home (*Heimkehr*), the sojourn (*Aufenthalt*). (Will you talk about that? I have skirted around it a lot myself, I'm not sure where, probably in "Demeure, Athènes," around the subject of his trip to Greece and his *Aufenthalte.*) I think I remember that soon after, in *Sein und Zeit,*[13] as he often does, he critiques the meager evidence of the inside, of being-in: space isn't *in* the subject nor the world *in* space. That, for him, is the underiveable, what can't drift. For every drift or derivation has its place or takes place there. Spacing itself, the spatiality of spacing, distancing, does not drift or derive, and what is a

---

12 [*Le mors,* thus also *le mort,* "the dead one/guy/body." (D.W.)]

13 §23 [In their translation of *Sein und Zeit,* Macquarrie and Robinson coin the term "de-severance" to express the complexity of distancing referenced here and discussed above. See Heidegger, *Being and Time,* 138–44. (D.W.)]. My right of reply: these learned references added after the event, designed to enrage I know not whom. For example that arrogant illiterate who, as usually happens these days, paraded about in some weekly, saying that all of us French who are too interested in Heidegger are, for him, "precious damsels [*précieuses ridicules*]." In other words, bad French. He thereby classifies on the one side and the other and then crowns his own favorite philosopher. You will never guess who. When we next see one another I'll tell you who gets the prize and we can laugh about it. I love laughing with you. (2 July 1998)

On a second reading I am adding this in order to change the subject as quickly as possible: orientation, the ability to *find one's way,* has always been a miraculous experience for me. An anxiety that is at the same time constant and dumbfounded. Is it possible? How does one do it? How do animals manage to *retrace their steps,* following such labyrinthine itineraries, infinitely better than "us"? The very power of the impossible. I know that there are "objective" responses to these questions, but that in no way changes the feeling of absolute marvel, of a talent above any other: *(re)finding* oneself, before faces or letters, before places even, *recognizing* paths, a way, a direction, a sense. Instead of giving learned references, I'll tell you this confidence, Catherine, yet another question: why do I think of my mother, mourning her, feeling sorry for her, watching her fade out of sight, whenever, without understanding it in the least, I admire my sense of orientation? Her fragility, the threat that seemed both to affect and protect her? Each time I tell myself—for example, in O'Hare Airport in the middle of the harrowing labyrinth of sub-terminals, concourses, and gates, or in Tokyo, where one can no longer read the street names, or in the alleyways of East Jerusalem—that my mother would be as lost here as a child. What would she do in my place? She wouldn't budge, she would put down her suitcase and wait for someone to save her. Moreover, at the end of her life she used to get lost like that, she used to "lose herself," as we say so strangely well; she no longer knew at which station to get off the train, for example between Versailles and Ris-Orangis. In the last years in Nice, her city of exile, she would ask every evening to leave her house so that she could go home (in fact, her childhood home, right in the center of Algiers, and not the one she had spent the greater part of her life in, in El Biar. A classic symptom among the old.). We would lie to her, take her for a walk around the block, and then, as submissive as a child, she would consent to be repatriated. The smart ones will conclude without delay that I always orient myself, even within the question of orientation, on the basis of my mother's disorientation (23 July 1998).

priori, originary, absolutely prior, is the "encounter (*Begegnen*)," the encounter with space as region (*Gegend*). We should stop to think travel on the edge of the encounter. Not everything comes down to the encounter, but can you imagine a traverse without encounter? Should we cultivate the virtualities of this lexicon, between "with" (*apud hoc, cum*) and "*contra.*" In Latin, therefore, contra Heidegger (I always travel, as I told you, and *I think counter to* Heidegger's order, I am on the side of his counter-example or his counterpart. The petty prosecutors will allege that it comes down to the same thing; perhaps, but not for sure.). I would have liked to write you postcards full of the memories of the hundreds of words derived from *contra*, from region [*contrée*] to *contrada* (Siena, 1981, the Palio: *L'Istrice*, hedgehog, name of one of the *contrada*, also comes to me by that route), to country. Contradictions, contretemps, and contracts would be there to point out the way, referring us to what, in the idea of the encounter or meeting sends us back out *en voyage*, and therefore sends us back [*renvoie*]. Moreover, I wonder if the reason I travel so much is not because (I have the feeling that from France) I have always been "sent down [*renvoyé*]," as happened to me at school. Does one travel because one is sent away or in order to go toward the *encounter*? What does "counter" mean? and counter-hospitality? and going by a counterpath? Is it really a question of travel? (There would thus be travel questions, like travel kits, travel bags, travel agencies.) But there you have it, if one travels *in view of* the meeting, there is no more encounter, nothing happens. The encounter is the undecided precipitation, without the least preparation, at the mercy of the other who decides, the irruption of what one has, above all, not seen coming—and that can arrive or happen, yes indeed, "at home."

In a certain way, there is perhaps no voyage worthy of the name except one that takes place there where, in all senses of the word, *one loses oneself*, one runs such a risk, without even taking or assuming this risk: not even of losing oneself but of getting *lost*. For oneself. No privilege given, *ergo*, to any of these three words: "Where am I?"

You see, I seek the accident of travel, and I seek to recount to you merely the little stories of a "catastrophe," as you call it, but which in the end would no longer resemble—I am almost quoting you here—the accident that "confirms" the essence. I would have liked to select for you everything insignificant, little anodyne things, anecdotal or anachronistic, that neither you nor I could *foresee* under the rubric of "travel." Such that whoever reads me after you, as third person, has but a single impression of them: it is *displaced*. Deferred [*renvoyé*] until later. Adjourned.

It is five o'clock in the morning, I am writing to you on the terrace, the sun is going to rise in front of me, over Lago Maggiore, everyone is sleeping, I made myself coffee all alone, without making a sound. And, as every morning, with only a cat for a witness. Here his name is Settembrino . . .

VERSION ("NON-ARRIVAL")

3

Foreword

Map

> The gap between the opening of this *possibility (as a universal structure)* and the *determinate necessity* of this or that religion will always remain irreducible; and sometimes within each religion, between on the one hand that which keeps it closest to its "pure" and proper possibility, and on the other, its own historically determined necessities or authorities. Thus, one can always criticize, reject, or combat this or that form of sacredness or of belief, even of religious authority, in the name of the most originary possibility. The latter can be *universal* (faith or trustworthiness, "good faith" as the condition of testimony, of the social bond and even of the most radical questioning) or already *particular*, for example belief in a specific originary event of revelation, of promise or of injunction, as in the reference to the Tables of the Law, to early Christianity, to some fundamental word or scripture, more archaic and more pure than all clerical or theological discourse. But it seems impossible to deny the *possibility* in whose name—thanks to which—the (derived) *necessity* (the authority or determinate belief) would be put into question, suspended, rejected or criticized, even deconstructed. One can *not* deny it, which means that the most one can do is to deny it. Any discourse that would be opposed to it would, in effect, always succumb to the figure or the logic of denial. Such would be the place where, before and after all the Enlightenments in the world, reason, critique, science, tele-technoscience, philosophy, **thought** in general, retain the *same* resource as religion in general.[1]

To neutralize invention, to translate the unknown into a known, to metaphorize, allegorize, domesticate the terror, to circumvent (with the help of circumlocutions: turns of phrase, tropes, and strophes) the inescapable catastrophe, the undeviating precipitation toward a remainderless cataclysm. What is unheard of here would be the abyssal, and, for the sleepwalker I am talking about, "passing to the side of" the chasm would amount to falling into it just the same, without seeing or knowing. But does one ever die otherwise?[2]

Before it's too late, go off to the ends of the earth like a mortally wounded animal. Fasting, retreat, departure, as far as possible, lock oneself away with oneself in oneself, try finally to understand oneself, alone and oneself.[3]

What are the chances of my losing at a game or for the neutron bomb to be dropped?[4]

Itinerary

"The world is going badly . . . "[5] What is happening to the world today is a catastrophe. Derrida never stops saying so, wherever he goes, on every one of his travels. Political, social, economic, and strategic analysis orients all his movements and all his texts.

A catastrophe: the disappearance of Eastern and Western blocs, the emergence of the "new world order" have done nothing to resolve economic wars, the inequality and injustice that result from them; on the contrary, those changes have accentuated such a state of affairs. The imposition of the free-market capitalist model as the only economic perspective and worldwide rejection of Marxism do not open up any new horizon. The wounds caused by unemployment and social distress, so-called ethnic conflicts and wars with civilian hostages, the return of nationalisms, fanaticisms, and xenophobias, are further than ever from being healed. However, new political and social stakes have been raised, there are new forms of life, in a word, new chances. The construction of Europe, for example, could be one such chance. Posing the question of the future of the European Union, Derrida asks precisely, in *The Other Heading,* how it might be possible for that Europe to be open to "the heading of the other."[6]

It is always from within the same discourse, according to the same logic, that he *denounces* the catastrophe and allows something else to *be announced* or appear. That is the logic that Pathway 3 seeks both to unfold and follow.

What logic and discourse are we talking about here, presuming such words are still pertinent? If travel, the experience of the other, the opening to the world can not, or no longer, respond to the "phenomenological motif" that allows one to establish diagnoses, to propose dogmatic solutions, to draw up assessments by relying on a truth or a sense of *presence*, then it must be shown that what has come to pass, what is coming to pass today, and what can come to pass tomorrow does not derive from any existing or assignable origin or cause. What has come to pass, what is coming to pass, or what can come to pass draws its resource from a non-place: the pure possibility—which can never present or *presentify* itself—of the event, something that no event can, could ever, will ever be able to fully satisfy [*saturer*]. To this non-place the text "Demeure, Athènes" gives the name of "non-arrival" or "non-arriver" [*le non arrivé*].[7]

Thinking arrival without derivation requires us to turn toward this sense of non-arrival. Pathway 1 explores that *version* or that *strophe* in its own way, under the heading of "destinerrance." The event always escapes teleology by dint of surprise. Whatever arrives misses or lacks its destination, in other words it doesn't arrive. Pathway 3 examines another aspect of the relation between arrival and non-arrival. Instead of insisting on whatever, by arriving or occurring, is bound neither to *telos* nor destination, it concerns what has never arrived, what will perhaps never arrive, but which is at the same time the determinant condition for anything whatsoever to arrive, happen, or be produced. If one wanted to risk summarizing in a few words one of the most subtle turns of Derrida's thinking, one could say that everything that happens owes its chance to non-arrival. "Owes its chance": this expresses at the same time a debt (every event is indebted with respect to non-arrival) and the relation of a possibility to its condition of possibility (what happens or arrives derives from nothing, owes its existence to non-arrival).

Pathway 3 proposes exploring more precisely the distance between what arrives and what hasn't arrived. What is between them takes place. *Its place is the world,* the world of *today.* But what does "today" signify in such a case? When does today date from? Interrogating the sense of today's date is an enterprise that, in many respects, might seem absurd: today is ageless. But it remains that "agelessness" always has a today and in that sense it allows itself to be dated. In what respect can our today be said to mark its date? In "No Apocalypse, Not Now" Derrida shows that the today of our world is the "nuclear age." All the catastrophes that affect the world are produced in the imminence or the threat of the radical event that is atomic warfare. An event without precedent: "Here we are dealing hypothetically with a total and remainderless destruction of the archive."[8] The possibility of this catastrophe, which has emerged only in the twentieth century, is that of the absolute destruction of the world. Yet at the same time this war has not taken place. It is what has not arrived. It has no place. It exists only through prophetic, scientific, or phantasmatic versions of its potential break-out. A non-place (the war that has not taken place) gives rise to the event; everything that happens today stands out against the background of its possibility.

The relation between arrival and non-arrival is thereby clarified. But Derrida postulates it in a more radical way still: what if, at bottom, every event, whatever its age, owed its possibility to a non-place, to non-arrival? And what if at bottom nuclear war was itself only a *version* (a certain occurrence, a certain face, a certain interpretation) of an *atopia* that was paradoxically constitutive of the world, a non-place of place, so old as to be ageless? In Plato's *Timaeus,* the name for this non-place is *khōra.* The womb or matrix of all forms, itself impassive and indifferent to all form, *khōra* is the nothing that gives birth to everything.

Derrida recalls the current senses of *khōra* in Greek: " 'place,' 'location,' 'placement,' 'region,' 'country'."[9] This is a most important point for thinking the voyage, namely that what gives rise to or makes place for place, country, region, land is itself stateless, without a place of origin. *Khōra* does not make a world, is nothing in itself, but it makes a place for everything that is. It is for Derrida the most splendid name for non-arrival. Pathway 3 will therefore attempt to bring to light the surprising relation that unites *khōra* and nuclear war and allows this *atopia* to be conceived of as "mother," "nurse," or "receptacle" for travel.

Is not non-arrival also, by definition, (1) what could have arrived or happened? (2) what can still arrive or happen? Is it not the other of everything that has taken place, that remains to come, the other possibility, the wholly other chance? Derrida affirms that catastrophe has to be thought of together with promise, the promise of justice, the promise of democracy. Non-arrival is the very possibility of the arrival of every wholly other (thing), the worst along with the best, and there is therefore no contradiction in thinking of non-arrival as the "*absolute* arrivant." This absolute *arrivant* does not wait, it exceeds every horizon of waiting, every apocalypse, all visibility; turning toward it also means turning away from it; the *arrivant* undoes any such *vers(at)ion*. Derrida refers to a messianicity "without messianism,"[10] thereby linking thought and philosophy to the possibility of an opening to the other that does not involve waiting, to the promise of a coming without any Messiah. The third stage of our trajectory will question precisely the political dimension of the "messianic," analyzing the chance of a world as "*heading of the other,* but also . . . the *other of the heading.*"[11]

Finally, with the title "Island, Promised Land, Desert," the fourth and final rendering of the trajectory forged by Pathway 3 will examine the sense of this "credit" or faith accorded the wholly other. Such a *belief* orients, like the need for reason, both voyage and thinking.

[6]

4

From One Catastrophe
to Another (Amazon–Paris)

Two catastrophic voyages, two itineraries that lead to the country or to the heart of catastrophe intersect here. The first is that of Lévi-Strauss in the Amazon forest, among the Nambikwara Indians. The second is that of Derrida interpreting the first. The staging of this scene is now famous, found in the second part of *Of Grammatology*, entitled "Nature, Culture, Writing," and in its first chapter, "The Violence of the Letter: From Lévi-Strauss to Rousseau." In those passages Derrida comments on two episodes from *Tristes Tropiques*, extracted from the chapters "The Writing Lesson" and "On the Line," first of all bringing to the attention of the reader "the art of composition of this travelogue. In accordance with eighteenth-century tradition, the anecdote, the page of confessions, the fragment from a journal are knowledgeably put in place, calculated for the purposes of a philosophical demonstration of the relationships between nature and society, ideal society and real society, most often between the *other* society and *our* society."[1]

Reading "The Writing Lesson"

It is unnecessary to point out that the Nambikwara have no written language, but they do not know how to draw either, apart from making a few dotted lines or zigzags on their gourds. . . . I handed out sheets of paper and pencils. At first they did nothing with them, then one day I saw that they were all busy drawing wavy, horizontal lines. I wondered what they were trying to do, then it was suddenly borne upon me that they were writing or, to be more accurate, were trying to use their pencils in the same way as I did mine, which was the only way they could conceive of, because I had not yet tried to amuse them with my drawings. The majority did this and no more, but the chief had further ambitions. No doubt he was the only one who had grasped the purpose of writing. So he asked me for a writing-pad, and when we both had one, and were working together, if I asked for information on a given point, he did not supply it verbally but drew wavy lines on his paper and presented them to me, as if I could read his reply. He was half taken in by his own make-believe; each time he completed a line, he examined it anxiously as if expecting the meaning to leap from the page, and the same look of disappointment came over his face. But he never admitted this, and there was a tacit understanding between us to the effect that his unintelligible scribbling had a meaning which I pretended to decipher, his verbal commentary followed almost at once, relieving me of the need to ask for explanations.

As soon as he had got the company together, he took from a basket a piece of paper covered with wavy lines and made a show of reading it, pretending to hesitate as he checked on it the list of objects I was to give in exchange for the presents offered me: so-and-so was to have a chopper in exchange for a bow and arrows, someone else beads in exchange for his necklaces. . . . This farce went on for two hours. Was he perhaps hoping to delude himself? More probably he wanted to astonish his companions, to convince them that he was acting as an intermediary agent for the exchange of goods, that he was in alliance with the white man and shared his secrets. We were eager to be off, since the most dangerous point would obviously be reached when all the marvels I had brought had been transferred to native hands. So I did not try to explore the matter further, and we began the return journey with the Indians still acting as our guides.[2]

My hypothesis, if correct, would oblige us to recognize the fact that the primary function of written communication is to facilitate slavery. The use of writing for disinterested purposes, and as a source of intellectual and aesthetic pleasure, is a secondary result, and more often than not it may even be turned into a means of strengthening, justifying or concealing the other.[3]

If we look at the situation nearer home, we see that the systematic development of compulsory education in the European countries goes hand in hand with the extension of military service and proletarianization. The fight against illiteracy is therefore connected with an increase in governmental authority over the citizens. Everyone must be able to read, so that the government can say: Ignorance of the law is no excuse.[4]

By themselves, the above quotes create a whole economy in which a solidarity of relations among deriving, arrival, and catastrophe is clearly defined. That solidarity becomes evident in the reversal that proceeds the dénouement of the plot, as in a theatrical tragedy. After having "grasped" the "purpose" of writing, the chief reverses his situation of ignorance—he doesn't know how to write—in order to extract from it the best possible advantage. He pretends to know how to write in order to oppress and deceive the other members of the tribe. This *accidental inversion*—by chance, thanks to a concurrence of circumstances or an *event*, absence of knowledge produces an excess of power—confirms an *inversion of principle*: what seems to be merely the *effect* of writing (subjugation) in fact reveals itself as the "primary function of written communication." Writing thus appears as it has always appeared in the metaphysical tradition, a pure derivation from speech, something that comes to affect speech from the outside, however much it remains dependent on it.

First derived catastrophe: the intrusion of writing allows the chief to deceive the other members of the group even though he lags behind what is really going on. He doesn't master writing but simply uses a technique imported by the traveler.

Second derived catastrophe: this scene is itself a derived reproduction of a more originary structure, namely the violent intrusion of writing as instrument of oppression within the primary innocence of orality. Thus, the accident of the writing lesson is able to confirm a general law.

Third derived catastrophe: the fact of drawing "wavy lines" appears as the "metaphoric" sense of writing, derived from its proper sense, namely the use it is put to by the anthropologist.

The "Innocence" of the Nambikwara

Lévi-Strauss thus presupposes that the evil of writing necessarily "comes from without," harming the integrity of a community judged originarily good and innocent. Indeed, for him, according to Derrida:

Only an innocent community, and a community of reduced dimensions (a Rousseauist theme that will soon become clearer), only a micro-society of non-violence and freedom, all the members of which can by rights remain within range of an immediate and transparent, a "crystalline" address, fully self-present in its living speech, only such a community can suffer, as the surprise of an aggression coming *from without*, the insinuation of writing, the infiltration of its "ruse" and of its "perfidy." Only such a community can import *from abroad* "the exploitation of man by man."[5]

The Nambikwara, around whom the "Writing Lesson" will unfold its scene, among whom evil will insinuate itself with the intrusion of writing come from *without* . . . , the Nambikwara, who do not know how to write, are *good*, we are told. The Jesuits, the Protestant missionaries, the American anthropologists, the technicians on the telegraph line who believed they perceived violence or hatred among the Nambikwara are not only mistaken, they have probably projected their own wickedness upon them. And even provoked the evil that they then believed they saw or wished to perceive.[6]

Epigenesis and Ethnocentrism

The derivative schema put in place by Lévi-Strauss (writing derives from speech, metaphoric sense derives from literal sense) is authorized by an *epigenetist* conception of writing, according to which the latter would be capable of suddenly appearing, being born all at once from spoken language. Thus, for Lévi-Strauss, the chief did not take long to understand the function of writing, the spirit if not the letter of it. Between anthropologist-traveler and tribal chief graphic contamination occurs almost instantaneously. Derrida identifies in that analysis the very principle of ethnocentrism:

The colloquial difference between language and writing, the rigorous exteriority of one with respect to the other, is admitted. This permits the distinction between peoples using writing and peoples without writing. Lévi-Strauss is never suspicious of the value of such a distinction. This above all allows him to consider the passage from speech to writing as a *leap*, as the instantaneous crossing of a line of discontinuity: passage from a fully oral language, pure of all writing—*pure*, innocent—to a language appending to itself its graphic "representation" as an accessory signifier of a new type, opening a technique of oppression. Lévi-Strauss needed this "epigenetist" concept of writing in order that the theme of evil and of exploitation suddenly coming about with the *graphie* could indeed be the theme of a surprise and an accident affecting the purity of an innocent language from without. Affecting it *as if by chance*. At any rate the epigenetist thesis repeats, in connection with writing this time, an affirmation that we could have encountered five years previously in the *Introduction a l'oeuvre de Marcel Mauss* (p. 47): "Language could only have been born suddenly." We might well find numerous questions to raise about this paragraph, which ties sense to signification and more narrowly to linguistic signification in *spoken* language. . . .

The traditional and fundamental ethnocentrism which, inspired by the model of phonetic writing, separates writing from speech with an ax, is thus handled and thought of as anti-ethnocentrism. It supports an ethico-political accusation: man's exploitation by man is the fact of writing cultures of the Western type. Communities of innocent and unoppressive speech are free from this accusation.[7]

Two significances are quickly drawn from the incident itself.

1. The appearance of writing is *instantaneous*. It is not prepared for. Such a leap would prove that the possibility of writing does not inhabit speech, but the outside of speech. "So writing had made its appearance among the Nambikwara! But not at all, as one might have supposed, as the result of a laborious apprenticeship." From what does Lévi-Strauss arrive at this epigenetism that is indispensable if one wishes to safeguard the exteriority of writing to speech? From the incident? But the scene was not the scene of the *origin*, but only that of the *imitation* of writing. Even if it were a question of writing, what has the character of suddenness here is not the passage to writing, the invention of writing, but the importation of an already constituted writing. It is a borrowing and an artificial borrowing. As Lévi-Strauss himself says: "The symbol had been borrowed, but the reality remained quite foreign to them." Besides, this character of suddenness obviously belongs to all the phenomena of the diffusion or transmission of writing. It could never describe the appearance of writing, which has, on the contrary, been laborious, progressive, and

differentiated in its stages. And the rapidity of the borrowing, when it happens, presupposes the previous presence of the structures that make it possible.

2. The second significance that Lévi-Strauss believes he can read in the very text of the scene is connected to the first. Since they learned without understanding, since the Chief used writing effectively without knowing either the way it functioned or the content signified by it, the end of writing is political and not theoretical, *"sociological, rather than . . . intellectual."* This opens and covers the entire space within which Lévi-Strauss is now going to think writing.[8]

The "Imitation of Writing"

Ethnocentrism is manifested yet again through the way in which the anthropologist considers that the Indians possess only metaphors for expressing the act of writing: "making a few dotted lines or zigzags," "drawing wavy, horizontal lines." Derrida asks whether the "literal" sense of writing is not indeed always metaphoric:

It is quite evident that a literal translation of the words that mean "to write" in the languages of peoples with writing would also reduce that word to a rather poor gestural signification. It is as if one said that such a language has no word designating writing—and that therefore those who practice it do not know how to write—just because they use a word meaning "to scratch," "to engrave," "to scribble," "to scrape," "to incise," "to trace," "to imprint," etc. As if "to write" in its metaphoric kernel, meant something else. Is not ethnocentrism always betrayed by the haste with which it is satisfied by certain translations or certain domestic equivalents? To say that a people do not know how to write because one can translate the word which they use to designate the act of inscribing as "drawing lines," is that not as if one should refuse them "speech" by translating the equivalent word by "to cry," "to sing," "to sigh"? Indeed "to stammer." By way of simple analogy with respect to the mechanisms of ethnocentric assimilation/exclusion, let us recall with Renan that, "in the most ancient languages, the words used to designate foreign peoples are drawn from two sources: either words that signify 'to stammer,' 'to

mumble,' or words that signify 'mute.'" And ought one to conclude that the
Chinese are a people without writing because the word *wen* signifies many
things besides writing in a narrow sense? As in fact J. Gernet notes:

> The word *wen* signifies a conglomeration of marks, the simple symbol in
> writing. It applies to the veins in stones and wood, to constellations, rep-
> resented by the strokes connecting the stars, to the tracks of birds and
> quadrupeds on the ground (Chinese tradition would have it that the obser-
> vation of these tracks suggested the invention of writing), to tattoo and
> even, for example, to the designs that decorate the turtle's shell. . . . The
> term *wen* has designated, by extension, literature and social courtesy. Its
> antonyms are the words *wu* (warrior, military) and *zhi* (brute matter not yet
> polished or ornamented).[9]

In taking to task the presuppositions implicit in anthropological discourse, Derrida is not re-establishing a hierarchy of subordination by being
content to invert certain priorities. If one is to follow the voyage of gram-
matological reading, one must abandon the very principle of inversion,
which is merely an inverse derivation, in favor of opening up to a different
thinking of the event and the accident. At the same time, *outside* changes
its meaning. Indeed, the violence of writing does not come from outside:

> [It] *does not supervene* from without upon an innocent language in order to
> surprise it, a language that suffers the aggression of writing as the accident of
> its disease, its defeat and its fall; but is the originary violence of a language
> which is always already a writing. Rousseau and Lévi-Strauss are not for a
> moment to be challenged when they relate the power of writing to the exer-
> cise of violence. But radicalizing this theme, no longer considering this vio-
> lence as (*derivative*) with respect to a naturally innocent speech, one reverses
> the entire sense of a proposition—the unity of violence and writing—which
> one must therefore be careful not to abstract and isolate.[10]

Reading "On the Line": There Is No Society "Without Writing"

Although the Nambikwara were easy-going and unperturbed by the presence
of the anthropologist with his notebook and camera, the work was complicated

by linguistic difficulties. In the first place, the use of proper names is taboo; in order to identify individuals, we had to follow the custom adopted by the telegraph workers, that is, come to an agreement with the natives about arbitrary appellations such as Portuguese names—Julio, Jose-Maria, Luiza, etc.—or nicknames like *Lebre* (hare) or *Assucar* (sugar). There was one Indian who had been christened Cavaignac by Rondon, or one of his companions, because he had a goatee, a very rare feature among Indians, who are usually beardless.

One day, when I was playing with a group of children, a little girl who had been struck by one of her playmates took refuge by my side and, with a very mysterious air, began to whisper something in my ear. As I did not understand and was obliged to ask her to repeat it several times, her enemy realized what was going on and, obviously very angry, also came over to confide what seemed to be a solemn secret. After some hesitation and questioning, the meaning of the incident became clear. Out of revenge, the first little girl had come to tell me the name of her enemy, and the latter, on becoming aware of this, had retaliated by confiding to me the other's name. From then on, it was very easy, although rather unscrupulous, to incite the children against each other and get to know all their names. After which, having created a certain atmosphere of complicity, I had little difficulty in getting them to tell me the names of the adults. When the latter understood what our confabulations were about, the children were scolded and no more information was forthcoming.[11]

This text shows in negative terms that since a society presumes, as its condition of possibility, a hierarchy and economy of power, institutions, and structures of parenthood, in other words, *differences*, the source of that power is classification, order, the taxonomy of individuals, in other words, already, the effacement of their individuality. Derrida refers to this as the "erasure of the proper name." Every social group exists as what it is only to the extent that it is able to use proper names as common nouns, inasmuch as a proper name is used, as the ambiguity of the term suggests, to "call" individuals but also at the same time to classify them. In this way the name becomes a label and loses its vocative value. Every society is therefore violent to the extent that it proceeds on the basis of the death of the proper, or what is one's "own." This obliteration is precisely what Derrida calls "writing in the broad sense," "arche-writing," or else "differance." Arche-writing is anterior to what actually occurs as the emergence of writing in the usual sense, or in the narrow sense. It is not something that happens to the original innocence of speech, it is neither the deadly double nor the exotic storehouse of speech. The possibility of obliterating properness or "ownness" inhabits speech itself. Because of that, communities that do not know writing in the usual sense (as technique for the notation of the spoken word) cannot for all that be said to be "without writing": "But above all, how can we deny the practice of writing in general to a society capable of obliterating the proper, that is to say, a violent society?"[12]

If writing is no longer understood in the narrow sense of linear and phonetic notation, it should be possible to say that all societies capable of producing, that is to say of obliterating, their proper names, and of bringing classificatory difference into play, practice writing in general. No reality or concept would therefore correspond to the expression "society without writing." This expression is dependent on ethnocentric oneirism, upon the vulgar, that is to say ethnocentric, misconception of writing.[13]

From the moment that the proper name is erased in a system, there is writing, there is a "subject" from the moment that this obliteration of the proper is produced, that is to say from the first appearing of the proper and from the first dawn of language. This proposition is universal in essence and can be produced *a priori*. How one passes from this *a priori* to the determination of empirical facts is a question that one cannot answer in general here. First because, by definition, there is no general answer to a question of this form.

It is therefore such a *fact* that we encounter here. It does not involve the structural effacement of what we believe to be our proper names; it does not involve the obliteration that, paradoxically, constitutes the originary legibility of the very thing it erases, but of a prohibition heavily superimposed, in certain societies, upon the use of the proper name: "They are not allowed . . . to use proper names," Lévi-Strauss observes [p. 270].

Before we consider this, let us note that this prohibition is necessarily (derivative) with regard to the constitutive erasure of the proper name in what I have called arche-writing, within, that is, the play of difference. It is because the proper names are already no longer proper names, because their production is their obliteration, because the erasure and the imposition of the letter are originary, because they do not supervene upon a proper inscription; it is because the proper name has never been, as the unique appellation reserved for the presence of a unique being, anything but the original myth of a transparent legibility present under the obliteration; it is because the proper name was never possible except through its functioning within a classification and therefore within a system of differences, within a writing retaining the traces of difference, that the interdict was possible, could come into play, and, when the time came . . . could be easily transgressed; transgressed, that is to say restored to the obliteration and the non-self-sameness [*non-propriété*] of the origin.[14]

If the primary innocence of speech, of the indigenous group or community, has always already been corrupted by the trace, it must be concluded that any originary voyage *delocalizes* from the outset any proximity to self. Starting out from the origin, there is transfer, transference, transport, that is to say, literally, metaphor.

There is no ground for objecting that "trace" is not the literal sense of writing. Writing, in the sense of "knowing how to write," as mastery of a technique, can hardly be the literal sense of what a pseudo-writing derived from an esthetic function (making a few dotted lines or zigzags on their gourds, drawing wavy, horizontal lines), is supposed to imitate. The literal sense of writing is always already metaphoric, for it always refers back to this same "aesthetic" value, or to a "rather poor gestural signification." As Derrida argues, writing is metaphor itself:

A writing that is sensible, finite, and so on, is designated as writing in the literal sense; it is thus thought on the side of culture, technique, and artifice; a human procedure, the ruse of a being accidentally incarnated or of a finite creature. Of course, this metaphor remains enigmatic and refers to a "literal" meaning of writing as the first metaphor. This "literal" meaning is yet unthought by the adherents of this discourse. It is not, therefore, a matter of inverting the literal meaning and the figurative meaning but of determining the "literal" meaning of writing as metaphoricity itself.[15]

Writing and Roadway

Contesting the *catastrophic* and *catastrophist* drift of writing vis-à-vis speech, and metaphoric sense vis-à-vis literal sense calls into question in a number of ways the traditional definition of the voyage. In the first place, it becomes impossible to separate point of departure from point of arrival, localization and abstraction, proper and foreign, with the trenchancy or critical knife of a hierarchical demarcation. In the second place, to speak of arche-writing or *differance*, that is to say once more, of originary metaphoricity, amounts to disturbing the very notion of the outside. To say that writing does not come out of speech means saying that there is no pure exteriority that would have produced that writing. Accident does not come from elsewhere, it only happens by not happening (manages only not to arrive). Thirdly, the immense question of the West's relation with its others comes to be posed and deconstructed once one takes into account a certain number of ethnocentric, logocentric, and phonocentric presuppositions.

For Derrida it is a matter of positing a voyage that would not proceed from assured limits between inside and outside. Thinking the absolute *arrivant* can only arise out of a new conception of what happens or *emerges*— the accident and the event—according to which catastrophe does not occur or *arrive*, that is to say does not breach any integrity or affect any innocence.

The roadway along which being, and the savage, are led outside of themselves, is an originary one:

Penetration in the case of the Nambikwara. The anthropologist's affection for those to whom he devoted one of his dissertations, *La vie familiale et sociale des Indiens Nambikwara* (1984). Penetration, therefore, into "the lost world" of the Nambikwara, "the little bands of nomads, who are among the most genuinely 'primitive' of the world's peoples" on "a territory the size of France," traversed by a *picada* (a crude trail whose "track" is "not easily distinguished from the bush"; one should meditate upon all of the following together: writing as the possibility of the road, of the rupture, of the *via rupta*, of the path that is broken, beaten, *fracta*, of the space of reversibility, and of repetition traced by the opening, the divergence from, and the violent spacing of nature, of the natural, savage, salvage, forest. The *silva* is savage, the *via rupta* is written, discerned, and inscribed violently as difference, as form is imposed on the *hylē*, in the forest, in wood as matter; it is difficult to imagine that access to the possibility of a road-map is not at the same time access to writing).[16]

[17]

5

Of Algeria

Ah, you want me to say things like "I was born in El Biar on the outskirts of Algiers in a petit bourgeois family of assimilated Jews but . . . " Is that really necessary? I can't do it. You will have to help me.[1]

First Traverse

. . . he runs, he flies so young and light futile subtle agile delivering to the world the very discourse of this impregnable inedible simulacrum, the theory of the parasite virus, of the inside/outside, of the impeccable *pharmakos*, terrorizing the others through the instability he carries everywhere, one book open in the other, one scar deep within the other, as though he were digging the pit of an *escarre* in the flesh . . .[2]

Who would have thought that one day the same Derrida who, as a child, was terrified at the idea of going any distance at all away from his house and his mother, would write such a self-portrait? Was he not destined to lead a sedentary life, this "scared child who up until puberty cried out 'Mummy I'm scared' every night until they let him sleep on a divan near his parents"?[3] It was only at the age of nineteen, in 1949, that Derrida left on his first "real" voyage, aboard the *Ville d'Alger*, heading for Marseilles and "metropolitan" France. He was on his way to Paris, to enroll for the final preparatory year for the *agrégation* exams [*khâgne*] at the Lycée Louis-le-Grand.

Rue Saint-Augustin, 1932.
(Jacques Derrida Archives)

Between the model called academic, grammatical, or literary, on the one hand, and spoken language, on the other, *the sea* was there: symbolically an infinite space for all the students of the French school in Algeria, a chasm, an abyss. I did not cross it, body and soul, or body without soul (but will I ever have crossed it, crossed it otherwise?), until, for the first time, sailing across on a boat, on the *Ville d'Alger*, at the age of nineteen. First journey, first crossing of my life, twenty hours of sea-sickness and vomiting—before a week of distress and a child's tears in the sinister boarding house of the "Baz'Grand" (in the *khâgne* of the Louis-le-Grand lycée, in a district I have practically never left since that time).[4]

Childhood and Fear

The child cries, therefore, when he has to leave home. Home, in the first place, means both the holiday home in El Biar, where he was born, and the primary family residence, rue Saint-Augustin in Algiers, where they lived until 1934.

The rue Saint-Augustin, in town, where I lived with my parents until I was 4 except in the summer, I remembered a few months ago, in the middle of my facial paralysis, I was driving in Paris near the Opéra and I discovered that other rue Saint-Augustin, homonym of the one in Algiers where my parents lived for 9 years after their marriage, my elder brother René was born there, Paul-Moïse, whom I replaced, was born and then died there before me, . . . I remembered this . . . a dark hallway, a grocer's down from the house. . . . [5]

Then it was back to El Biar, in a house the family moved into at 13, rue d'Aurelle-de-Paladines, with its "orchard, the intact PaRDeS,"[6] "on the edge of an Arab quarter and a Catholic cemetery, at the end of the Chemin du Repos."[7]
The child cries when he is lost:

I walked for more than two hours in the same neighborhood crying, a lost child. I have rather precise memories of this experience, I don't know if I ever told you about it, I was eight or nine, a fair in El Biar. I could no longer find my parents and blinded by tears I had been guided toward my father's car, up behind the church, by the creatures of the night, guardian spirits.[8]

But he also cries out of a sense that his native country is already lost to him. His resistance to leaving it and to traveling is perhaps a reaction to the prescience of an inevitable exile provoked by his double experience of war, of World War II and the Algerian war for independence:

I came to France at the age of nineteen. I had never left El Biar. The war of 1940 in Algeria, and thus the first underground rumblings of the Algerian war. As a child, I heard them coming in an animal fashion, with a feeling of the end of the world which was at the same time the most natural habitat, in any case the only one I had ever known. Even for a child who was unable to analyze things, it was clear that it would all end in fire and blood. No one could escape that violence and that fear.[9]

Dissociation of Identity

But what does he mean by "end[ing] in fire and blood"? What is Algeria? A French province, a country in Africa?

For we knew by way of an obscure but certain form of knowledge that Algeria was in no manner of speaking the province, nor Algiers the working-class district. Right from childhood, Algeria was, for us, also a country, and Algiers, a city within a country in a fuzzy sense of this word which coincides neither with the state, nor with the nation, nor with religion, nor even, dare I say, with an authentic community. And in this "country" of Algeria, besides, we were witnessing the reconstitution of the spectral simulacrum of a capital/province structure ("Algiers/the interior," "Algiers/Oran," "Algiers/Constantine," "Algiers-city/Algiers-suburbs," residential districts generally on hilltops/poor districts often further below).[10]

Very early on, Derrida had the feeling that his identity was divided: "at once a Maghrebian (which is not a citizenship) and a French citizen. One and the other at the same time. And better yet, at once one and the other *by birth*."[11] French, Maghrebian, and Jewish. The triple dissociation that dislocated the situation of his birth was itself subdivided in turn. The community that Derrida belonged to "will have been three times dissociated by what, a little hastily, we are calling interdicts. (1) First of all, it was cut off from both Arabic or Berber (more properly Maghrebian) language and culture. (2) It was also cut off from French, and even European language and culture, which, from its viewpoint, only constituted a distanced pole or metropole, heterogeneous to its history. (3) It was cut off, finally, or to begin with, from Jewish memory, and from the history and language that one must presume to be their own, but which, at a certain point, no longer was."[12]

"Where then *are we*? Where do we find ourselves?" the child asks, "With whom can we still *identify* in order to affirm our own identity and to tell ourselves our own history?"[13] In the same text, Derrida writes: "To be a Franco-

El Biar in the second decade of the twentieth century.
(Collection LL–Viollet)

Maghrebian, one 'like myself,' is not, not particularly, and particularly not, a surfeit or richness of identities, attributes, or names. In the first place, it would rather betray a *disorder of identity* [trouble d'identité]."[14]

Algerian without Arabic

A French Algerian was most often "someone to whom . . . access to any non-French language of Algeria (literary or dialectal Arabic, Berber, etc.) was *prohibited*."[15] High school students certainly had the "right" to study Arabic, but very few made a choice that was both devalued and downgrading with respect to the cultural norms imposed by metropolitan France.

We had the choice, the formal right, to learn or not learn Arabic or Berber. Or Hebrew. It was not illegal, or a crime. At the *lycée*, at least—and Arabic rather than Berber. I do not recall anyone ever learning Hebrew at the *lycée*. The in-

The Derrida-Safar family. "Souvenir of our outing to Fort de l'Eau on 20 August 1933." J.D. is the second child from the left, seated between his mother's legs. (Jacques Derrida Archives)

terdict worked therefore through other ways. More subtle, peaceful, silent, and liberal ways. It took other forms of revenge. In the manner of permitting and giving, for, in principle, everything was given, or at any rate permitted.[16]

Without having statistics at my disposal, I remember that the percentage of *lycée* students who chose Arabic was about zero. Those who, in extremely limited numbers, enrolled in it by a choice that at that time seemed unusual or even bizarre did not even form a homogeneous group. Among them, there were at times students of Algerian origin (the "natives," according to the official appellation), when in exceptional cases, they gained access to the *lycée*—but not all of them, at that time, turned toward Arabic as a linguistic discipline. Among those who chose Arabic, it seems to me that there were little French Algerians of non-urban origin, children of settlers, who came from the "interior." Following the counsel or desire of their parents, necessity being the law, they thought in advance of the need they would one day have of this language for technical and professional reasons: among other things, to make themselves heard, which means also listened to, and obeyed by their agricultural workers. All others, including myself, submitted passively to the interdict. It massively represented the cause, as well as the effect—well, the much sought-after effect—of the growing uselessness, the organized marginalization of those languages, Arabic and Berber. Their weakening [*exténuation*] was calculated by a colonial policy that pretended to treat Algeria as a group of three French departments.[17]

Arabic, an optional foreign language in Algeria![18]

Jewishness minus Jewishness

This young Jew's access to his Jewishness (language, culture, religion) was itself subject, in its own way, to a type of prohibition.

As for language in the strict sense, we could not even resort to some familiar substitute, to some idiom internal to the Jewish community, to any sort of language of refuge that, like Yiddish, would have ensured an element of intimacy, the protection of a "home-of-one's-own" [*un "chez-soi"*] against the language of official culture, back-up assistance for different socio-semiotic situations. "Ladino" was not spoken in the Algeria I knew, especially not in the big cities like Algiers, where the Jewish population happened to be concentrated.[19]

In the milieu where I lived, we used to say "the Catholics"; we called all the non-Jewish French people "Catholics," even if they were sometimes Protestants, or perhaps even Orthodox: "Catholic" meant anyone who was neither a Jew, Berber, nor an Arab.[20]

This incapacity, this handicapped memory, is the subject of my lament here. That is my grievance. For as I thought I perceived it during my adolescent years, when I was beginning to understand a little what was happening, this heritage was already ossified, even necrotized, into ritual comportment, whose meaning was no longer legible even to the majority of the Jews of Algeria. I used to think then that I was dealing with a Judaism of "external signs." But I could not rebel—and believe me, I was rebelling against what I took to be gesticulations, particularly on feast days in the synagogues—I could not lose my temper, except from what was already an insidious Christian contamination: the respectful belief in inwardness, the preference for intention, the heart, the mind, mistrust with respect to literalness or to an objective action given to the mechanicity of the body, in short, a denunciation, so conventional, of Pharisaism.

. . . I was not the only one to be affected by this Christian "contamination." Social and religious behavior, even Jewish rituals themselves were tainted by them, in their tangible objectivity. Our practices mimicked those of Christian churches, the rabbi would wear a black cassock, and the verger [*chemasch*] a Napoleonic cocked hat; the "bar mitzvah" was called "communion," and circumcision was named "baptism."[21]

Elie: my name—not inscribed, the only one, very abstract, that ever happened to me, that I learned, from outside, later, and that I have never felt, borne, the name I do not know, like a number . . . anonymously designating the hidden name, and in this sense, more than any other, it is the given name, which I received without receiving in the place where what is received must not be received, nor give any sign of recognition in exchange (the name, the gift), but as soon as I learned, very late, that it was my name, I put into it, very distractedly, on one side, in reserve, a certain nobility, a sign of election, I am he who is elected [celui qu'on élit], this joined to the story about the white taleth (to be told elsewhere) and some other signs of secret benediction.[22]

Before speech, among the Jews alone, there is circumcision, the sacred tongue will have slipped over me as though over a polished stone, perhaps, but I bury the deep things, I must have pretended to learn Hebrew, I lied to them about language and school, I pretended to learn Hebrew so as to read it without understanding it, like the words of my mother today, at one moment, in 1943, with a Rabbi from the rue d'Isly, just before the *bar-mitzvah*, which they also called "communion," at the moment when French Algeria in the person of its Governor-General, without the intervention of any Nazi, had expelled me from school and withdrawn my French citizenship . . . , so that thus expelled, I became the outside, try as they might to come close to me they'll never touch me again, they masculine or feminine, and I did my "communion" by fleeing the prison of all languages, the sacred one they tried to lock me up in without opening me to it, the secular they made clear would never be mine, but this ignorance remained the chance of my faith as of my hope, of my taste even for the "word," the taste for letters.[23]

One day I will write a long narrative for you, not a detail will be missing, not a candle light, not a flavor, not an orange, a long narrative about the Purim cakes in El-Biar, when I was ten years old and already understood nothing.[24]

French without Citizenship

This acculturation, product of colonialism, was at the same time masked and reinforced by the influence of France, most often called the "Metropole."

For the pupils of the French school in Algeria, whether they were of Algerian origin, "French Nationals," "French citizens of Algeria," or born in that environment of the Jewish people of Algeria who were at once or successively the one and the other ("indigenous Jews," as one used to say under the Occupation without occupation, indigenous Jews and nevertheless French during a certain period), for all these groups, French was a language supposed to be maternal, but one whose source, norms, rules, and law were situated elsewhere. . . . Elsewhere, that means in the Metropole. In the Capital-City-Mother-Fatherland. Sometimes, we would say "France," but mostly "the Metropole," at least in the official language, in the imposed rhetoric of speeches, newspapers, and school. As for my family, and almost always elsewhere, we used to say "France" among ourselves ("Those people can afford vacations in France"; "that person is going to study in France"; "he is going to take the waters in France, generally at Vichy"; "this teacher is from France"; "this cheese is from France").

The *metropole*, the Capital-City-Mother-Fatherland, the city of the mother tongue: that was a place which represented, without being it, a faraway country, near but far away, not alien, for that would be too simple, but strange, fantastic, and phantomlike [*fantomal*]. Deep down, I wonder whether one of my first and most imposing figures of spectrality, of spectrality itself, was not France; I mean everything that bore this name (assuming that a country and what bears the name of a country is ever anything else, even for the least suspect of patriots, perhaps for them especially).

A place of fantasy, therefore, at an ungraspable distance. As a model of good speech and good writing, it represented the language of the master.

(What's more, I do not think I have ever recognized any other sovereign in my life.) The master took the form, primarily and particularly, of the school-teacher. The teacher could thus represent, with dignity, the master in general, under the universal features of the good Republic. In an entirely different way than for a French child from France, the Metropole was Elsewhere, at once a strong fortress and an entirely other place. From the irreplaceable placement of this mythical "Overthere," it was necessary to attempt, in vain of course, to measure the infinite distance or the incommensurable proximity of the invisible but radiant hearth from which came to us paradigms of distinction, correctness, elegance, literary or oratory language. The language of the Metropole was the mother tongue; actually, the substitute for a mother tongue (is there ever anything else?) as the language of the other.[25]

In the middle of the war, just after the landing of the Allied forces in North Africa in November 1942, we witnessed the constitution of a sort of literary capital of France in exile in Algiers: a cultural effervescence, the presence of "famous" writers, the proliferation of journals and editorial initiatives. This also bestows a more theatrical visibility upon Algerian literature of—as they call it—French expression, whether one is dealing with writers of European origin (such as Camus and many others) or with writers of Algerian origin, who constitute a very different mutation. Several years later, in the still-sparkling wake of this strange moment of glory, I seemed to be harpooned by French philosophy and literature, the one and the other, the one or the other: wooden or metallic darts [flèches], a penetrating body of enviable, formidable, and inaccessible words even when they were entering me, sentences which it was necessary to appropriate, domesticate, coax [amadouer], that is to say, love by setting on fire, burn ("tinder" [amadou] is never far away), perhaps destroy, in all events mark, transform, prune, cut, forge, graft at the fire, let come in another way, in other words, to itself in itself.[26]

The country that the child loves so much is, however, the same country that rejects him. This is the sinister episode of the Occupation, during which Algerian Jews were stripped of their French nationality:

It is an experience that leaves nothing intact, an atmosphere that one goes on breathing forever. Jewish children expelled from school. The principal's office: You are going to go home, your parents will explain. Then the Allies landed, it was the period of the so-called two-headed government (de Gaulle–Giraud): racial laws maintained for almost six months, under a "free" French government. Friends who no longer knew you, insults, the Jewish high school with its expelled teachers and never a whisper of protest from their colleagues. I was enrolled there but I cut school for a year.[27]

They expelled from the Lycée de Ben Aknoun in 1942 a little black and very Arab Jew who understood nothing about it, to whom no one ever gave the slightest reason, neither his parents, nor his friends.[28]

Along with others, I lost and then gained back French citizenship. I lost it for years without having another. You see, not a single one. I did not ask for anything. I hardly knew, at the time, that it had been taken away from me, not, at any rate, in the legal and objective form of knowledge in which I am explaining it here (for, alas, I got to know it another way). And then, one day, one "fine day," without, once again, my asking for anything, and still too young to know it in a properly political way, I found the aforementioned citizenship again. The state, to which I never spoke, had given it back to me. The state, which was no longer Pétain's "French State," was recognizing me anew. That was, I think, in 1943; I had still never gone "to France"; I had never been there.

In essence, a citizenship does not sprout up just like that. It is not natural. But, as in a flash of a privileged revelation, the artifice and precariousness of citizenship appear better when it is inscribed in memory as a recent acquisition: for example, the French citizenship granted to the Jews of Algeria by the Crémieux decree in 1870. Or, better yet, in the traumatic memory of a "degradation," of a loss of citizenship: for example, the loss of French citizenship, less than a century later, for the same Jews of Algeria.

Such was, indeed, the case "under the Occupation," as we say.

Yes, "as we say," for it is actually a legend. Algeria was never occupied. I mean that if it was ever occupied, the German Occupant was never responsible for it. The withdrawal of French citizenship from the Jews of Algeria, with everything that followed, was the deed of the French alone. They decided that all by themselves, in their heads; they must have been dreaming about it all along; they implemented it all by themselves.

I was very young at the time, and I certainly did not understand very well—already, I did not understand very well—what citizenship and loss of citizenship *meant to say*. But I do not doubt that exclusion—for example, from the school reserved for young French citizens—could have a relationship to the disorder of identity of which I was speaking to you a moment ago. I do not doubt either that such "exclusions" come to leave their mark upon this belonging or non-belonging *of* language, this affiliation *to* language, this assignation to what is peacefully called a language.

But who exactly possesses it? And whom does it possess? Is language ever in possession, ever a possessing or possessed possession? Possessed or possessing in exclusive possession, like a piece of personal property? What of this being-at-home [*etre-chez-soi*] in language . . . ?

I have just emphasized that the ablation of citizenship lasted for two years, but it did not, *strictu sensu*, occur "under the Occupation." It was a Franco-French operation, one even ought to say an act of French Algeria in the absence of any German occupation. One never saw a German uniform in Algeria. No alibi, denial, or illusion is possible: it was impossible to transfer the responsibility of that exclusion upon an occupying alien.

We were hostages of the French, abidingly [*à demeure*]; something of it remains with me, no matter how much I travel.[29]

"My Mother Tongue," for Others

Something of this experience remains, namely being deprived of the mother tongue: "Never was I able to call French, this language I am speaking to you, 'my mother tongue.' These words do not come to my mouth; they do not come out of my mouth. I leave to others the words 'my mother tongue.'"[30]

The monolingual of whom I speak speaks a language of which he is *deprived*. The French language is not his. Because he is therefore deprived of *all* language, and no longer has any other recourse—neither Arabic, nor Berber, nor Hebrew, nor any languages his ancestors would have spoken—because this monolingual is in a way *aphasic* (perhaps he writes because he is an aphasic), he is thrown into absolute translation, a translation without a pole of reference, without an originary language, and without a source language [*langue de départ*]. For him, there are only target languages [*langues d'arrivée*], if you will, the remarkable experience being, however, that these languages just cannot manage to reach themselves [*n'arrivent pas à s'arriver*], because they no longer know where they are coming from, *from what starting point* they are speaking, and what the sense of their journey is. Languages without an itinerary and, above all, without any superhighway of goodness knows what information.

As if there were only arrivals [*arrivées*], and therefore only events without arrival.[31]

At the same time—this is in no way a contradiction—Derrida admits that he has never managed to "inhabit" any language other than French, and confesses his "old liaison with that foreigner, she who is called the French language."[32]

I feel lost outside the French language. The other languages which, more or less clumsily, I read, decode, or sometimes speak, are languages I shall never inhabit. Where "inhabiting" begins to mean something to me. And dwelling [*demeurer*].[33]

For it is *on the shores* of the French language, uniquely, and neither inside nor outside it, on the unplaceable line of its coast that, since forever, and abidingly [*à demeure*], I wonder if one can love, enjoy oneself [*jouir*], pray, die from pain, or just die, plain and simple, in another language or without telling anyone about it, without even speaking at all.[34]

Although he recognizes that he has "never ceased calling into question the motif of 'purity' in all its forms," Derrida confesses to a constitutive "purism" when it comes to his relation to French, a "purism" that very early on required him to repress his "accent" (an accent that has always "indicate[d] a hand-to-hand combat with language in general" and that says "more than just accentuation,")[35] to hold back his voice with a floodgate.

One entered French literature only by losing one's accent. I think I have not lost my accent; not everything in my "French Algerian" accent is lost. Its intonation is more apparent in certain "pragmatic" situations (anger or exclamation in familial or familiar surroundings, more often in private than in public, which is a quite reliable criterion for the experience of this strange and precarious distinction). But I would like to hope, I would very much prefer that no publication permit my "French Algerian" to appear. In the meantime, and until the contrary is proven, I do not believe that anyone can detect *by reading*, if I do not myself declare it, that I am a "French Algerian." I retain, no doubt, a sort of acquired reflex from the necessity of this vigilant transformation. I am not proud of it, I make no doctrine of it, but there it is: an accent—any French accent, but above all a strong southern accent—seems incompatible to me with the intellectual dignity of public speech. (Inadmissible, isn't it? Well, I admit it.) Incompatible, a fortiori, with the vocation of a poetic speech: for example, when I heard René Char read his sententious aphorisms with an accent that struck me as at once comical and obscene, as the betrayal of a truth, it ruined, in no small measure, an admiration of my youth.[36]

I say "floodgate," a floodgate of the verb and of the voice. I have spoken a great deal about this elsewhere, as if a clever maneuverer, a cybernetics expert of the tone, still kept the illusion of governing a mechanism and of watching over a gauge for the time it took to pass through the lock. I could have spoken of a dam for waters that are not very navigable. This dam is always threatening to give way. I was the first to be afraid of my own voice, as if it were not mine, and to contest it, even to detest it.[37]

This floodgate that holds back the voice, holding back catastrophe while maintaining it in its imminence (a catastrophe that Derrida identifies in *Monolingualism of the Other* with the possibility of madness), is the result of an anti-colonialism, of a violence between self and self, the violence whereby one self necessarily submits itself to the other. Such an originary ordeal is that of a pluralization of languages within one's tongue. One always speaks more than one tongue. At the same time, it is from the perspective of this multiplicity of languages that one can indeed *resist colonization*. That is something Derrida makes evident at the time of his first trip to sub-Saharan Africa, in Cotonou (Benin), in the course of a seminar that brought together various Francophone and Anglophone African philosophers.

I would like to define . . . what I think can be proposed for your examination and debated during the discussion as the principle of a politics of language. . . . We will no doubt have to avoid a linguisticism or logocentrism that would claim to solve all problems by voluntary decisions concerning *langage, langue,* or discourse. Nonetheless, the position that making language a transparent medium or extrinsic accident makes the linguistic secondary is also, paradoxically, a logocentrist position. I will state this principle summarily: *there is no choice*, and the choice that does not exist is not between one language and another, one group of languages and another (with everything a language entails). Every monolingualism and monologism restores mastery or magistrality. It is by *treating* each language *differently*, by *grafting* languages onto one another, by *playing* on the multiplicity of languages and on the multiplicity of codes within every linguistic corpus that we can struggle at once against *colonization* in general, against the colonizing principle in general (and you know that it exerts itself well beyond the zones said to be subjected to colonization), against the domination of language or domination by language. The underlying hypothesis of this statement is that the *unity* of language is always a vested and manipulated simulacrum. There are always languages in language and the structural rigor of the system of language is at once a positivist dogma of linguistics and a phenomenon that can be found nowhere.[38]

(No) More than One Shore

It is therefore "impossible to count languages."[39] And the identity of the young Jewish-French-Maghrebian emerges from more than one shore.

The Other Side of the Mediterranean

From another edge:

For the child from Provence or Brittany, there is surely an analogous phenomenon [attraction and repulsion vis-à-vis the "Metropole"]. Paris can always fill this role of a *metropolis* and occupy that place for a provincial, as the posh districts may do for a certain suburb. Paris is also the capital of Literature. But the other, in this case, no longer has the same transcendence of the *overthere*, the distancing of *being-elsewhere*, the inaccessible authority of a master who lives *overseas*. A sea is lacking there.[40]

And you can hear yourself saying, here it is, here's the Mediterranean, keep it, it's nothing but it has no price, keep it like a ring, a vulgar aquamarine, it's nothing, above all not anything precious, it's priceless if you will, we have swum in it, and it forgets us at every instant.[41]

It ebbs and flows like a wave that sweeps everything upon the shores that I know too well. It carries everything, that sea, and on two sides; it swells, sweeps along, and enriches itself with everything, carries away, brings back, deports and swells up again with what it has dragged away.[42]

The Other Shore of Judaism

"The other shore of Judaism" refers to what Derrida perceives of his own Judaism seen from his coastal standpoint, the shores of the Mediterranean: "The other shore of Judaism, on another coastline of the Mediterranean, in places that, in another way, are even more alien to me than Christian France."[43] This other shore is not that of a country; it is not Israel. It skirts the coast of a symbolic archipelago formed by a family of linguistic travelers: Kafka, Lévinas, Scholem, Benjamin, Celan, Arendt, Rosenweig. All of them exiles or foreigners who write in order to invent their citizenship, a citizenship that has, in a sense, been lost since or from its origin.

Some years after his loss, then recovery of French citizenship, Derrida ends up "identifying," if you wish, his Jewish memory, *recognizing* it in the figure of the Marrano ("a universal Marrano, if one may say, beyond what may nowadays be the finished forms of Marrano culture").[44] This is something he "confides" to himself, precisely during a voyage to Spain:

I confided it to myself the other day in Toledo, [that] is that if I am a sort of *marrano* of French Catholic culture, and I also have my Christian body, inherited from SA in a more or less twisted line, *condiebar eius sale* ["seasoned with His salt," St. Augustine], I am one of those *marranos* who no longer say they are Jews even in the secret of their own hearts, not so as to be authenticated *marranos* on both sides of the public frontier, but because they doubt everything, never go to confession or give up enlightenment, whatever the cost, ready to have themselves burned, almost, at the only moment they write under the monstrous law of an impossible face-to-face.[45]

To that which lives without having a name, we will give an added name: Marrano, for example. Playing with the relative arbitrariness of every nomination, we determine this added name [*surnom*], which a name always is, in memory of and according to the figure of the Marrano (of the crypto-judaic, and of the crypto-X in general). As we suggested just a while ago, it is said that the history of the Marranos has just come to an end with the declaration by the Spanish court [in 1992]. You can believe that if you want to.[46]

Let us figuratively call Marrano anyone who remains faithful to a secret that he has not chosen, in the very place where he lives, in the home of the inhabitant or of the occupant, in the home of the first or the second *arrivant*, in the very place where he stays without saying *no* but without identifying himself as belonging to. Well then, in the unchallenged night where the radical absence of any historical witness keeps him or her, in the dominant culture that by definition has control over the calendar, this secret keeps the Marrano even before the Marrano keeps it.[47]

Neither . . . Nor

Coming at the same time from so many sides of the sea, Derrida hesitates: European, African, Latin? None of those "through and through":

. . . the sort of uprooted African [that] I am, born in Algiers in an environment about which it will always be difficult to say whether it was colonizing or colonized.[48]

I am a foreigner . . . because I am neither an American—whether of the North or of the South—nor a European, Northern or Southern. I am not even really a Latin. I was born in Africa, and I guarantee you that I retain something of that heritage.[49]

I am European, I am no doubt a European intellectual, and I like to recall this, I like to recall this to myself, and why would I deny it? In the name of what?

But I am not, nor do I feel, European *in every part,* that is, European through and through. By which I mean, by which I wish to say, or *must* say: I do not want to be and must not be European through and through, European *in every part.* Being a part, belonging as "fully a part," should be incompatible with belonging "in every part." . . . I feel European *among other things.*[50]

[I am] someone who, as early as grade school in Algeria, must have tried to capitalize, and capitalize upon, the old age of Europe, while at the same time keeping a little of the indifferent and impassive youth of the other shore.[51]

[13]

6

The Time of the World:
Peril and Promise

"The World Is Going Badly"

The world is going badly, the picture is bleak, one could say almost black.[1]

This painful statement resonates in *Specters of Marx*, as if echoing Hamlet's words: "The time is out of joint."[2] The sentence speaks literally of an evil, a disease, a disorder or dysfunction. The course of the world is out of kilter, limping. Time is disjointed.

In "The time is out of joint," time is either *le temps* itself, the temporality of time, or else what temporality makes possible (time as *histoire*, the way things are at a certain time, the time that we are living, nowadays, the period), or else, consequently, the *monde*, the world as it turns, our world today, our today, currentness itself, current affairs: there where it's going okay (whither) and there where it's not going so well, where it is rotting or withering, there where it's working [*ça marche*] or not working well, there where it's going okay without running as it should nowadays [*par les temps qui courent*]. Time: it is *le temps*, but also *l'histoire*, and it is *le monde*, time, history, world.[3]

Is "our world today" still a world, or has it lost its name in favor of a "new world order"?

A time of the world, today, in these times, a new "world order" seeks to sta-

Being photographed in Moscow, 1994.
(Jacques Derrida Archives)

bilize a new, necessarily new disturbance [*dérèglement*] by installing an unprecedented form of hegemony. It is a matter, then, but as always, of a novel form of war.[4]

The Dominant Discourse

This new order is accompanied by a discourse that shapes the consensus uniting all so-called "democratic" and "industrialized" countries. To a great extent, it relies on the rejection of communism and "at least resembles a great 'conjuration' against Marxism, a 'conjurement' of Marxism."[5] In

Villanova, 26 September 1997

Leave tomorrow for New York, after a meeting on "Postmodernism and Religion" (two things that are foreign to me, as you know, but they are always situating me between the two, as you also know, one has to get used to it, resist, it all goes too quickly. My atheism develops in the churches, all the churches, can you understand that, can you?). Here it's an Augustinian university. Feel better here than in certain other philosophy departments, my friend Caputo has something to do with that. . . .

Since my last card, as I continue to read you, I have been wanting to add these three or four things: 1. If I do everything to cause what you name so well the "metaphysics of the voyage" to be diverted from its normal track, to cause it to derail, I tremble as I do so. A trembling that nothing escapes and that nothing precedes. It doesn't just rock the boat, it is my body for traveling, my own itinerant body. I tremble all the time. 2. What I think I called in one letter the unmovable *here itself* of some endless immobility indeed resembles the truth of your formulation "the origin doesn't travel." And yet, that is not so, mine does, all the same, I make it travel, unless it be that, "she" alone, who invites me to travel. 3. "Arriving without deriving," that's great, but you throw out that thread with a type of inflexible rigor that I don't feel I'm capable of. 4. Finally, especially, what "travels" the furthest in what I write, I'd almost call it my "homing pigeon [*pigeon voyageur*]," is precisely the fact *that* I write. I'll explain. My "thought" of the voyage (yes, yes!! you can laugh), my experience, I should say my apprehension of it, cannot be shared "with" me ("traveling with") in those places where, in one way or another, I speak of it, of travel, there where I deal with the theme of travel and other associated motifs (metaphor, movement, *fort/da*, the *go* and the *come*, the multiplicity of languages, cultures, politics, with names of cities and countries, etc.), nor in my traveling "in life" from one end of the world to the other, no, but *where I write*, and, in the "heart" of what I write, where everything moves forward, everything begins to shake in the imminence of an unforeseeable event whose arrival will stop the form of writing, *from the outside*, be its decisive caesura. Passively signed. From the outside, that is to say where not even a "performative" can produce the event, nor any "omnipotence of thinking" (cf. "Telepathy"). This event could take the form of an arrival at a destination, for example a reading in the hands of another, a "reception." With the danger of a loss, therefore, a bet that signs the writing. The two recent examples of this are "Circumfession" (I could never be sure with each sentence whether my mother's death, the real subject of the text, wouldn't happen in the very middle of the itinerary, between two words; but I knew in advance, it is

"Back from Moscow," Derrida shows that since the collapse of the logic of political blocs, we are today witnessing a veritable "globalization" [*mondialisation*] of the Western democratic model. He recalls with humor the title of the Beatles song ("Back in the USSR") with its "play on the homonymy or the metonymy between US and USSR," and its staging of "a twinning or a specularity, more and more interesting today, between US and USSR."[6] The full English title, "Back from Moscow, in the USSR," reinforces this. During a visit to Moscow that took place in the middle of the period of "perestroika," in February 1990, Derrida was present during the first tremors that signaled the destruction of the entity then still called the USSR.[7] Whereas one can celebrate this destruction from diverse perspectives, one should not for all that lose from view the fact that the now dominant discourse concerning democracy and free-market capitalism masks an imperialism of a new type. The capitalist good conscience that today reigns uniformly throughout the West authorizes rich countries to wage war against "recalcitrant" ones, to impose economic sanctions on them, or else, quite simply, to insist that they are "backward."

Today, the dominant discourse, in the West and for the travelers it dispatches in the Eastern countries, too often consists in asking oneself: Are these people going to succeed—at what cost, at what rhythm—in resembling us by entering the now more than ever assured space of democracies and their market (whether it is called capitalist, neocapitalist, or mixed or whether its autoregulation is named in another fashion)? Are they finally going to enter history? . . . This discourse (which I would like, of course, at all costs to escape, along with what it overturns: the whole historic difficulty of the task, the difficulty of thinking the history of this history) can be maintained on occasion by the citizens of the Eastern countries, as we know so well; it almost always implies that democracy is not *to come* but already given in the presence of its concept or its fact. It is my perplexity on this subject that paralyzes me at the moment of speaking of my trip to Moscow. This perplexity does not concern only the concept or the fact of democracy; it also concerns, *and as a result*, the identification of the process that is happening and is known under the name of *perestroika*. In the debates that I will try to report, certain of my Muscovite interlocutors and myself rather easily fell into agreement in saying that

Improvisation with Ornette Coleman at La Villette Jazz Festival, 1997.
(Christian Ducasse)

true, that in any case my mother would never read it), and "A Silkworm of One's Own": a certain verdict was controlling everything there, I couldn't do anything about it, it was deciding everything right inside the sentences but it also came from an absolute outside, from the other (the other can be lodged in my very body), beyond any possible reappropriation. The fact that in those texts I speak of so many crossings, and that the second is a sort of travel diary (Buenos Aires, Santiago, Valparaiso, São Paulo), remains contingent with respect to what suspends the course of the writing, the rhythm of the text itself, contingent to the arrival of the event, of a taking-place that no longer depends on me, that risks *losing me* and makes me hold my breath, in the breathlessness of an absolute voyage: the irreversible passage of what is going to have to come to pass while passing me by. So of course I can subsequently pretend to reappropriate this outside of writing, to repatriate it, but that is a ruse that I could not, in front of you, claim to be "inessential."[14] That could have been the case for *The Post Card*, I

[14] Upon reflection I think that the most recent example of this will have been my experience at the beginning of July, this year, at La Villette with Ornette Coleman. It was in Paris, but no voyage will ever have taken me so far away, myself and my body and my words, onto an unknown stage, without any possible rehearsal or repetition. Music always travels "further closer" than words. The brief "rehearsal" that preceded the improvisation, Coleman's or my own, in no way resembled what took place before the audience, in the conditions I've told you about. You know what happened subsequently, the event comes, as always, after the event. [Derrida's text, "*Joue—le prénom*," which Coleman "accompanied" by improvising, along with the interview that preceded the session ("La Langue de l'autre"), was published in *Les Inrockuptibles* 115, 20 August–2 September 1997. See also *Jazz Magazine* 473, 1997. (C.M.)]

no one yet knows what something like *perestroika* is, which is to say what it will have been.[8]

In reality, the function of the label "new world order" is to occlude "a new world disorder [that] is attempting to install its neo-capitalism and neo-liberalism."[9] Never before has economic and social violence been unleashed at such a level as that of the present time.

For it must be cried out, at a time when some have the audacity to neo-evangelize in the name of the ideal of a liberal democracy that has finally realized itself as the ideal of human history: never have violence, inequality, exclusion, famine, and thus economic oppression affected as many human beings in the history of the earth and of humanity. Instead of singing the advent of the ideal of liberal democracy and of the capitalist market in the euphoria of the end of history, instead of celebrating the "end of ideologies" and the end of the great emancipatory discourses, let us never neglect this obvious macroscopic fact, made up of innumerable singular sites of suffering: no degree of progress allows one to ignore that never before, in absolute figures, never have so many men, women, and children been subjugated, starved, or exterminated on the earth.[10]

The Plagues of the Earth

Derrida draws up a "black picture on a blackboard [*tableau noir*]" of this global situation, enumerating a list of "ten plagues": unemployment, the massive exclusion of the homeless, the relentless economic war, the inability to master the contradictions of this war (protectionism or opening of borders), the worsening of external debt, arms trafficking, the extension and dissemination of nuclear weapons, interethnic wars, the omnipotence of phantom-states (Mafia, narco-traffic), the inequality of states before the law (international law being largely dominated by particular nation-states).[11]

The New International

Political, legal, and ethnic *delocalization* has created a general spectrality which gives the traveler the feeling he is losing his grounding, as if the

am not sure. Since you quote the "Envoi" of 2 October 1977, twenty years ago already, good God ("For the day that there will be a reading of the Oxford card, the one and true . . . "), I can tell you that that reading has never taken place. As far as I know. Not entirely unexpected to my mind, at least if one really wants to read. Do I dare say that I delight in that every day? Contrary to the most commonly held certainty, I doubt that one writes to be read, really read, within a calculable delay, so that letters arrive at their destination. It is only from the perspective of this indecision that the *cause of the voyage* will return to that of *destinerrance*, and that there will arrive the history of the letter as literature . . .

world had ceased constituting a community. However, this violent deterritorialization also appears as a promise. There is thus a second sense that Derrida finds in the sentence "The time is out of joint," one which no longer amounts to finding something wrong, but which instead announces the possibility of discontinuing things as they are. As if a present other than that of catastrophic current events were refusing to keep step with the latter even while accompanying it as its shadow or detachable lining. For every present harbors within itself a reserve of the possible.

Even beyond the regulating idea in its classic form, the idea, if that is still what it is, of democracy to come, its "idea" as event of pledged injunction that orders one to summon the very thing that will never present itself in the form of full presence, is the opening of this gap between an infinite promise (always untenable at least for the reason that it calls for the infinite respect of the singularity *and* infinite alterity of the other as much as for the respect of the countable, calculable, subjectal equality between anonymous singularities) and the determined, necessary, but also necessarily inadequate forms of what has to be measured against this promise. To this extent, the effectivity or actuality of the democratic promise, like that of the communist promise, will always keep within it, and it must do so, this absolutely undetermined messianic hope at its heart, this eschatological relation to the to-come of an event *and* of a singularity, of an alterity that cannot be anticipated.[12]

The *dis*adjusted present allows one to trace a strange and improbable line of separation between what arrives or happens (the "plagues" of the "black picture") and non-arrival, the non-place as promise. This non-place would outline, like a negative, the territory of those who suffer, and exist as the paradoxical site of a "New International" comprising all those travelers who consent to experience a dis-jointed time and space, thus opening themselves to the resource of such a dis-adjustment. This would be the double possibility of catastrophe and surprise.

[The New International] is a link of affinity, suffering, and hope, a still discreet, almost secret link, as it was around 1848, but more and more visible, we have more than one sign of it. It is an untimely link, without status, without title, and without name, barely public even if it is not clandestine, without contract, "out of joint," without coordination, without party, without country, without national community (International before, across, and beyond any national determination), without co-citizenship, without common belonging to a class. The name New International is given here to what calls to the friendship of an alliance without institution among those who, even if they no longer believe or never believed in the socialist-Marxist International, in the dictatorship of the proletariat, in the messiano-eschatological role of the universal union of the proletarians of all lands, continue to be inspired by at least one of the spirits of Marx or Marxism (they now know that there is *more than one*) and in order to ally themselves, in a new, concrete, and real way, even if this alliance no longer takes the form of a party or of a workers' international, but rather a kind of counter-conjuration, in the (theoretical and practical) critique of the state of international law, the concepts of State and nation, and so forth: in order to renew this critique, and especially to radicalize it.[13]

What remains to be questioned in this context is the articulation between place and non-place that organizes every voyage.

[11]

Poets' Alley, Central Park, New York, September 1998.
(Jacques Derrida Archives)

New York, 2 October 1997

Not my *Immémoriaux* but . . . when I am a hundred years old, I'll publish the Memoirs of my New York memories. I'll exhibit their *stays* (do you like this word?).[15] The "thing" doesn't resemble anything: a more vertiginous set of props than all the towers in the world, those of New York in particular, a theatre of memory suspended over the void, virtual, unconstructible, undeconstructible therefore, *not* even by me, who remains incapable of making one *step* follow the last. I begin with the arrivals, always in September. After the first trip by boat, in 1956, I now land every year on a Saturday afternoon at JFK. The sweetness of this eternal return is like a blessed ecstasy for my soul, my effusion soothed, the first Sunday morning in Central Park. Then, almost out loud I speak to all the poets in Poets' Alley, cousins of my friends the birds of Laguna Beach. Not to be missed and something I wait all year for, this moment has to retain first of all the traits of a return, already. Since I don't like to call that a pilgrimage, it is as if, visiting my memory, each time for a first and the last time, I have been loving along this timeless alley in order to salute it—from a *contre-allée*. Salute it by dreaming of saving it: Hi! *Salut les poètes!* But like a lover accompanying me, the *contre-allée* doesn't come after the alley, it doesn't skirt it from afar or from the outside. The *contre-allée* of my memory traces the outline of its edges within the alley itself. Draw: it is the shape of my heart.

[15] [Or "struts (*étais*)," thus also my "I-was-heres," and, by extension, my "summers (*étés*)." (D.W.)]

Another moment of autumnal euphoria, often the day before I leave: a promenade in Brooklyn Heights. In the interval, I retrace all my migrations, from Battery Park to Columbia, one end of Manhattan to the other. A city I venerate—that's the word—and know better, especially downtown (Gramercy Park, Union Square, Washington Square, Soho, South Street Seaport), I mean that I know it differently well than Paris, at whose altar I nevertheless worship unconditionally. I cry to think that I will die without having celebrated and kissed her every stone to give her thanks. There is not the smallest lane in Paris that doesn't say to me, literally, I hear myself whispering with each step, "I will survive you." And I love her lane [*ruelle*], like everything I love, on the basis of this melancholic declaration, or, if you prefer the mask, this triumphant, gracious, and merciless avowal. *Rue* Montague, in Brooklyn Heights, *elle* for example, she tells me the same thing in another language. You see, Catherine, I only become "sentimental" and can only reconcile myself to that word, all the way to its suspect mawkishness, for the time of a voyage (read "journey").

To continue: from travel to the letter as literature. Is it literature that we are writing in this book, along roads we will never have traveled with one another? (That is what they are asking us.) If I, as sole available witness, were now to underline the fact that what you quote, at least from the postcards of 25 September 1977 ("I'm destroying my own life," etc.) and 10 June 1977 ("I burned everything, slowly, at the side of a road"), *really happened* to me, Catherine, who would be obliged to believe me? And if that testimony remained a literary fiction? I swear to you that it's true, however, I swear, you believe me, don't you . . .

7

The Greek Delay

The text "Demeure, Athènes (Nous nous devons à la mort)" was written to accompany a series of photographs and is entirely devoted to analysis of the delay effect, to a type of inopportunity or contretemps, the non-coincidence of self with self, or of self with the other. The analysis is all the more striking because its context—a trip to Greece—itself bears witness to an astonishing delay, to the fact that Derrida went to Greece for the first time late in life. Derrida's "Greek miracle" is perhaps due to the way in which a delay mechanism, similar to a camera's shutter delay, revealed to him the Athens, Mykonos, Ephesus, or Patmos sun as if after the event.

CLICHÉ IX

That day I was coming back to Athens from Brauron with friends. It was about midday and we were going to take a swim after paying our respects to the procession of young women on their way to the Altar of Artemis. I had come back to Athens the day before, but that time from Cape Sounion, where we had also been to swim, and it was then that I had remembered Byron's other signature, the other petroglyph that marks his having been there, at Lerici near Porto Venere. And I also remembered the time Socrates took to die after the verdict that condemned him (as we know, the name Sounion cannot be separated from that event). This was my third sojourn in Greece. Hardly "so-

Monastery of Kaisariani, Mt. Hymettus, 1996.
(Jacques Derrida Archives)

journs," alas, rather visits, multiple, brief, and late, so late. Why so late? Why had I waited so long before coming to Greece, so late in life?

But from now on I love a delay as something that gives me the most to think about, more than the present instant, more than the future or eternity, a delay *before* time itself. To think the *at-present* of the now (present, past, or future), to rethink instantaneity on the basis of delay rather than the inverse. Delay [*retard*] is not the right word in fact, a delay doesn't really exist. It will never be a subject or an object. What I would rather cultivate is "holding off abidingly" [*retardement à demeure*], the chronodissymmetrical process of the moratorium, the delay that carves out its calculation in the incalculable.

CLICHÉ X

I have always associated holding-off with the experience of the photographic. Not with photography but with the photographic experience of an "image-hunter." Before the instant of the shot which, almost for eternity, freezes what is naively called an image, there would be this *retardement*. And thoughtful reflection concerning it has always been woven, and veiled, in me along the lines of two Athenian threads: *photography* (the writing of light, could there be a word that was more Greek?) and the enigmatic thought of the αἰών (the full interval of a duration, an incessant space of time, also sometimes called eternity). The *intriguing* possibility of a holding-off is woven in advance along these threads. Incessantly.

Incessantly, what a word.

Whence my passion for delay, and for the delay within delay (periphrasis for the advance, one would need time to make that turn), the reason why I love to distraction all the figures of this moratorium *en abyme* that is organized within photographic invention—with the sole aim, almost, of illustrating it or bringing it to light—by the technique called trigger-delay, delayed action, or automatic delay. It is at once banal in its possibility and yet singularly unprecedented as an operating relation, and today it gives rise to machinery that is more sophisticated than so many imaginable sophistries. Everything will be held in place in the instant, incessantly, presently or at present, so that later, in a few more instants, sometimes a long time, very long after, another present to come will be surprised by the click of the shutter and fixed forever, reproducible, archivable, saved, or lost for this present time. We don't yet know what the image will give, but the interval must be objectively *calculable*, there must be a technique, and that is perhaps the origin or essence of technique.[1]

Derrida sketches out a chronology of trips to Greece: "There was Athens three times, and Mykonos, and Rhodes—which is where I think I swam for the first time—then Ephesus, Patmos, with Georges and Myrto, then the Kaisariani monastery with Catherine Velissaris and Demosthene Agrafiotis."[2] And his writing grasps in a single movement the delay that constitutes photography and his own experience as a traveler:

When in fact does a *shot* [prise de vue] take place? And then, where? Given the shutter delay, the time lag, can it be said that the photograph is taken when the photographer sets the thing in his sights, when he sets the aperture and releases the shutter, or when the click signals the capturing of the impression, or even later still, at the time of development?[3]

We were coming back from Brauron, where we had seen the Saint George Chapel, the little craters for the ritual of naked maidens running or again a procession of virgins toward the altar of Artemis . . . and we were going to

"Photographer on the Acropolis."
(Jean-François Bonhomme)

take a swim. I had to catch a plane but delays were on the agenda and we laughed about that, my friends know that I love delay, the smallest delay kills me, especially when it is time to leave for the station or the airport, in truth at the moment of arriving, of arriving to or managing to leave.[4]

One photograph in particular holds Derrida's attention. It is entitled "Photographer on the Acropolis" and shows a man sleeping or musing in front of his camera, which is set on a tripod. Derrida compares it to the tripod that the Pythia sat on at Delphi and sees the scene as a scene of mourning, the "advance mourning" that is the unanticipatable anticipation of death.

Delay appears thus as the ridiculous reprieve separating the traveler from his own end.

CLICHÉ XI

Let us come back to the "Photographer on the Acropolis," whom you can see meditating or sleeping with his head down, in the center of this book. Hasn't he installed an archaic figure of the delayed action mechanism there in front of him, in front of you? Hasn't he decided, upon reflection, to photograph photography and its photographer, in order to show everything there is to see in photography, and deliver everything there is in this book? He seems to have arranged the animal-machine on a Delphic tripod. Eyes closed, look, he is protecting them from the light with sunglasses, he has even sought out the shade from his sun umbrella, unless it be a reflector . . .

CLICHÉ XIII

Imagine him, through the images he has "taken." By skirting the abyss of those images, as I was saying before, I retrace the steps of the photographer. *In advance*, he brings mourning for Athens, mourning for a city that is owed to death, and two or three times rather than a single one, according to different temporalities: mourning for an ancient, archeological, or mythological Athens, no doubt, mourning for an Athens that has disappeared and that shows the body of its ruins; but also mourning for an Athens that he knows— because he has photographed it, in the present of the instants of his shots— will disappear tomorrow, is already condemned to expire, and whose witnesses (the Adrianou Street Market, Café Neon on Omonia Square, the Street Piano) have in fact disappeared since he "took the shot"; and finally, third anticipated mourning, he knows that other photographs have captured spectacles that are still visible, today, presently, at the moment the book appears (Athinas Market, Meat Market, Fish Market), but which will have to be, "ought" to be, destroyed tomorrow. A question of debt or of necessity, of economy, of the "market," the landscape of these streets, cafés, markets, musical instruments having to die, *owed* to death. It is the law. They are threatened with or promised to death. Three deaths, three instances, three temporalities of death in sight of or in the business of photography . . . , three "presences" of disappearance, three phenomena of the "disappeared" being: the first *before* the shot is taken, the second *from the perspective of* [depuis] the shot, and the last later still, tomorrow, but it is imminent, *after* the appearance of the print. But if the imminence of what is thus owed to death suspends the moment it falls due, as does the *epoch* of all photography, at the same time it signs its verdict. It confirms it and seals it with an ineluctable authority: it will have to die, it is assigned to residence and the date is set [*la mise en demeure est en marche*], the countdown has begun, there is simply a delay, time to photograph, but no one dreams of escaping death, and nothing will be saved. I think of Socrates' death, of the *Phaedo* and *Crito*. Of the incredible reprieve that holds off the fatal day so many days after the judgment. They were waiting for sails to appear, for them to appear in the distance, to come into the light, at a precise, unique, and inevitable instant, as fatal as the click of a shutter.[5]

[15]

8

Cities

The City of Asylum

Walking through cities one finds that the city is indeed an open, non-totalizable set of idioms, singularities, styles: a place to welcome the other within oneself, a place open to what is coming, the very coming of what is to come, open to imminence.

What makes possible the living community of the generations who live in and construct the city, who are permanently exposed to the stress of even projecting a city to be de- or re-constructed, is the paradoxical renunciation of the absolute tower, of the total city which reaches the sky: it is the acceptance of what a logician would perhaps call the *axiom of incompleteness*. A city is a set which must remain indefinitely and structurally non-saturable, open to its own transformation, to the augmentations which alter and displace as little as possible the memory of its patrimony. A city must remain open to what it knows about what it doesn't yet know about what it will be. It is necessary to inscribe, and to thematize, the respect for this *non-knowledge* in architectural and urbanistic science or know-how. Otherwise, what would one do other than apply programs, totalize, saturate, suture, asphyxiate?[1]

The permanent de/re-construction that assures the survival of a city must

"The question 'What is a city?'" ("Generations of a City"). Boston.
(Eric Jacolliot)

inscribe this event within it, at the outside causing it, as a whole, to appear
as event.

If what we still call today the city consists less than ever of a petroglyphic
erection, but just as much one in glass, windows, telecommunications fibers,
and cables, electrical and acoustical networks—there is an urgency to thinking the city by privileging in it the elementary (but renewed) media of speech,
writing, and music.[2]

This is again the mechanism of the sluice and the jetty, this time structur-
ing the city: regulation and distribution of the flow of singularities, invention of a being-together based on an originary uprooting or exile. That is
why every city should as a matter of principle become a "city of asylum,"
and elaborate an "ethics of hospitality":

Hospitality is culture itself and not simply one ethic amongst others. Insofar
as it has to do with the *ethos*, that is, the residence, one's at-home, the famil-

iar place of dwelling, as much as the manner of being there, the manner in which we relate to ourselves and to others, to others as our own or as foreigners, *ethics is hospitality*; ethics is entirely coextensive with the experience of hospitality, whichever way one expands or limits that.[3]

Cities of asylum, created as a network by the International Parliament of Writers, on which Derrida serves as a Vice-President, are cities that have agreed to welcome and protect intellectuals persecuted in their home countries. This presumes a city's autonomy vis-à-vis the state and implies a rethinking of the role of the capital.

The question "What is a city?" and "What is a capital?" takes on today an all the more melancholic or eschatological appearance when, I believe (and this would be the implicit hypothesis which orients these modest proposals), the city, the metropolis, the *polis*, the town are already no longer the steadfast and ultimate unities, topological unities of habitat, of action, of communication, of strategy, of commerce—in a word, of sociality and of human politics, of a *politics* which will have to change its name as soon as the city as *polis* or *acropolis* no longer provides the measure of the *res publica*. But the fact that this "*post-city age*" has begun does not mean that we should forget the city.[4]

Whether it be the foreigner in general, the immigrant, the exiled, the refugee, the deported, the stateless or the displaced person (all of which categories need to be prudently differentiated), we would ask these new cities of asylum to reorient the politics of the state. We would ask them to transform and refound the modalities of membership by which the city [*cité*] belongs to the state, as in a developing Europe or in international juridical structures still dominated by the inviolable rule of state sovereignty—an intangible rule, or one at least supposed such, which is becoming increasingly precarious and problematic nonetheless. This neither can nor should still be the ultimate horizon for cities of asylum. Is this possible?[5]

What we have been calling the city of asylum, it seems to me, bridges several traditions or several moments in Western, European, or para-European traditions. We shall recognize in the Hebraic tradition, on the one hand, those cities which would welcome and protect those who sought refuge there when pursued by a blind or avenging justice, from what the texts of that time call 'bloody vengeance', for a crime of which they were innocent (or otherwise had committed accidentally). . . . In the medieval tradition, on the other hand, one can identify a certain sovereignty of the city: the city itself could determine the laws of hospitality, the articles of predetermined law, both plural and restrictive, with which they meant to condition *the* Great Law of Hospitality—an unconditional Law, both singular and universal, which ordered that the gates be open to each and every one, male and female, to every other, to all who might come [*tout arrivant*], without question or without their even having to identify who they are or whence they come. . . . Finally, at this same juncture, we could identify the cosmopolitical tradition common to a certain Greek Stoicism and a Pauline Christianity, whose inheritors were the figures of the Enlightenment, and to which Kant will doubtless have given the most rigorous philosophical formulation in his famous *Definitive Article in View of Perpetual Peace*: 'The law of cosmopolitanism must be restricted to the conditions of universal hospitality'.[6]

Strasbourg, "This Generous Border City"

This eminently European city, the capital city of Europe, and the first of our cities of asylum.[7]

A city which, while it does not, as it once very symbolically did, lie outside of France, is nevertheless not just any French city. This frontier city is a place of passage and of translation, a buffer zone, a privileged site for encounter or competition between two immense linguistic territories, two also among the most densely populated worlds of philosophical discourse.[8]

Paris as Capital

Regarding Paris, Valéry used to say that it thinks us more than we think it, even before we form the project of thinking it.[9]

Prague, De/Re-constructed City

There is a city. We are there. We inhabit it, we pass through it. Today, still, by law, it is a capital. It bears a proper name which the whole world recognizes and about which no legal challenge has arisen. It is *Praha*, Prague for a French speaker. One can raise legal questions, one could one day contest its identity as a political capital whether national or international (for example Czecho-slovakian), or cultural (for example European or Central European). But no one would be able to raise the slightest admissible challenge to the fact that it is a question of a city and that it does bear the name of Prague. This city is like a juridical person or like a character in a novel, the *persona* of a theatrical, dramatic, tragic, comic fiction, together with the fact that *persona* can signify also the mask behind which the identity of the actor or of the personal subject can remain secret as on a day of masquerade, of festival or campaign [*opération*], indeed, of revolutionary opera. What has been the identifiable, self-identical subject persisting throughout the discontinuous history which has run through the epochs of Gothic and Baroque architecture, the destruction of the ghetto, the institution of Czechoslovakia, the German and then the Soviet protectorate, the Prague Spring, the normalization and finally the last revolution which is now underway? Is it the same city which responds to this name? Is it to the same city that we are responding? How does one respond to a city? How is one to *answer* for, assume responsibility for, a city?[10]

In a passage where Prague speaks for itself, the city whose name means "threshold" says:

I am one, but I am only the threshold of myself, guard me, protect me, save me, save therefore the order which I give you, heed my law, it is one, but for this construct me, thus de- and re-construct me, you are at the threshold, expand me, transform me, multiply me, don't leave me intact, take the risk of deconstructing me. If you leave me intact, and one, you will lose me. It is necessary both to protect me and break and enter me, both to safeguard me *and* to transfigure me, to transform me precisely in order to save me: it is necessary both to love me *and* to violate me—but in a certain manner and not in another. It is necessary to affirm me as I affirm myself, and, in order for this, to invent the impossible, which consists in respecting my past body, in telling my age, but also, and out of respect, in giving me enough life so as not to confuse me with a conservatory of archives, a library of lithographic legends, a museum, a temple, a tower, a centre of administrative or political decisions,

"L.A. is not anywhere, but it is a singular organization of the experience of 'anywhere'" ("Fax-itexture"). (Eric Jacolliot)

a parliamentary enclosure, a tourist hotel, a chamber of commerce, an investment centre, a hub of railway or information connections, a computerized stock exchange, or even a habitable, laborious, and productive hive. I include all these within me, in my great, moving body, but you must never reduce me to this, I am the threshold of something else again: I have never been, and a city will never have been, simply that.[11]

Los Angeles and the "Post-Political Age"

L.A. is not anywhere, but it is a singular organization of the experience of "anywhere." What would also merit some reflection on our part, in this place, is first the fact that it is not a question of just any city in the world but of this municipal space, that of Los Angeles, for which the name of a city, *polis*, or even urban structure probably no longer fits to the same degree as for many cities in the world. It is a remarkable example of decentralization in a pre-capitalist, capitalist, and neo-capitalist human agglomeration (I want at all

In Los Angeles with Sam Weber, 1995.
(Jacques Derrida Archives)

costs to avoid the expression post- or late-capitalism). L.A. is an experimental place for numerous so-called modern or postmodern architectural investigations. Some of you here can testify better than others that they had more than a little to do with its richness and visibility in this respect. In this sense, and this is why I privileged this example so far from and so close to Japan, L.A. is not anywhere in the life of the majority of you. Nor in mine. And L.A. belongs perhaps already, without belonging completely, to what one could call the "post-city age," which perhaps also announces a "post-*polis*" and therefore a "post-political age," which would not necessarily be an apolitical or depoliticized age (therein lies the difficulty and the concern that orient these remarks). Los Angeles is therefore not *anywhere,* but it is also an unclassifiable and, at the same time, exemplary kind of anywhere. I do not have time in this introduction, but a useful exercise would be to test with this example the remarkable taxonomy that Asada and Isozaki proposed to order *architectural space* (1. sedentary, 2. nomad, 3. nomad-immobile), architecture in urban space (1. real—with the mediation of *genius loci* or of *fen sui*; 2. unreal; 3. simulated), and architecture in universal space (hermetic or cryptic space and postal or telegraphic, telephonic, televisual space), that is to say, also telefaxual. One will see that Los Angeles is, certainly, a mix that *participates* in all of

these opposed models (of Venice, which it mimes, includes, and also reduces; of Tokyo and Disneyland, taking up two of the examples illustrating
this taxonomy); but Los Angeles also corresponds, and precisely in the polit-
ical-social violence of what is called a "rebuilding," to a third term not reducible to any of the types or modes of the taxonomy. It excludes therefore
that in which it seems to participate. (I note in passing that this logic, that
consists in being at the same time a mixture that participates in two opposing
extremes and a third irreducible term, is also the paradox in the Platonic presentation of the Khōra).[12]

Geneva and the Becoming-Postal of the Museum

Did you know that the biggest postal museum is to be found here in Geneva?
As soon as I can walk I will get myself there (I am continuing my investigations, more or less continuously). In the "modern" period of postal becoming
(in my language I intend by that the period that follows the epoch of "impe-
rial" territory and of politico-military investment—Persian or Roman empires,
Cyrus and Caesar—then the epoch that I really would like to name the "university" period, because in the 13th century in France, during the long
process of remonopolization, of the renationalization of a dispersed network,
the University of Paris had been granted a privilege, I'll tell you about it, in
the circulation of the mail. Louis XI puts an end to it, little by little reproduces
centralization—of the Roman type, with his own censorship and his "black
cabinet"—and the process, fatal to the University's privilege, winds up, in our
day, with the monopolistic regime, in 1681 I believe), yes, in the "modern"
period the country of the Reformation played a rather important role, it seems
to me, in postal reform—and I believe the fact is significant. The Universal
Postal Union was born in Berne (1874–78), and is now an institution under
the jurisdiction of the U.N. No, I don't have any big hypothesis about the
conjoint development of capitalism, Protestantism, and postal rationalism,
but all the same, things are necessarily linked. The post is an instance of the
banking system. Don't forget that in the great reformation of the "modern" period another great country of the Reformation played a spectacular role: in

1837 Rowland Hill publishes his book, *Post-Office Reform: Its Importance and Practicability*. He is an educator; and a reformer of the fiscal system. What was he proposing? but the stamp, my love, what would we have done without it? The adhesive stamp, that is, the uniformization of payment, the general equivalent of the tax, and above all the bill before the letter, payment in *advance* (*the uniform rate and a system of prepayment*, which were adopted in 1840 after great popular agitation, the famous battle of the pp, "*popular agitation for the 'penny post'*"). And under the proviso of *further investigations*, I believe that the post card comes to us from there too, very recently (from Australia, 1869, to England, 1870, but the private *picture post card* was authorized only in 1894).[13]

Bordeaux and the Becoming-Museum of the Postal

There is a center in France which assembles all lost letters, all the letters sent P.R. that are not picked up by their addressee after a certain date (the time limit is shorter than you would think), the letters whose addressees and senders cannot be found. I don't know how long they keep them, before destroying them I suppose. It is in Bordeaux, I would very much like to know why. A very, very long time ago, I had to deal with this machinery. On a trip, I had sent to myself, Poste Restante, a packet of letters that I did not want to keep on myself. I thought that I had a very wide interval at my disposal for picking them up, after my return. Mistake: when I presented myself at the post office, they could not be found. Personnel confused: they had doubtless been sent to Bordeaux (since this time I hadn't put my address on the back; which was precisely what I wanted to avoid in this case). And in Bordeaux, it is always difficult to refind anything. In any event, everything is opened and read in order to divine, with the best intentions in the world, the name of a sender or of an addressee. When I came back into possession of these letters two months later, they had in fact been opened. Once more become the post cards that at bottom they already were. I have destroyed them since, and quite sincerely I no longer recall which letters were in question.[14]

Unknown Antwerp

The train is approaching Antwerp. We are barely three-quarters of an hour from Brussels, and I had intended, even before the lecture, to come here alone for several hours. Want cities unknown to you, to which you could have accompanied me, and I no longer know whether I am taking them in order to give them to you or to take them away from you. I had told you that I would come to Antwerp, this morning, and why, in this city about which I know only the name and a few clichés. If you were crazy you would have come to wait for me like someone hallucinating, I would have run toward you on the platform, right next to the track, I would have done everything so as not to fall.[15]

Amsterdam and the Floodgate of Its Tympan

Tympanum, Dionysianism, labyrinth, Ariadne's thread. We are now traveling through (upright, walking, dancing), included and enveloped within it, never to emerge, the form of an ear constructed around a barrier, going round its inner walls, a city, therefore (labyrinth, semicircular canals—warning: the spiral walkways do not hold) circling around like a stairway winding around a lock, a dike (dam) stretched out toward the sea; closed in on itself and open to the sea's path. Full and empty of its water, the anamnesis of the concha resonates alone on a beach. How could a breach be produced, between the earth and sea?[16]

Athens and Photography: A Mourned-for Survival

CLICHÉ II

Who is this, death? The question can be asked for each instance of this Athenian photographic crossing, and not only in the cemeteries, before the mounds or rows of tombstones, funerary steles, columns and crosses, archeological sites, decapitated statues, ruined temples, chapels, antique stores in the flea market, the displays of dead animals, meat or fish, along the street of a market. For the one who took the time to take these images of Athens over a period of about fifteen years did not simply give himself over to producing a photographic *statement* [relevé] of certain sites that *already* constituted hypomnestic ruins, like so many monumental signs of death (Acropolis, Agora, Kerameikos, Tower of the Winds, Theater of Dionysos). He also saw, with the passage of time, the *disappearance* of places he photographed when they were, as it were, "living," but which have since "disappeared," like the sort of flea market on Adrianou Street, for example, or Café Neon on Omonia Square, most of the player pianos, etc. This world, which was the Athens of yesterday, and which represented already a certain modernity of that city, the Athens photographed one day like any other day, suddenly that Athens is no longer Athens. Its soul might be even less present, if that can be said, than the archeological vestiges of ancient Athens. The ruin of those vestiges, their sole speaking archive, of this market, this café, this piano, the best memory of that culture resides in these photographs. One has therefore to meditate upon such an invasion of photography within the history of the city. It is an absolute transformation, but one that was prepared in the most distant past. . . . This book bears the signature of one who keeps a vigil, involved in more than one mourning, a doubly surviving witness, a lover gently infatuated with a city that has died several times, at several times, a city busy keeping watch over its *contretemps*, but living. A living Athens is here seen guarding, regarding, and reflecting its deaths.[17]

"The New York Thread"

Day after tomorrow, New York, appointments on arrival—at lunch time (at MoMA) and the lecture at night at Columbia. I'll call you from there, from the station one is not obliged to telephone *"collect"* (this calculation is completely ridiculous in our case, as if one could know who pays for the communication, and who decides it).[18]

6 October 1978.

I am writing you in a taxi. I avoid the subway, here too, precisely because I like it. And because I get lost in the *correspondances*, although the system is much simpler than in Paris. It's like an express fact. Last night, after the lecture, I crossed the entire city in a taxi, all the way to Washington Square, this was after the reception (it was already very late, it was nice, I was drunk, I loved, I went home almost immediately after).

Tomorrow, return to Yale, day after tomorrow excursion in Hillis's sailboat.[19]

Last week in the East. Thursday, New York again, this time I'll be at the Hotel Barbizon. Departure for Cornell the next morning very early.

from the very first *envoi*: no gift, gift step [*pas de don*], without absolute forgetting (which also absolves you of the gift, *don*, and of the dose), forgetting of what you give, to whom, why and how, of what you remember about it or hope. A gift, if there is one, does not destine itself.[20]

. . . *the desire to name New York, where 21 years ago, on notebooks lost in Algeria in '62 unless they're hidden here, I had begun again, at the Hotel Martinique, to write "for myself"—follow the New York thread, from trip to trip, up to this one, the Kippours of N.Y., the cut with Kippour, the noncircumcision of the sons—up to that year when, coming out of a restaurant near MOMA I enter a "reformed" synagogue . . . circumcision remains the threat of what is making me write here.*[21]

"Am I in Jerusalem?"

The war for the "appropriation of Jerusalem" is today the world war. It is happening everywhere, it is the world, it is today the singular figure of its being "out of joint."[22]

According to 2 Chronicles, chapters 3 and 8, the place where this occurs, where the sacrifice of Abraham or of Isaac (and it is the sacrifice of both of them, it is the gift of death one makes to the other in putting *oneself* to death, mortifying oneself in order to make a gift of this death as a sacrificial offering to God) takes place, this place where death is given or offered, is the place where Solomon decided to build the House of the Lord in Jerusalem, also the place where God appeared to Solomon's father, David. However, it is also the place where the grand Mosque of Jerusalem stood, the place called the Dome of the Rock near the grand El-Aksa mosque where the sacrifice of Ibrahim is supposed to have taken place and from where Muhammad mounted his horse for paradise after his death. It is just above the destroyed temple of Jerusalem and the Wailing Wall, not far from the Way of the Cross. It is therefore a holy place but also a place that is in dispute, radically and rabidly, fought over by all the monotheisms, by all the religions of the unique and transcendent God, of the absolute other.[23]

Am I in Jerusalem? This is a question to which one will never respond in the present tense, only in the future or in the past anterior. . . . Am I in Jerusalem or elsewhere, very far from the Holy City? Under what conditions does one find oneself in Jerusalem? Is it enough to be there physically, as one says, and to live in places that carry this name, as I am now doing? What is it to live in Jerusalem? This is not easy to decide. Allow me to cite Meister Eckhart. . . . Like that of Denys, his work sometimes resembles an endless meditation of the sense and symbolism of the Holy City: a logic, a rhetoric, a topology, and a tropology of Jerusalem. Here is an example among many others:

> Yesterday I sat in a place where I said something [dâ sprach ich ein wort] that sounds incredible—I said that Jerusalem is as near to my soul as the place where I am now [mîner sele als nâhe als diu stat, dâ ich nû stân]. In truth, that which is a thousand miles beyond Jerusalem is as near to my soul as my own body; I am as sure of this as of being a man (*Adolescens, tibi dico: surge, in Meister Eckharts Predigten*, 2:305).[24]

[3]

REVERSAL

1. ii. "Envoyage" *and* "Setting Out"

9

Foreword

Wer zeigt uns den Weg?
(Who will show us the way?)

. . . in der Geschichte waltet das Geschick
(in history the *envoi* makes the law).[1]

Map

. . . as if I had attempted more than an extension or a *continuous* radicalization of the Heideggerian movement. . . . Everything takes place as if I had only generalized what Ricoeur calls Heidegger's "limited criticism" and as if I had stretched it inordinately, beyond all bounds. A passage, Ricoeur says, "from the limited criticism of Heidegger to Jacques Derrida's unbounded 'deconstruction' in 'White Mythology'". . . . A little further on, in the same gesture of assimilation or at least of continuous (derivation), Ricoeur resorts to the figure of a "theoretical core common to Heidegger and to Derrida, namely, the supposed collusion between the metaphoric couple of the proper and the figurative and the metaphysical couple of the visible and the invisible."[2]

Retreat [*retrait*] of metaphor. I have made a story of voyages (and not a narration of a voyage) and of the very very divided trait (*Riss*) out of it, in commemoration of us. What I said passed, as always, as you well know, unnoticed. Last trip to Geneva, to which you never will have accompanied me, finally.[3]

In other words: if one wished that *withdrawal-of* be understood as a metaphor, this would be a curious, inverting—one would say almost *catastrophic*, catastropical—metaphor: its end would be to state something new, something still unheard of about the vehicle and not about the apparent subject of the trope.[4]

Such a catastrophe inverts therefore the metaphoric passage at the moment when, having become excessive, metaphoricity no longer allows itself to be contained in its so-called "metaphysical" concept.[5]

This is serious because it upsets Heidegger's still ("derivative") schema (perhaps).[6]

. . . following in the steps of Heidegger, who, precisely near this orthodox Greek temple [Monastery of Kaisariani], did not fail, in his *Aufenthalte*, to incriminate once more not only Rome, its church, its law, its state, and its theology, technics, machines, tourism, and the spectacle designed for visitors—and above all, photography, the clicking and whirring of still or movie cameras which, on guided tours, "replaces" the authentic experience of the visit.[7]

Itinerary

It is common to consider, as does Ricoeur in particular, that the reversal effected by Derrida's work simply radicalizes a gesture that was already contained in Heidegger's thought, as though it were a continuous derivation from it. Without going into the details of this unacceptable interpretation, it remains necessary to clarify certain points that contradict it, and which relate directly to the question of travel. In fact, it is perhaps that question—the sense that one will give to travel, to the way or path, to *viability* in general—which constitutes the site of the most serious confrontation between Heidegger and Derrida.

It is indeed Heidegger who was first to show that the concept of metaphor only made sense within the field of a traditional metaphysics. In *The Principle of Reason* he declares that "the metaphorical exists only within metaphysics."[8] As Derrida comments: "'Metaphysics' would not only be the enclosure in which *the* concept of metaphor *itself* would be produced and enclosed."[9] It is indeed Heidegger again who is first to apply himself to the task of a "destruction" [*Destruktion*] of the metaphysical tradition and hence to a *Destruktion* of the concept of metaphor circumscribed by it. And this *Destruktion*, finally, proceeds from a clarification of the question of Being, a question that henceforth cannot be dissociated from a thinking of the path or way [*Weg*]. In this sense, Heidegger would be the first thinker of the originary voyage (away from itself) of the origin.

Derrida's undertaking quite clearly follows in the wake of such thinking. It is impossible to comprehend the stakes of the "initial catastrophe"[10] without taking into account this progression. But it is also clear that Derrida follows Heidegger only with "style," with, as he himself says:

the weight of some pointed object. At times this object might be only a quill or a stylus. But it could just as easily be a stiletto, or even a rapier. Such objects might be used in a vicious attack against what philosophy appeals to in the name of matter or matrix, an attack whose thrust could not but leave its mark, could not but inscribe there some imprint or form. But they might also be used as protection against a threatening form, in order to keep it at a distance, to repel it—as one bends or recoils before its force, in flight, behind veils and sails (*des voiles*).[11]

In other words, Derrida follows Heidegger *without deriving from him*, repelling the "threatening form" that, for him, is precisely that borrowed by Heidegger's concept of "path," and which still remains too attached to the *derivative logic* that it nevertheless claims to "destroy." But how is it possible to follow something without deriving from it? Derrida proposes a name for this strange gesture or disturbing posture: the *retrait* (re/withdraw[al]). The word, analyzed fully and precisely in "The *Retrait* of Metaphor," is, if one wishes, a *portmanteau word*. One has to understand *retrait* in the sense of a noun taken from the verb *retirer* (pull back, take back, withdraw), as well as—following the "violence to" or "abuse of"[12] the word that Derrida admits to—a noun based on "to retrace," a retreat or withdrawal, therefore, that also signifies a retracing of the trait or line, a supplement to it.

This fold or twist of the *retrait* already indicates the way in which Derrida intends to situate himself with respect to Heidegger's work. He will follow it by retreating from it and retracing it at the same time, while setting off on an incredible voyage of reading in the form of the task he also sets himself, namely of analyzing the very destiny of the word *retrait* in Heidegger: "I presumed the word retrait—at once intact (and forced, except in my language) and simultaneously altered—to be the most proper to capture the greatest quantity of energy and information in the Heideggerian text."[13]

The Sense of the "Withdrawal [*Retrait*] of Being" in Heidegger

Metaphysics (the philosophical tradition that extends from the Pre-Socratics to Husserl) is deployed, according to Heidegger, from the basis of a *retrait* [*Entziehung, retrait* in the suspensive sense] of Being. In *The Principle of Reason* he declares: "Being proffers itself to us, but in such a way that at the same time it, in its essence, already withdraws."[14] It withdraws to the very extent that it is not (a) present. In fact, in its essence Being [*Sein, être*] is not a being ["entity," *Seiendes, étant*]. It is the means by which a being comes to be being, it indicates the provenance and sense of "beingness" without ever being confused with it. The Being by which a being comes to be being is not itself a being. Heidegger applies the term "ontological difference" to this difference between Being and being. The philosophical tradition proceeds by occluding this difference, and that is what founds the unity of the tradition as metaphysical, fundamentally determining the sense of being as a form of presence (*Ousia, Anwesenheit*), a presence that is itself understood as presence of what is present.

Metaphysics involves a forgetting of being, or a retreat from the withdrawal of Being, since it conceives of Being as something that can present itself, hence as a being. The graph of the withdrawal of being in Heidegger is therefore a double line: the mode of being of the dispensation of Being (which exceeds the categories of presence and absence), as well as the supplement or doubling of withdrawal described by metaphysics' "fall" into a tradition. But the occlusion of ontological difference does not obey a conscious intention on the part of philosophy. It corresponds to the very withdrawal of Being. It is neither present nor absent and can only come to be in withdrawal. It *is* not, but dispenses itself, and this dispensation constitutes its history, its destiny and destination, its *Geschick*, which Derrida translates as *envoi* (*schicken* signifies both "destine" and "send"):

Geschick is destiny, of course, and therefore everything that touches on the destination as well as on destiny, and even on *sort* ["fate"]—it means *sort*, as you know, and there we are close to the *fortune-telling book*. I also like that this word *Geschick*, which everything ends up passing through, even the thinking of the history of Being as dispensation, and even the gift of the *"es gibt Sein"* or *"es gibt Zeit,"* I like that this word also says address, not the address of the addressee, but the skill of whoever's turn it is, in order to pull off this or that, chance too somewhat, one dictionary says the *"chic"*—I'm not making it up! And *schicken* is to send, *envoyer*, to "expedite," to cause to leave or to arrive, etc.[15]

Now with this thinking regarding the *envoi*, Heidegger really starts philosophy off on a voyage, *en voyage*, and metaphor goes *on leave*.

Cutting a Path

Indeed, in and by its withdrawal, through its destining and sending, *Being sets out on a path*. Heidegger's thinking of Being cannot be separated from a thought that involves marking the way (*Bahn*) or path (*Weg*). Heidegger calls *Geschick* a *Be-Wëgung*, which can be translated as *setting out on the path* [mise en chemin]: "We hear the words 'give way' [*Be-Wëgung*] in this sense: to be the original giver and founder of ways. . . . Following the ancient usage of the Alemannic Swabian idiom, the verb *wegen* can mean 'to forge a path,' for example through countryside deep in snow."[16] And he points out how close *Be-Wëgung* is to the *Tao*: "The key word in Laotse's poetic thinking is *Tao*, which, 'properly speaking' means way. . . . *Tao* could be the way that gives all ways. . . . and makes way for everything. All is way."[17]

We need to be attentive to the quotation marks around "properly speaking." *Be-Wëgung* is not a metaphor for Heidegger, it does not partake of the play between literal and figurative. To the extent that Being is not a being, it is precisely impossible for a trope to describe it; no figure can represent it. Metaphorical transport (*re-ference*, or sending back, and substitution of one entity for another) cannot function as the vehicle for what, originarily, has rendered it possible, namely *Geschick*. Metaphor cannot

"Heidegger's thinking of Being cannot be separated from
a thought that involves marking the way (*Bahn*) or path
(*Weg*)." Heidegger in Todtnauberg, June 1968. (Digne
Meller Marcovicz)

transgress the limits of metaphysics. Bringing the pathmaking [*chemine-
ment*] of Being, or Being as path, into view, which can take place the moment the metaphysical tradition reaches its limit, demands precisely the
abandoning, or withdrawal, of metaphor: "'Metaphor' as a normative conception [*massgebende Vorstellung*] also becomes untenable."[18]

Heidegger thus draws out a completely unheard of sense of voyage; neither literal, nor proper, the originary opening of all paths, of all destinations and all destinies. The means by which setting out on the path exceeds

the metaphoricity and literality of the pathway is not a fact of any over-abundance nor of any plenitude of the origin, but rather of the tracing of a *trait, Aufriss*, which Derrida translates as *entame* ("broaching/breaching").[19] Heidegger calls this *trait* a "signature," a "cut" that "assigns poetry and thinking to their nearness to one another," also referred to as their "neighborhood."[20] It can no more be a case of subordinating figurative sense, which derives traditionally, and necessarily, from the poetic resources of language, to the purity or propriety of the philosophical concept. Poetry and thinking are given originarily one to the other, they approach each other always already, without the one being older than the other, and without one being presumed simply to derive from the other. As a consequence of their proximity, which provides for language itself, there can be no hierarchical separation between literal and metaphoric. Because the neighboring *trait*, which gives poetry to thinking and vice versa, is the opening of a path, the path through which Being sets out on its voyage, and that voyage itself, have neither proper nor figurative sense. Metaphor, therefore, withdraws.

Derrida's *Envoyage*

By having the word *retrait* "capture the energy" of Heidegger's text, Derrida is able to begin analyzing the structural link between the suspensive withdrawal of Being and the suspensive withdrawal of metaphor. But he shows that the *retrait* is barely captured before that suspensive withdrawal is itself doubled by a *retrait* that is a retracing or supplement of the *trait* (*Aufriss*).

Metaphor withdraws, granted. But what remains, says Derrida, is the metaphoricity of Heidegger's text, beginning with the word *retrait* and formulations such as "withdrawal of Being" or "withdrawal of metaphor" themselves. The suspensive withdrawal of Being is doubled with a "supplementary fold" which "repeat[s] the intra-metaphysical metaphor in displacing it,"[21] which *reverses* it (which constitutes a supplementary sense and a retracing of the "metaphorical catastrophe"). We must insist on this double writing of the *retrait*, suspension and *overabundant remaining*, for it is what leads, as if to its originary articulation, to the question of the trait or the broach/breach that sets thinking and poetry on their way.

Derrida declares that it is necessary to take into account Heidegger's writing, "his treatment of language and, more rigorously, his treatment of the trait, of 'trait' in every sense, and more rigorously still of 'trait' as a word in his language, and of the trait as a tracing incision (*entame*) of language."[22] In other words one has to explore "the apparently metaphoric power of a text, whose author no longer wishes that what happens in that text and what claims to get along without metaphor there be understood precisely as 'metaphoric,' nor even under any concept of metalinguistics or rhetoric."[23] Derrida's proposal is that we think the *retrait* at the level of Heidegger's text, thinking through this re-*trait* (return) of metaphor liberated by the (suspensive) *retrait* of metaphor-metaphysics.

Retrait/ trait/ tracing: Derrida's wordplay allows him to *follow* as closely as possible Heidegger's thinking of the pathmarking or setting out and voyage of Being. In fact, an understanding of the originary cutting of the path is not possible without this polysemy of the word "trait." To say that the origin is breached as it is broached, broken open and into by the *trait*, amounts to saying that the origin is in *retrait* or retreat from the (moment of the) origin. That means that nothing can derive from it; nothing can happen to it. Heidegger's *trait* is thus very close to arche-writing. The path along which being is dispensed is not an Odyssey; it unfolds on the order of epochs or ages (*Zeitalter*) which periodize its dispensation: the Greek era, the modern era or era of representation, etc. But this periodization doesn't obey any teleology. It has no pre-assigned sense, no predetermined identity, nor does it form any totality or system. It is thus that thinking the *envoi* of being exceeds the metaphysical sense of a voyage as drift, a drift that is always derived from an originary *Geschick*. Being is neither the point of departure nor the place of arrival of its history. Nor is it a transcendental signified that would send some set of tropical signifiers charged with representing it off on their mission.

This originary retreat or withdrawal of the origin is at the same time a retracing of the conceptual limits of the voyage. It is not, or no longer, possible to envisage setting out on the way as a movement from indigenous to allogenous, from an inside to an outside. Setting out on the path renounces demands of *presentification* made to the other or to the foreigner, or at least renounces bringing that presence closer. Traveling therefore implies an experience of proximity of what is distant that results from being distanced from proximity.

Derrida follows Heidegger, but distinguishes himself as he follows and retraces. By proposing that Heidegger's text be read on the basis of the motif of the retrait, something that Heidegger himself never configured or organized *in the same way*, he is already displacing it. He displaces it toward a thinking of the dissemination of the trait that wrenches the path—*Weg* or *Tao*—from what still has to be called its *destinal unity*, from whatever, within it, *resists traveling*. Derrida will in fact show that the *Geschick* or *envoi* of being remains dependent upon a traditional logic of destination. That sense of Being never gets lost along the road and always ends up arriving at or being moored to *truth*. In the same manner, it will always be possible for poetry and thinking to recollect themselves or reassemble in the unity of this *envoi* which becomes a *putting into operation* of their truth. With Heidegger, the originary *trait* does not end by being effaced. In this sense the dispensation of being still obeys, in its own way, the derivative schema of metaphysics.

Given that, the *Be-Wëgung* doesn't travel far enough. Derrida remains therefore very suspicious of the path, of everything with respect to it that still depends on a *methodical derivation*. This explains why he never characterizes his own project as a path or as pathmaking. In borrowing a formula from *The Post Card*, I would propose calling this non-pathmaking project his *envoyage*.[24] *Envoyage* has us understand at the same time a being-away [*l'être-en-voyage*] without pause or stopover, and the cutting of a path or a sending along the way without that leading back to its own truth or proper sense.

The four stages of the journey that follow are all organized to explore this *envoyage*, set in motion by these words: "I have tried to retrace a path opened on a thinking of the *envoi* which . . ."[25]

[10]

"We Can't Bypass Freiburg"

"We can't bypass [*contourner*] Freiburg."[1] It is in these terms that Derrida affirms the unavoidable aspect of Heidegger's thinking without that in any way preventing him from displacing it or retracing its contours. The reader is invited to travel through this long extract from "The *Retrait* of Metaphor" without any further commentary:[2]

What, then, would happen with metaphor? Everything: the totality of what is (*l'étant*). And it would happen that we should get along without it, without being able to dispense with it (*il se passerait ceci qu'on devrait se passer d'elle sans pouvoir s'en passer*), and this defines the structure of withdrawals which interests me here. On the one hand, we must be able to dispense with it because the relation of (ontotheological) metaphysics to the thought of Being, this relation (*Bezug*) which marks the withdrawal (*retrait, Entziehung*) of Being, can no longer be named—*literally*—metaphoric as soon as the usage (I do say usage, the becoming-usual of the word and not its original meaning to which no one has ever referred, in any case not me) was fixed by way of this couple of metaphysical opposition to describe relations among beings. Being nothing, not being a being, it can not be expressed or named *more metaphorico*. And therefore it does not have, in such a context of the dominant metaphysical usage of the word 'metaphor,' a proper or literal meaning which could be alluded to (*visé*) metaphorically by metaphysics. Consequently, if we cannot speak metaphorically on its subject, neither can we speak properly or literally. We will speak of being only *quasi*-metaphorically, according to a metaphor of metaphor, with the surcharge of a supplementary trait, of a double trait (*re-trait*), of a supplementary fold of metaphor articulating this withdrawal, repeating the intra-metaphysical metaphor in displacing it, the very one that the withdrawal of Being would have made possible. The graphics of this withdrawal would then take the following turn (*allure*), which I describe very dryly:

1. What Heidegger calls metaphysics *itself* corresponds to a withdrawal of Being. Therefore metaphor, as a so-called metaphysical concept, corresponds to a withdrawal of Being. Metaphysical discourse, producing and containing the concept of metaphor, is itself quasi-metaphoric with respect to Being: therefore it is a metaphor englobing the narrow-restrained-strict concept of metaphor which itself therefore has only strictly metaphoric sense.

2. The so-called metaphysical discourse can only be exceeded (*débordé*) insofar as it corresponds to a withdrawal of Being, according to a withdrawal of metaphor as a metaphysical concept, according to a withdrawal of metaphysics, a withdrawal of the withdrawal of Being. But as this withdrawal of the metaphoric leaves no place free for a discourse of the proper or the literal, it will have at the same time the sense of a re-fold (*re-pli*), of what retreats like a wave on the shoreline, and of a re-turn (*re-tour*), of the overcharging repetition of the supplementary trait, of yet another metaphor, of a double trait (*re-trait*) of metaphor, a discourse whose rhetorical border is no longer determinable according to a simple and indivisible line, according to a linear and indecomposable trait. This trait has the internal multiplicity, the folded-re-folded structure of a double trait (*re-trait*). The withdrawal of metaphor gives place to an abyssal generalization of the metaphoric—metaphor of metaphor in two senses—which splays (*évase*) the borders, or rather, invaginates them. I do not wish to be overabundant in the developments of this paradoxy; I only draw from it, very quickly, two provisional conclusions.

1. The word *retrait*, which is 'French'" up to a certain point, is not too abusive, I believe, as a translation of *Enziehung*, the *Sich-Entziehen* of Being, insofar as, suspending, dissimulating, giving way, and veiling itself, etc., Being withdraws into its crypt. To the extent of being 'not too abusive' (a 'good' translation must always *abuse*), the French word is suitable in order to desig-

nate the essential and in itself double, equivocal movement which makes possible all that I am speaking about at this moment in the text of Heidegger. The withdrawal of Being, in its being-with-drawn, gives place to metaphysics as onto-theology producing the concept of metaphor, coming forth and naming itself in a quasi-metaphoric manner. In order to think Being in its withdrawal it would be necessary to allow a withdrawal of metaphor to come forth or to *vanish away* (*se* réduire) which however (leaving room for nothing which might be *opposed*, opposable to the metaphoric) will spread out without limit and will charge any metaphoric trait with supplementary surplus value. Here the word *re-trait* (a trait in addition to supplement the subtracting withdrawal, the *re-trait* expressing at once, at one stroke [*d'un trait*] the plus and the minus) designates the generalizing and supplementary return only in a sort of quasi-catachrestic violence, a sort of abuse I impose on language, but an abuse that I hope is overjustified by what is required for good, economic formalization. *Retrait* is neither a translation nor a non-translation (in the current sense) in relation to the text of Heidegger; it is neither proper nor literal, neither figurative nor metaphoric. . . .

2. Second provisional conclusion: because of this chiasmatic invagination of borders—and if the word *retrait* functions here neither literally nor by metaphor—I do not know what I mean (*veux dire*) before having thought, so to speak, the withdrawal of Being *as* withdrawal of metaphor. Far from proceeding by way of a word or a known or determinate meaning (the withdrawal) to think where the question of Being or of metaphor stands, I will come to comprehend, understand, read, think, allow the withdrawal in general to manifest itself, only from the withdrawal of Being as a withdrawal of metaphor in all the polysemic and disseminal potential of withdrawal. In other words: if one wished that *withdrawal-of* be understood as a metaphor, this would be a curious, inverting—one would say almost *catastrophic*, catastropical—metaphor: its end would be to state something new, something still unheard of about the vehicle and not about the apparent subject of the trope. *Withdrawal-of-Being-or-of-metaphor* would put us on the way of thinking less Being or metaphor than the Being or the metaphor *of withdrawal*, by way of leading us to think about the way and the vehicle, or their forging of the path [*frayage*]. Habitually, usually, a metaphor claims to procure access to the unknown and to the indeterminate by the detour of something recognizably fa-

miliar. 'The evening,' a common experience, helps us to think 'old age,' something more difficult to think or to live, as 'the evening of life,' etc. According to this common schema, we would know in a familiar way what *withdrawal* means, and we would try to think the withdrawal of Being or of metaphor by way of it. Now what arises here is that for once we can think of the trait of *re-trait* only from the thought of this ontico-ontological difference on whose withdrawal would have been traced—with the borders of metaphysics—the current structure of metaphoric usage.

Such a catastrophe inverts therefore the metaphoric passage at the moment when, having become excessive, metaphoricity no longer allows itself to be contained in its so-called "metaphysical" concept. . . . I will therefore underline . . . Heidegger's statements on the so-called metaphysical concept of metaphor, and, on the other [hand], his own text insofar as it appears more 'metaphoric' or *quasi*-metaphoric than ever, at the very moment when he defends himself from it. How is that possible?

In order to find the path, the form of the path, between the two, it is necessary to glimpse what I have just called the generalizing catastrophe. I will draw two examples from among a number of possibilities. It is still a question of these typical moments when, resorting to formulas which one would be tempted to accept as metaphors, Heidegger specifies that these are not metaphors and throws suspicion on what we believe assured and clear in this word. . . . In the "Letter on Humanism," a movement which I cannot reconstitute here includes this sentence: *"Das Denken baut am Haus des Seins,"* "Thought works at (constructing) the house of Being," the adjoinment of Being (*Fuge des Seins*) coming to assign, enjoin (*verfugen*) man to inhabit the truth of Being. And a little further, after a citation from Hölderlin:

> *Discourse about the house of Being* (Die Rede vom Haus des Seins) *is not a metaphor* (Übertragung) *transporting the image of the 'house' toward Being, but* [by implication: conversely] *it is by way of appropriating thinking the essence of Being* (sondern aus dem sachgemäss gedachten Wesens des Seins) *that we will one day be able to think what 'house' and 'to inhabit' are.* (pp. 189/236–37)

"House of Being" would not operate, in this context, in the manner of a metaphor in the current, usual, that is to say, literal meaning (*sens*) of metaphor, if there is one. The current and cursive meaning—I understand it also in the sense of direction—would transport a familiar predicate (and here nothing is more familiar, familial, known, domestic and economic, one would think, than the house) toward a less familiar, more remote, *unheimlich* (uncanny) subject, which it would be a question of better appropriating for oneself, becoming familiar with, understanding, and which one would thus designate by the indirect detour of what is nearest—the house. Now what happens here *with* the quasi-metaphor of the house of Being, and what does *without* metaphor in its cursive direction, is that it is Being which, from the very moment of its withdrawal, would let or promise to let the house or the habitat be thought. . . . In the inversion considered, Being has not become the proper of this supposedly known, familiar, nearby being, which one believed the house to be in the common metaphor. And if the house has become a bit *unheimlich*, this is not for having been replaced, in the role of 'what is nearest,' by "Being." We are therefore no longer dealing with a metaphor in the usual sense, nor with a simple inversion permutating the places in a usual tropical structure. All the more since this statement (which moreover is not a judicative statement, a common proposition, of the constative type S is P) is no longer a statement among others bearing on relations between predicates and ontic subjects. First of all because it implies the economic value of the domicile and of the proper, both of which often (or always) intervene in the definition of the metaphoric. Then, because the statement speaks above all *of* language and therefore in it *of metaphoricity*. In fact, the house of Being, we will have read above in the "Letter," is *die Sprache* (a particular language or language in general). . . . Another way of saying that one will be able to think the proximity of the near (which, itself, is not near or proper: proximity is not near, propriety is not proper) only from and within language. . . .

This movement is no longer simply metaphoric. 1. It bears on language in general and on a particular language as an element of the metaphoric. 2. It bears on being which is nothing and which one must think according to ontological difference which, with the withdrawal of Being, makes possible both its metaphoricity and its withdrawal. 3. Consequently there is no term which may be proper, usual, and literal in the separation without divergence (*dans l'écart sans écart*) of this phrasing. Despite its aspect (*allure*) or resemblance, this phrasing is neither metaphoric nor literal. Stating non-literally the condition of metaphoricity, it frees both its unlimited extension and its withdrawal. Withdrawal by which what is distanced (*entfernt*) in the non-near of proximity is withdrawn and sheltered in it. As said at the beginning of "The Nature of Language," no more metalanguage, no more metalinguistics, therefore no more meta-rhetoric and no more metaphysics. Always yet another metaphor the moment metaphor withdraws in expanding (*évasant*) its limits.

This torsion, this twist of the gait and of the step, this *detour* of the Heideggerian path, one finds its trace everywhere where Heidegger writes and writes about the path. Its trail can be followed everywhere and can be deciphered according to the same rule which is neither simply from a rhetoric nor from a tropical system. I will situate only one other occurrence, because it enjoys some privileges. 1. In "The Nature of Language" (1957–58), it precedes, from quite a distance, the passage cited a while ago on "*Worte wie Blumen*" (words like flowers). 2. It concerns not only the claimed metaphoricity of some statements on language in general, and on metaphor in language. It initially pursues an ostensibly metaphoric discourse bearing on the relation between thought and poetry (*Denken und Dichten*). 3. It determines this relation as one of neighborliness (*voisinage, Nachbarschaft*), according to this type of proximity (*Nähe*) called neighborhood, in the space of the home and the economy of the house. Now there again, to call metaphor, as if we knew what it was, any value of neighborliness between poetry and thought, to act as if one were first of all assured of the proximity of proximity and of the neighborliness of neighborhood (*voisinage du voisinage*), is to close oneself to the necessity of the other movement. Inversely, in renouncing the security of what we believe we recognize under the name of metaphor and of neighborhood, we will perhaps approach the proximity of neighborliness. . . .

What therefore is the trait (*Riss*) of this *Bezug* between *Denken* and *Dichten*? It is the trait of an 'incision' (*entame*), of a tracing, *fraying* opening (the word *Bahnen* [path, groove] appears often in this context with the figures of *Bewegen* [to open a way]), of an *Aufriss*. The word *incision* [entame] which I have used a good deal elsewhere, appears to me the most approximate (*approchant*) for translating *Aufriss*, a decisive word, a word of decision in this context of the non-'voluntary' decision, and one that French translators render sometimes by *tracé-ouvrant* (opening sketch) and sometimes by *gravure* (engraving).

Incised, the two parallels cut each other at infinity, re-cut, split and sign in some way the one in the body of the other, the one in the place of the other, the contract without contract of their neighborliness. If the parallels cut one another (*schneiden sich*: intersect) at infinity (*im Un-endlichen*) in this cut or this split (*entaille, Schnitt*), they do not do it to themselves, they re-cut without touching each other, without affecting each other, without wounding each other. They only incise each other and are cut (*geschnitten*) in the incision (*Aufriss*) of their proximity (*avoisinement*), of their neighboring essence (*nachbarlichen Wesens*). And via this incision which leaves them intact, they are *eingezeichnet*, "signed" as the published French translation says: designed, characterized, assigned, consigned. Heidegger then says *Diese Zeichnung ist der Riss*. It incises (*er reisst auf*), it traces in opening *Dichten* and *Denken* in the approximating (*approchement*) of one to the other. This approximating does not draw them into proximity again from another place where they would already be themselves and then would allow themselves to be drawn (*ziehen*) to each other. The approximating is the *Ereignis* which sends *Dichten* and *Denken* back into the proper (*in das Eigene*) of their essence (*Wesen*). The trait of the incision, therefore, marks the *Ereignis* as propriation, as an event of propriation. It does not precede the two properties which it causes to come to their propriety, for it is nothing without them. In this sense it is not an autonomous, originary instance, itself proper in relation to the two which it incises and allies. Being nothing, it does not appear itself, if has no proper and independent phenomenality, and in not disclosing itself it withdraws, it is structurally in withdrawal, as a divergence (*écart*: splitting aside), opening, differentiality, trace, border, traction, effraction, etc. From the moment that it withdraws in drawing itself out, the trait is *a priori* withdrawal, unappearance, and effacement of its mark in its incision.

Its inscription, as I have attempted to articulate it in the trace or in differance, *succeeds only in being effaced* (n'arrive qu'à s'effacer*).

It arrives, happens, and comes about only in effacing itself. Inversely, the trait is not (derived.) It is not secondary, in its arrival, in relation to the domains, or the essences, or to the existences that it cuts away, frays, and refolds in their re-cut. The *re-* of *re-trait* is not an accident occurring to the trait. It rises up (*s'enlève*) in allowing any propriety to rise up, as one says of a figure against a ground. But it is lifted neither before nor after the incision which permits it to be lifted up, neither substantially, accidentally, materially, formally, nor according to any of the oppositions which organize so-called metaphysical discourse. If metaphysics had a unity, it would be the regime of these oppositions which appears and is determined only *by way of, by starting out from* (à partir de), the withdrawal of the trait, the withdrawal of the withdrawal, etc. The "starting out from" is itself engulfed in it (*s'y abime*).[3]

[12]

The *Khōra*-Nuclear Catastrophe

In other words, what remains to be questioned is the articulation between the event—what comes to pass or arrives—and its very possibility, or *eventness* [événementialité]. We must remember that every event owes its chance to non-arrival, to the imminence of the wholly other in the voyage toward arrival.

Non-arrival can indeed be thought of as a point of departure, as departure from and resource for every event. But this chance is precisely not an origin from which what arrives derives. Non-arrival designates a non-place in the place and stead of the origin. In a sense this non-place is a *principle*. But it is a matter of a non-archeological *arkhē*, an an-archic archaism, in the double sense of a-principial and an-archivable. A principle without being (one), an *arkhē* that resists and excludes itself from all archivation, non-arrival resists and at the same time excludes itself from the order of arrival. An origin from which nothing can derive is obviously *atopian* and *anachronic*: it has neither place nor time. The origin of the event allows itself to be conceived of, therefore, as a non-place in space and as a non-time in time, as the very possibility, for the present of the now, of disjointing itself and detaching itself from itself.

Paradoxically, this non-place and non-time are inscribed deep within the metaphysical discourse of the origin, and from the very beginning. In fact, we find the perspective of another thinking, another origin, another thinking of the origin, breaking itself off from Platonic philosophy at the very level of its foundation. Its name is *khōra*, the impassiveness of the *Timaeus*, an-archic and an-archivable.[1] *Khōra* becomes more and more insistent in Derrida's texts, developed as the wholly other of what derives. Although very ancient, *khōra* haunts our present time. Freed from chronological order it belongs to an "ageless contemporaneity."[2] This is what explains its capacity to appear or reappear, phantomatically, in our era, threatened as it is by a radical event, namely nuclear catastrophe, an event that is itself an-archivable. *Khōra*, which originarily referred to place and earth without either occupying place or being found on earth, calls for thinking of and in this very moment when the danger of destruction of every single place has spread across the earth. Khōra *and atomic fission go* [envoyagent] *together without following one from the other*, in an unheard-of complicity that forms—without giving it form—the constitutive anachrony of all history, the fantastic and phantasmatic memory of every voyage today, the invisible face of the world, not yet come, still to come.

Khōra "in Which Country?"

In everyday Greek *khōra* means "country" or "region":

Khōra, spacing, can also simply mean, in so-called current language, country, village, birthplace, indeed, the earth. *Pou tes khoras*: "in which place on the earth?" but also "in which country?" It would be necessary to study elsewhere the grammar, logic, and the uses of the Greek *pou*. This word entitles one of Aristotle's ten ontological categories, and its function is sometimes that of an interrogative adverb of place (one searches to know, to determine, in posing the anxious question "where?"), sometimes that of an indefinite adverb that abandons things to the negativity of their indeterminacy (*quelque part*, I don't know, somewhere, anywhere—from which comes the meaning of "in some manner, perhaps, it is possible, it is not impossible, difficult to decide, in a way, somehow, why not," etc. And the "et cetera" itself raises the stakes of the indefiniteness of *any*).[3]

Inasmuch as *khōra* means in Greek an inhabited place, post, or position—point of departure and destination of every voyage—it can also refer to the origin, the source of what is; it could even designate the very basis of being, its cause, principle, the taking- or being-place of every place. Now, when it appeared for the first time on the philosophical scene in Plato's *Timaeus*, it distanced itself from the ontological dignity that its name nevertheless invokes. Indeed, by means of its impassiveness or neutrality it resisted all foundational logic. Mother of all forms—"[it] figures the place of inscription of *all that is marked on the world*"[4]—it remains itself foreign to form.

Khōra receives, so as to give place to them, all the determinations, but she/it does not possess any of them as her/its own. She possesses them, she has them, since she receives them, but she does not possess them as properties, she does not possess anything as her own. She "is" nothing other than the sum or the process of what has just been inscribed "on" her, on the subject of her, on the subject, right up against her subject, but she is not the *subject* or the *present support* of all these interpretations, even though, nevertheless, she is not reducible to them.[5]

Beyond the retarded or johnny-come-lately opposition of *logos* and *mythos*, how is one to think the necessity of that which, while *giving place* to that opposition as to so many others, seems sometimes to be itself no longer subject to the law of the very thing which it *situates*? What of this *place*? Is it nameable? And wouldn't it have some impossible relation to the possibility of naming? Is there something to *think* there, as I have just so hastily said, and to think according to *necessity*?[6]

In "Faith and Knowledge" Derrida declares that "Chora *is nothing (no being, no present)*."[7] Given that, one cannot even speak about it in terms of metaphor. For *khōra* there is neither metaphor nor literal sense; no first sense which, in, by, or through it, could let itself figure as something that would become a concept. Because it disturbs every dialectic polarity (sensible/intelligible, same/other), *khōra* subverts the derivative economy of literal and metaphorical, of essential and contingent. It does not even make sense on the horizon of being.

Seminar on religion on Capri, 1995. *Clockwise, from left to right:* Vitiello, Gadamer, Gargani, Ferraris, Trias, Derrida, Vattimo (*back to camera*). (Jacques Derrida Archives)

Turin-Pisa, 25 November 1997

. . . Spoke again about the animal in Kant and Heidegger, Lévinas and Lacan. And of a certain globalization [*mondialisation*] in the "Cartesian" treatment of the animal. If I had to describe my travels, rhetoric, performance, and locommotions in a word, I'd call it the "*critical* experience of *mondialatinisation*" (this term came to me on Capri, as you know).[16] . . . And I'm still reading you. You know and say just about everything, algebraically yet beautifully. Let me add that Italy is the country in Europe, probably the only one in the world, where I would like to eternally return. Just in order to remind me of my returns. My trips through memory by counterpath. It is one of the rare countries I have sometimes visited without any public or academic "pretext," just "with" friends of the heart or the head. It is true that I have traveled very little without such pretexts, but, I think I can say it, I have never decided on any destination of my own accord, by

16 [See "Faith and Knowledge." (C.M.)]

We shall not speak of metaphor. . . . And this . . . would not be because it [*khōra*] would inalterably be *itself* beyond its name but because in carrying beyond the polarity of sense (metaphorical or proper), it would no longer belong to the horizon of sense, nor to that of meaning as the meaning of being.[8]

We would never claim to propose the exact word, the *mot juste*, for *khōra*, nor to name it, *itself*, over and above all the turns and detours of rhetoric, nor finally to approach it, *itself*, for what it will have been, outside of any point of view, outside of any anachronic perspective. Its name is not an exact word, not a *mot juste*. It is promised to the ineffaceable even if what it names, *khōra*, is not reduced to its name. Tropology and anachronism are inevitable. And all we would like to show is that it is structure which makes them thus inevitable, makes of them something other than accidents, weaknesses, or provisional moments. It is this structural law which seems to me never to have been approached *as such* by the whole history of interpretations of the *Timaeus*. It would be a matter of structure and not of some essence of the *khōra*, since the question of essence no longer has any meaning with regard to it. Not having an essence, how could *khōra* stand beyond its name? The *khōra* is anachronistic; it "is" the anachrony within being, or better: the anachrony of being. It anachronizes being.[9]

Khōra marks a place apart, the spacing which keeps a dissymmetrical relation to all that which, "in herself," beside or in addition to herself, seems to make a couple with her. In the couple outside of the couple, the strange mother who gives place without engendering can no longer be considered as an origin. She/it eludes all anthropo-theological schemes, all history, all revelation, and all truth. Preoriginary, *before* and outside of all generation, she no longer even has the meaning of a past, of a present that is past. *Before* signifies no temporal anteriority. The relation of independence, the nonrelation, looks more like the relation of the interval or the spacing to what is lodged in it to be received in it.[10]

If there is place, or, according to our idiom, *place given*, to give place here does not come down to the same thing as to make a present of a place. The expression *to give place* does not refer to the gesture of a donor-subject, the support or origin of something which would come to be given to someone.[11]

myself, never. That can be interpreted however one wishes. Invitation, call, suggestion, whatever name one gives to it, and even if there has each time been a type of consent on my part, necessarily, the decision will always have come from the *other*.[17] I never said, of my own accord, never: "I am going to go here or there." If it were up to me I would never have budged. Even for Italy, whose most beloved names for my memory are not those of big cities—I know all of them—but rather Fano, for example, Assisi, Gubbio, Perugia, Lerici, Lucca, Sovicile, near Siena, Meina. . . . Since you quote that old phrase ("in a text where we already believe ourselves to be"), I wonder whether today, at the end of a long road, I wouldn't make the word "believe [*croyons*]" carry the whole weight of it. In the polysemy, indeed the homonymy of the verbs *croire* (*believe that* this is going to happen, *believe* someone's word, *believe in* someone, so many different things, but most often *possible*, likely, thus credible beings, and hence independent of any *pure* belief), I would insist on that *other* belief, the credence par excellence, which is possible only by *believing in the impossible*. A miracle is in the realm of the ordinary for *pure* belief. And the "text where we believe ourselves to be," another name for this place, place in general, interests me only where the impossible, that is to say the incredible, encircles and harries it, making my head turn, leaving an illegible trace within the taking-place, there, in the vertigo, "where we believe ourselves to be." . . . Place is always unbelievable for me, as is orientation. *Khōra* is incredible. That means: one can *only* believe in it, coldly, impassively, and nothing else. As in the im-possible. Absolute faith. Believe—travel. . . .

17 This *vocation* (only travel on the other's initiative) no doubt speaks *conjointly* of the essence (without essence, precisely) *both* of decision (about which I maintain that it depends on and comes *from the other*, holds and comes *to the other*), *and* traveling. The call of this vocation would be the very *same* traveling, the *first* voyage, if one can still say "same" and "first." The fact that one is not authorized to do so signifies precisely that before any vocation-to-travel (nothing will have been more foreign to me, finally), a voyage always responds to some convocation—and come from some one, some day, one day or another [*un jour ou l'autre*]. In this, the voyage (*journey*), always at the mercy of the other, becomes a birth (the eve and wake of a death), a coming to daylight which, were it able to depend solely on me, would risk being forever adjourned.

From the open interior of a corpus, of a system, of a language, or a culture, chora *would situate the abstract spacing,* place itself, *the place of absolute exteriority.*[12]

The Hypothesis of a "Remainderless Destruction of the Archive"

Nothing therefore derives from *khōra*. There is no starting out from *khōra*. Nothing proceeds from it for it conceals itself from what it situates, from the possibility of going somewhere, of leaving and returning, in a word, of traveling. That does not prevent a certain trajectory—neither method nor *Bewëgung*—from being sketched out between the antiquity of the *khōra*, forever older than every past and every archive, and the present-day [*actuelle*], contemporary imminence of the an-archivable. What responds to the immemorial seniority of the Greek-speaking *khōra*—without this response echoing the teleology of a sending—is the radical novelty of a destitution of the *arkhē*, the possibility that emerged only in the twentieth century of a total destruction of the world by means of nuclear catastrophe. However, between the absolute exteriority that opens wide its womb or matrix to the dawn of philosophy, and the risk of a the total destruction of every possible matrix in a nuclear conflict, there passes, but in an aporetic way which means that it *impasses*, some sort of strange alliance, like that linking fellow travelers. This complicity comes from the fact of their both pointing in the direction of the archive. The possibility of every archive being destroyed leads back to *khōra* as the very possibility of the an-archivable. Conversely, the nuclear threat invites us to reread the *Timaeus*. *Khōra* takes place in the precipitate manner of a catastrophe, and every catastrophe carries the memory of *khōra*. Therefore, today's traveler is always destined, in every place traveled, to have the joint experience of these two non-places.

Here we are dealing hypothetically with a total and remainderless destruction of the archive. This destruction would take place for the first time and it would lack any common proportion with, for example, the burning of a library, even that of Alexandria, which occasioned so many written accounts and nourished so many literatures. The hypothesis of this total destruction watches over destruction, it guides its footsteps; it becomes possible to recognize, in the light, so to speak, of that hypothesis, of that fantasy, or phantasm, the characteristic structures and historicity of the discourses, strategies, texts, or institutions to be deconstructed. That is why deconstruction, at least what is advanced today in its name, belongs to the nuclear age.[13]

We say the "nuclear age," and doesn't a reference to age still imply a reference to history, to an era or epoch, inasmuch as nuclear war, this "irreducibly new phenomenon,"[14] is made possible by a certain state of modern technology, thus appearing undeniably *dated*? Doesn't speaking of the nuclear age mean returning to a model of derivation, in terms of which catastrophe, or rather the risk of catastrophe would occur as an accident derived from a cause? In order to understand these questions we have to clearly understand that, like *khōra*, nuclear war has no real referent in that it hasn't taken place. Like *khōra*, it hasn't arrived. It only exists by not being produced and in this way remains in imminence. It is a matter of "a phenomenon whose essential feature is that of being, through and through, *fabulously textual*."[15]

For the moment, a nuclear war has not taken place: one can only talk and write about it. You will say, perhaps: but it is not the first time; the other wars, too, so long as they hadn't taken place, were only talked about and written about. And as to the fright of imaginary anticipation, what might prove that a European in the period following the war of 1870 would not have been more terrified by the "technological" image of the bombings and exterminations of the Second World War (even supposing he had been able to form such an image) than we are by the image we can construct for ourselves of a nuclear war? The logic of this argument is not devoid of value, especially if one is thinking about a limited and "clean" nuclear war. But it loses its value in the face of the hypothesis of a totally nuclear war, which, as a hypothesis, or, if you prefer, as a fantasy, or phantasm, conditions every discourse and all strategies. Unlike the other wars, which have all been preceded by wars of more or less the same type in human memory (and gunpowder did not mark a radical break in this respect), nuclear war has no precedent. It has never occurred, itself; it is a non-event. The explosion of American bombs in 1945 ended a "classical," conventional war; it did not set off a nuclear war. The terrifying "reality" of nuclear conflict can only be the signified referent, never the real referent (present or past) of a discourse or a text. At least today. And that sets us to thinking about *today*, our day, the presence of this present in and through that fabulous textuality. Better than ever and more than ever. The growing multiplication of discourses—indeed, of the literature—on this subject may constitute a process of fearful domestication, the anticipatory assimilation of that unanticipatable entirely-other. For the moment, today, one may say that a non-localizable nuclear war has not occurred; it has existence only through what is said of it, only where it is talked about. Some might call it a fable then, a pure invention: in the sense in which it is said that a myth, an image, a fiction, a utopia, a rhetorical figure, a fantasy, a phantasm, are inventions. It may also be called a speculation, even a fabulous specularization. The breaking of the mirror would be, finally, through an act of language, the very occurrence of nuclear war. Who can swear that our unconscious is not expecting this? dreaming of it, desiring it?[16]

The Future of Truth

Derrida's statements do not, once again, indicate any *catastrophism*. Firstly, because they neither prophesy nor foresee anything. Non-arrival is unpresentable; even if it were to arrive or occur, it wouldn't present anything. Non-arrival doesn't refer to a not yet realized, or not yet real or present, possibility. It always remains what it is: possible, and in this way, unanticipatable. Its truth is without apocalypse: "No truth, no apocalypse."[17] A truth that reveals nothing escapes unveiling and visibility. We will not see the catastrophe arrive. As a result, and because one cannot turn one's back on it, the threat of the worst is also the possibility of chance and the injunction to come: "The absolute effacement of any possible trace . . . is thus the only ineffaceable trace, it is so as the trace of what is entirely other, '*trace du tout autre*'."[18] While we certainly risk "look[ing] like suicidal sleepwalkers, blind and deaf alongside the unheard of,"[19] this risk is itself the resource of the future: "This invention of the wholly other is the only invention possible."[20] It can be seen that non-arrival harbors as much the possibility of the worst as the possibility of justice or democracy:

Beyond right, and still more beyond juridicism, beyond morality, and still more beyond moralism, does not justice as relation to the other suppose . . . the irreducible excess of a disjointure or an anachrony, some *Un-Fuge*, some "out of joint" dislocation in Being and in time itself, a disjointure that, in always risking the evil, expropriation, and injustice (*adikia*) against which there is no calculable insurance, would alone be able to *do justice* or to *render justice* to the other as other? A *doing* that would not amount only to action and a *rendering* that would not come down just to restitution? . . . Here . . . would be played out the relation of deconstruction to the possibility of justice . . . to what must (without debt and without duty) be rendered to the singularity of the other, to his or her absolute *precedence* or to his or her absolute *previousness*, to the heterogeneity of a *pre-*, which, to be sure, means what comes before me, before any present, thus before any past present, but also what, for that very reason, comes from the future or as future: as the very coming of the event. The necessary disjointure, the de-totalizing condition of justice, is indeed here that of the present—and by the same token the very condition of the present and of the presence of the present. This is where deconstruction would always begin to take shape as the thinking of the gift and of undeconstructible justice.[21]

[What] . . . never fails to happen . . . happens only in the trace of what would *happen otherwise* and thus also happens, like a specter, in that which does not happen.[22]

It is there that differ*a*nce, if it remains irreducible, irreducibly required by the spacing of any promise and by the future-to-come that comes to open it, does not mean only (as some people have too often believed and so naively) deferral, lateness, delay, postponement. In the incoercible differ*a*nce the here-now unfurls. Without lateness, without delay, but without presence, it is the precipitation of an absolute singularity, singular because differing, precisely [*justement*], and always other, binding itself necessarily to the form of the instant, in *imminence and in urgency*: even if it moves toward what remains to come, there is the *pledge* [gage] (promise, engagement, injunction and response to the injunction, and so forth). The pledge is given here and now, even before, perhaps, a decision confirms it. It thus responds without delay to the demand of justice. The latter by definition is impatient, uncompromising, and unconditional.[23]

[22]

The Postal Principle

"In the Beginning Was the Post"

If "starting out from" [*à partir de*] falls into its own abyss as *re-trait* of the origin, what is it that starts sending up [*le moteur de l'envoi*]? It is possible in these terms to add urgency to the fundamental question that Derrida asks Heidegger. The question clearly does not aim at some founding instance but insists on a certain sense—neither proper nor literal—of the motor, that is to say the machine. If the trait of sending is nothing, it therefore has to be understood in one sense as *automomatique*, that is to say as *technique*. Sending is not possible without the post.

Heidegger perhaps never went to the very end of his expedition and never managed to think the *envoi* as "postal principle."[1] But that is the dominant motif haunting *The Post Card*, a text whose "Envois" play on the possibility of creating a departure between the current understanding of the formula "postal principle"—post (office) as institution, technique, telecommunication center, etc.—and its wider sense, "arche-post," in other words, mode of dispensation of the *trait* and of the cutting of a path. Derrida shows quite precisely that one cannot point to the post as "ontological" ("the post without support [in the usual and strict sense], the post without post, without 'document,' and even without wires, without cables"),[2] without also pointing to postal technics, what is ordinarily understood by the word "post." What relates to the machine and what relates to destiny have become inseparable and travel together in adestination. Everything begins with the post, which is to say, doesn't begin.

The thing is very serious, it seems to me, for if there is first, so to speak, the *en-voi*, the *Schicken* reassembling itself into *Geschick*, if the *envoi* (derives) from nothing, then the possibility of posts is always already there, in its very retreat [*retrait*]. As soon as *there is*, as soon as it gives (*es gibt*), it destines, it tends . . . it destines and it tends (I will show this in the preface, if I write it one day, by reading the play of *Geben*, *Schicken*, and *Reichen* in *Zeit und Sein*). If I take my "departure" from the destination and the destiny or destining of Being (*Das Schicken im Geschick des Seins*), no one can dream of then *forbidding me to speak* of the "post," except on the condition of making of this word the element of an image, of a figure, of a trope, a post card of Being in some way. But to do it, I mean to accuse me, to forbid me, etc., one would have to be naively certain of knowing what a postcard or the post is. If, on the contrary (but this is not simply the contrary), I think the postal and the post card on the basis of the destinal of Being, as I think the house (of Being) on the basis of Being, of language, and not the inverse etc., then the post is no longer a simple metaphor, and is even, as the site of all transferences and all correspondences, the "proper" possibility of every possible rhetoric. Would this satisfy Martin? Yes and no. No, because he doubtless would see in the postal determination a premature(?) imposition of *tekhnē* and therefore of metaphysics (he would accuse me, you can see it from here, of constructing a metaphysics of the posts or of postality); and above all an imposition of the *position* precisely, of determining the *envoi* of Being as position, posture, thesis or theme (*Setzung*, *thesis*, etc.), a gesture that he alleges *to situate*, as well as technology, within the history of metaphysics and within which would be given to think a dissimulation and a retreat [*retrait*] of Being in its *envoi*. This is where things are the most difficult: because the very idea of the retreat (proper to destination), the idea of the halt, and the idea of the epoch in which Being holds itself back, suspends, withdraws, etc., all these ideas are immediately homogenous with postal discourse. To post is to send by "counting" with a halt, a relay, or a suspensive delay, the place of a mailman, the possibility of going astray and of forgetting (not of repression, which is a moment of keeping, but of forgetting). The *ēpokhē* and the *Ansichhalten* which essentially scan or set the rhythm of the "destiny" of Being, or its "appropriation" (*Ereignis*), is the place of the postal, this is where it comes to be and where it takes place (I would say *ereignet*), where it gives place and also lets come to be.[3]

In the beginning, in principle, was the post, and I will never get over it. But in the end I know it, I become aware of it as of our death sentence: it was composed, according to all possible codes and genres and languages, as a declaration of love. . . . And it begins with a destination without address, the direction cannot be situated in the end. There is no destination, my sweet destiny

you understand, within every sign already, every mark or every trait, there is distancing, the post, what there has to be so that it is legible for another, another than you or me, and everything is messed up in advance, cards on the table. The condition for it to arrive is that it ends up and even that it begins by not arriving. This is how it is to be read, and written, the *carte* of adestination.[4]

In Heidegger the *envoi* retains the sense of a *sending of the self* and is not exposed to divisibility. *Envoyage*, on the other hand, refers to the path to the extent that the latter bears off, is erased, gets posted as it gets traced.

I have tried to retrace a path opened on a thought of the *envoi* which, while (like the *Geschick des Seins* of which Heidegger speaks) of a structure as yet foreign to representation, did not as yet gather itself to itself as an *envoi* of being through *Anwesenheit*, presence and then representation. This as it were pre-ontological *envoi* does not gather itself together. It gathers itself only in dividing itself, in differing itself. It is neither originary nor originarily a sending-from [*envoi-de*] (the *envoi* of a being or of a present which would precede it, still less of a subject, or of an object by and for a subject). It is not one and does not begin with itself although nothing present precedes it; and it issues forth only in already sending back, it only issues forth starting from the other, *the other in itself without itself*. Everything begins by sending or referring back [*par le renvoi*], that is to say, does not begin. . . . But as these *renvois* from the other and to the other, these traces of differ-

In front of the Yale Post Office ("and in order to really feel what I am talking about, I mean about my body, you must recall what an American mailbox standing in the street is like. . . . I go over to the other end of the mall, the large, all-white post office" [*The Post Card*]). (Jacques Derrida Archives)

ance, are not original and transcendental conditions on the basis of which philosophy traditionally tries to (derive) effects, not subdeterminations or even epochs, it cannot be said, for example, that representative (or signifying or symbolic, etc.) structure *befalls* them; we shall not be able to assign periods or have some epoch of representation follow upon these *renvois*. As soon as there are *renvois*, and it is always already, something like representation no longer waits and we must perhaps arrange to tell this story differently, from *renvois* to *renvois* of *renvois,* in a destiny which is never certain of gathering itself up, of identifying itself, or of determining itself. I don't know if that can be said with or without Heidegger, and it does not matter.[5]

Epochs of the Postal

The problematic of the divisibility of the *trait*, which threatens the unity of destination, accounts for the distance separating the *envoi* of being from the adestination of the letter. Derrida makes clear that differance "offers itself to thought . . . *beyond the question of being*, of a gathered destiny or of the *envoi* of being,"[6] beyond the place thought by Heidegger, for whom "the place . . . is always a place of collecting together (*Versammlung*)."[7] A unity of emission can be deciphered in Heidegger's conception of the dispensation of being, even if it has neither point of departure or arrival: "the being-together of the originary *envoi* in a way arrives at or moors itself [*s'arrive*] to itself, closest to itself."[8] Whereas the epochs of being are not deployed in response to any teleology, they do nevertheless follow the ontological thread of the *Geschick*, and are collected in an originary *legein*. They are relayed through a unity, through the duction or *ductility* of the question of the *sense* of being, which remains for Heidegger, as is known, the question that directs and sets us right [*rectrice et directrice*].[9]

This question ensures and is at the same time ensured by a "sort of indivisibility of what is destined [*du destinal*]"[10] that keeps and safeguards this sense, that is to say the path. Indeed, for Heidegger, "Sense is always the direction (*sens*) of a road (*sent* and *set* in Indo-European)."[11] This is a road that never gets lost en route. Derrida finds proof of this indivisibility of what is destined in Heidegger's *periodization* of the history of being—"It is in basing itself on this gathered indivisibility of the *envoi* that Heidegger's reading can single out epochs"[12]—a periodization that still obeys, in its very structure, the *derivative schema* that governs the tradition. The epochs of being would still *be derived* from the *envoi* of being.

This is serious because it upsets perhaps Heidegger's still ("derivative") schema (perhaps), upsets by giving one to think that technology, the position, let us say even metaphysics do not come about, do not come *to determine* and to dissimulate an "*envoi*" of Being (which would not yet be postal), but would belong to the "first" *envoi*—which obviously is never "first" in any order whatsoever, for example a chronological or logical order, nor even the order of the *logos* (this is why one cannot replace, except for laughs, the formula "in the beginning was the logos" by "in the beginning was the post"). If the post (technology, position, "metaphysics") is announced at the "first" *envoi*, then there is no longer *LA métaphysique*, etc. (I will try to say this one more time and otherwise), nor even THE *envoi*, but *envois* without destination.[13]

In other words, postal technics does not happen to being; its catastrophe is not derived. Heidegger would not have admitted that but rather would have considered the "postal principle" as a determination proper to an epoch of being.

Tekhnē (and doubtless [Heidegger] would have considered the postal structure and everything that it governs as a *determination* (yes, precisely, your word), a metaphysical and technical determination of the *envoi* or of the destinality (*Geschick*, etc.) of Being, and he would have considered my entire insistence on the posts as a metaphysics corresponding to the technical era that I am describing, the end of a certain post, the dawn of another, etc.); now, *tekhnē*, this is the entire—infinitesimal and decisive—*differance*, *does not arrive*. No more than metaphysics, therefore, or than positionality; always, already it parasites that to which he says it happens, arrives, or that it succeeds in happening to [*arrive à arriver*]. This infinitesimal nuance changes everything in the relation between metaphysics and its doubles or its others.[14]

Derrida replies by showing that taking the postal principle out of the regime of ontological periodization certainly does not amount to excluding it from history (or from travel stories).

There is not even the post or the *envoi*, there are *posts* and *envois*. And this movement (which seems to me simultaneously very far from and very near to Heidegger's, but no matter) avoids submerging all the differences, mutations, scansions, structures of postal regimes into one and the same great central post office. In a word (this is what I would like to articulate more rigorously if I write it one day in another form), as soon as there is, there is *differance* (and this does not await language, especially human language, and the language of Being, only the mark and the divisible trait), and there is postal maneuvering, relays, delay, anticipation, destination, telecommunicating network, the possibility, and therefore the fatal necessity of going astray, etc. There is strophe (there is strophe in every sense, apostrophe and catastrophe, address in turning the address [always toward you, my love], and my post card is strophes). But this point of clarification gives one the possibility of assimilating none of the differences, the (technical, eco-political, phantasmatic etc.) differentiation of the telecommunicative powers. By no longer treating the posts as a metaphor of the *envoi* of Being, one can account for what essentially and decisively occurs, everywhere, and including in language, thought, science, and everything that conditions them, when the postal structure makes a shift, *Satz* if you will, and posits or posts itself otherwise. This is why this history of the posts, which I would like to write and to dedicate to you, cannot be a history of the posts: primarily because it concerns the very possibility of history, of all the concepts, too, of history, of tradition, of transmission or interruptions, going astray, etc. And then because such a "history of posts" would be but a minuscule *envoi* in the network that it allegedly would analyze (there is no metapostal), just a card lost in a bag, that a strike, or even a sorting accident, can always delay indefinitely, lose without return. This is why I will not write it, but I dedicate to you what remains of this impossible project. The (eschatological, apocalyptic) desire for the history of the posts worldwide is perhaps only a way, a very infantile way, of crying over the coming end of our "correspondence."[15]

There are therefore posts and sendings, and this disseminative pluralization of the *envoyage* robs the postal principle of its unity of sense, that is to say of its path. The postal principle does not have the sense of a question, nor is it a question about sense. The catastrophe—simple sorting accident—anodyne and banal, yet threatening or fatal, can compromise an *envoi*, the safe arrival and safe haven for a letter or traveler, for ever.

Such a catastrophe is too far from the truth, perhaps, for Heidegger to have conceived of its trait and for him to recognize it as initial catastrophe, as the machination of writing, a "difference unable to be repatriated within the envoi *of self.*"[16] In the end, Heidegger would remain naively on his *path*, within the *order of what is derived*, like Nietzsche, Freud, and all the others:

The charter is the contract for the following, which quite stupidly one has to believe: Socrates comes *before* Plato, there is between them—and in general—an order of generations, an irreversible sequence of inheritance. Socrates is before, not in front of, but before Plato, therefore behind him, and the charter binds us to this order: this is orientation in thinking, this is the left and this is the right, march. Socrates, he who does not write, as Nietzsche said (how many times have I repeated to you that I also found him occasionally or even always somewhat naive *on the edges*; remember that photograph of him with his "good guy" side, at the beginning in any event, before the "fit [*mal*]," before the disaster?). He understood nothing about the initial catastrophe, or at least about this one, since he knew all about the others. Like everyone else he believed that Socrates did not write, that he came before Plato who more or less wrote at his dictation and therefore let him write by himself, as he says somewhere. From this point of view, N. believed Plato and overturned nothing at all. The entire "overturning" remained included in the program of this credulity. This is true *a fortiori*, and each time with a different *a fortiori*, ready to screw everything up otherwise, of Freud and Heidegger.[17]

[25]

13

Italy and the *Countertime* of Love

The other side is also the side of the other, whom or which it is impossible to reach altogether. Once again, a floodgate controls access. The lovers' voyage—the memory of which traverses in particular "Envois" in *The Post Card*—is composed of inopportunities, contretemps, *countertimes.* The lovers of Verona live on and die of this separation within proximity.

It was near the Italian border, coming back from Florence, customs was not far off, you gave me a very greasy cheese to eat while I was driving, and I told you that you transfigured everything, you did not hear me, you made me repeat while turning the radio dial (I still see your finger, the greasy paper of the cheese, and the ring . . . [1]

(You remember, we had spoken of taking the plunge with a side trip to Sicily that summer, we were right near it, you were against it when, misfortune would have it that, on the coast south of Rome, that accursed phone call broke out over us, truly a blow—and the worst is that nothing had obliged me to call that night myself.)[2]

What happens to Romeo and Juliet, and which remains . . . an accident whose aleatory and unforeseeable appearance cannot be effaced, at the crossing of several series and beyond common sense, can only be what it is, accidental, insofar as it has *already* happened, in essence, before it happens.

The desire of Romeo and Juliet did not encounter the poison, the contretemps or the detour of the letter by chance. In order for this encounter to take place, there must *already* have been instituted a system of marks (names, hours, maps of places, dates and supposedly "objective" place-names) to thwart, as it were, the dispersion of interior and heterogeneous durations, to frame, organize, put in order, render possible a rendezvous: in other words to deny, while taking note of it, non-coincidence, the separation of monads, infinite distance, the disconnection of experiences, the multiplicity of worlds, everything that renders possible a contretemps or the irremediable detour of a letter. But the desire of Romeo and Juliet is born in the heart of this possibility. There would have been no love, the pledge would not have taken place, nor time, nor its theater, without discordance. The accidental contretemps comes to *remark* the essential contretemps. Which is as much as to say it is not accidental. It does not, for all that, have the signification of an essence or of a formal structure. This is not the abstract condition of possibility, a universal form of the relation to the other in general, a dialectic of desire or consciousness. Rather the singularity of an imminence whose "cutting point" spurs desire at its birth—the very birth of desire. I love because the other is the other, because its time will never be mine. The living duration, the very presence of its love remains infinitely distant from mine, distant from itself in that which stretches it toward mine and even in what one might want to describe as amorous euphoria, ecstatic communion, mystical intuition. I can love the other only in the passion of this aphorism. Which does not happen, does not come about like misfortune, bad luck, or negativity. It has the form of the most loving affirmation—it is the chance of desire. And it not only cuts into the fabric of durations, it spaces. Contretemps says something about topology or the visible; it opens theater.[3]

[7]

14

In the Field

Of little meaning or direction, in one sense. There are multiple orientations within this strange landscape that promises the perilous chance of an arrival without deriving, but which in promising keeps itself in reserve, that is to say always reserves the possibility of a surprise. Poem-hedgehog, no more one than the other, destined to know nothing of its *trait* of belonging, the traveler embarks upon a strange game: a textuality match with no offside rule, ordeal without limits.

Indeed, nothing outside the text, no origin, no indivisible mooring, no inviolable resting-place, no falling back into the house of being or into the sense of a pathway. Nothing, and for that very reason it amounts to an incessant journeying. It is a voyage that has its marks and points of reference, that doesn't fail to orient its hesitation in the face of divergent sense and direction. Derrida's work always lays out for the reader the topographical profile of the space it explores, that of a "countryside without country, opened onto the absence of a homeland, a marine landscape, space without territory, without private roads, without express locality [*lieu-dit*]."[1]

"There Is No Outside to the Text"

Derrida begins by disturbing the very concepts of opening and closing, interior and exterior. The difference between inside and outside is never given, it always remains to be produced.

If there is nothing outside the text, this implies, with the transformation of the concept of text in general, that the text is no longer the snug airtight inside of an interiority or an identity-to-itself . . . but rather a different placement of the effects of opening and closing.[2]

The movements of deconstruction are not brought to bear on structures from the outside. They are possible and effective, and able to take accurate aim, only by inhabiting those structures. Inhabiting them *in a certain way*, because one always inhabits and all the more when one does not suspect it. Operating necessarily from the inside, borrowing all the strategic and economic resources of subversion from the old structure, borrowing them structurally, that is to say without being able to isolate their elements and atoms, the enterprise of deconstruction always in a certain way falls prey to its own work.[3]

"Wherever We Are"

The point of departure cannot henceforth be justified in any absolute sense:

The opening of the question, the departure from the enclosure of a self-evidence, the putting into doubt of a system of oppositions, all these movements necessarily have the form of empiricism and of errancy. At any rate, they cannot be described, *as to past norms*, except in this form. No other trace is available, and as these errant questions are not absolute beginnings in every way, they allow themselves to be effectively reached, across the whole of their surface, by this description which is also a critique. We must begin *wherever we are* and the thought of the trace, which cannot not take the scent into account, has already taught us that it was impossible to justify a point of departure absolutely. *Wherever we are*: in a text where we already believe ourselves to be.[4]

The *departure* is radically empiricist. It proceeds like a wandering thought on the possibility of itinerary and of method. It is affected by nonknowledge as by its future and it *ventures out* deliberately.[5]

Belonging to a place, to any space of habitation whatsoever, in the world or in the text, can no longer be conceived of in terms of soil, blood, filiation, or descent.

What is a lineage in the order of discourse and text? If in a rather conventional way I call by the name of *discourse* the present, living, conscious *representation* of a *text* within the experience of the person who writes or reads it, and if the text constantly goes beyond this representation by means of the entire system of its resources and its own laws, then the question of genealogy exceeds by far the possibilities that are at present given for its elaboration. We know that the metaphor that would describe the genealogy of a text correctly is still *forbidden*. In its syntax and its lexicon, in its spacing, by its punctuation, its lacunae, its margins, the historical appurtenance of a text is never a straight line. It is neither causality by contagion, nor the simple accumulation of layers. Nor even the pure juxtaposition of borrowed pieces. And if a text always gives itself a certain representation of its own roots, those roots live only by that representation, by never touching the soil, so to speak. Which undoubtedly destroys their *radical essence*, but not the necessity of their *racinating function*. To say that one always interweaves roots endlessly, bending them to send down roots among the roots, to pass through the same points again, to redouble old adherences, to circulate among their differences, to coil around themselves or to be enveloped one in the other, to say that a text is never anything but a *system of roots*, is undoubtedly to contradict at once the concept of system and the pattern of the root. But in order not to be pure appearance, this contradiction takes on the meaning of a contradiction, and receives its "illogicality," only through being thought within a finite configuration—the history of metaphysics—and caught within a root system which does not end there and which as yet has no name.[6]

The Porousness of Borders

How does one cross a border if "the shore is divided in its very outline,"[7] if the trait is divisible, if there is a "crisis of versus,"[8] of the one against the other? Derrida shows that every border is perforated by a multiplicity of openings that render infractions of it ungovernable, uncontrol-

"The crossing of borders always announces itself according to the movement of a certain step [*pas*]—and of the step that crosses a line" (*Aporias*). Boundary stone marking the Tropic of Cancer, Baja California, Mexico. (Eric Jacolliot)

lable, even impossible. The frontier always intersects or breaches itself. Everything that is kept outside of it, expelled, not tolerated by it, comes back at it from the other side, confrontationally or indirectly.

The crossing of borders always announces itself according to the movement of a certain step [*pas*]—and of the step that crosses a line. An indivisible line. And one always assumes the institution of such an indivisibility. Customs, police, visa or passport, passenger identification—all of that is established upon the institution of the indivisible, the institution therefore of the step that is related to it, whether the step crosses it or not. Consequently, where the figure of the step is refused to intuition, where the identity or indivisibility of a line (*finis* or *peras*) is compromised, the identity to oneself and therefore the possible identification of an intangible edge—the crossing of the line—becomes a *problem*. There is a *problem* as soon as the edge-line is threatened. And it is threatened from its first tracing. This tracing can only institute the line by dividing it intrinsically into two sides. There is a *problem* as soon as this intrinsic division divides the relation to itself of the border and therefore divides identity or the being-one-self [*ipséité*] of anything whatsoever.[9]

Shibboleth

Oblique and transversal paths, interferences, contamination; every mark of belonging, every singularity or idiom is from its origin subject to migration [*transhumance*]; like a quotation or a translation, always expatriated, without habitat.

In principle, the quotation-translation that I am for a moment comparing to a transhumance always seems possible from any place to any other place, from anywhere to anywhere. A quotation-transhumance always seems possible. Starting from the translation, reception, and recycling of a thought, the movement of a quotation, like the incitement to the quotation, can seem to come from anywhere and thus to challenge its indigenousness, indeed its autochthony, the place of its origin, its habitat, its archivation, its library. Its idiom in sum and ownership in general. And the architects assembled here are not by chance today great artists of the quotational graft and experts in rhetoric. Place itself and, among all places, the place of habitat or possible residence, the end of a transhumance, is defined after the fact, like this *anywhere* that comes to be determined, to suspend its wandering or its organized migration, from what one imports to it or exports from it. Place then becomes a reach [*portée*] or a *port*, which in the French idiom also leads us to the musical staff [*la portée musicale*] as well as seaport, or comportment [*port de tête*], in other words, to the head [*chef, caput*], the place of capital or what one also calls in my language, the county seat [*chef-lieu*], indeed the capital: the privileged site of decision, of accumulated wealth, of authority or power, a centripetal and at the same time centrifugal hearth or focus. The port is sometimes a cape, and we are here, on this island, not far from a place where the port and the cape are one.[10]

Where do the dividing lines pass among the event of an inaugural statement, a quotation, paraphrase, commentary, translation, reading, interpretation?[11]

The "dividing line" or improbable limit does not exist other than as a password, as a mark having no sense in and of itself but which allows distinctions to be *made*, like a "shibboleth."

A *shibboleth*, the word *shibboleth*, if it is one, names, in the broadest extension of its generality or its usage, every insignificant arbitrary mark, for example the phonemic difference between *shi* and *si*, as that difference becomes discriminative, decisive, and divisive. The difference has no meaning in and of itself, but it becomes what one must know how to recognize and above all to mark if one is *to take the next step* [faire le pas], to get over the border of a place or the threshold of a poem, to see oneself granted asylum or the legitimate habitation of a language. So as no longer to be beyond the law. And to inhabit a language, one must already have a *shibboleth* at one's disposal: not simply understand the meaning of the word, not simply *know* this meaning or know how a word *should* be pronounced (the difference of *h* between *shi* and *si*: this the Ephraimites knew), but *be able* to say it as one ought, as one ought to be able to say it. It does not suffice to know the difference; one must be capable of it, must be able to do it, or know how to do it—and doing here means *marking*.[12]

Collapse of the Edges and *Accosting* the Other

Marking difference while acknowledging that it remains an improbable task means accepting to position oneself only in the *surrounds* [parages] of the other, renouncing *accosting* [aborder] them directly or face on.

The Unpresentable Approach

Accosting [aborder] is the slowness of a movement of approach, between gesture and discourse, a movement that doesn't yet reach its end, attain its goal—here that is the shore [*rive*]—doesn't yet arrive, hasn't yet arrived or occurred. As a movement (or step or not), it hasn't yet made contact with the edge [*bord*], which only remains an edge with respect to it to the extent that it isn't touched or that its contiguity doesn't totally erase what is distinct or distant. *Aborder* means hailing or signaling from afar; it thus also means calling to the distance from a distance and depends on the initiative and place of the other, who, being thus provoked, doesn't necessarily accept to be accosted. Come: in this suspense of a distancing proximity, the edge of the approach (or, to come back to the sea, of boarding for verification of identity) is dissimulated without for all that being presented elsewhere.[13]

The Step Not [pas]

The problematic of the approach to the other is inseparable from the logic of the *pas*, which has to be understood in two ways: the *pas* as noun relating to passage (step, advance), and the *pas* of negation. Both signal toward the act of crossing a border and at the same time the impossibility of passage. The sense of the formula "step not beyond" [*pas au-delà*] or what "goes for a certain *pas*" [*il y va d'un certain pas*] is therefore undecidable. The *step-not toward the other doesn't find its place.*

In our starting point, however, we will dogmatically begin with the axiom according to which no context is absolutely saturable or saturating. No context can determine meaning to the point of exhaustiveness. Therefore the context neither produces nor guarantees impassable borders, thresholds that no step could pass, *trespass*, as our anglophone friends would say. By recalling that this sentence, *il y va d'un certain pas*, is untranslatable, I am thinking not only of translatability into another language or into the other's language. For any translation into a non-French language would lose something of its potential multiplicity. And if one measures untranslatability, or rather the essential incompleteness of translating, against this remainder, well, then a similar border *already* passes between the several versions or interpretations of the same sentence *in French*. The *shibboleth* effect operates *within*, if one may still say so, the French language.[14]

For example, and to limit myself to just two possibilities, *first of all*, one can understand it, that is, one can paraphrase it in this way: he is going there at a certain pace [*il y va d'un certain pas*], that is to say, someone, the other, you or me, a man or a walking animal, in the masculine or the neuter, goes somewhere with a certain gait. Indeed, one will say: look, he is stepping out at a certain pace [*il y va d'un certain pas*], he is going there (to town, to work, to combat, to bed—that is to say, to dream, to love, to die) with a certain gait [*pas*]. Here the third person pronoun "he" [*il*] has the grammatical value of a masculine personal subject.

But, *secondly*, one can also understand and paraphrase the same sentence, *il y va d'un certain pas*, in another way: what is concerned—neuter and impersonal subject—what one is talking about here, is the question of the step, the gait, the pace, the rhythm, the passage, or the traversal. . . .

Thirdly, and finally, this time in inaudible quotation marks or italics, one can also mention a mark or negation, by citing it: a certain "not" [*pas*] (*no, not, nicht, kein*).[15]

[The *pas*] is accomplished in its very impossibility, it enfranchises itself with respect to itself.[16]

The step [*pas*] that approaches steps away [*é-loigne*], at the same time and in the same step that denies itself and takes itself off, it reduces and extends its own distance.[17]

Spur

This strange *advance* has the form of a spur:

Thus, the style would seem to advance in the manner of a *spur* of sorts [*éperon*]. Like the prow, for example, of a sailing vessel, its *rostrum*, the projection of the ship which surges ahead to meet the sea's attack and cleave its hostile surface.

Or yet again, and still in nautical terminology, the style might be compared to that rocky point, also called an *éperon*, on which the waves break at the harbor's entrance.[18]

The *éperon*, which is translated *sporo* in Frankish or High German, *spor* in Gaelic, is pronounced *spur* in English. In *Les mots anglais* Mallarmé relates it to the verb *to spurn*, that is, to disdain, to rebuff, to reject scornfully. Although this may not be a particularly fascinating homonym, there is still a necessary historic and semantic operation from one language to the other evident in the fact that the English *spur*, the *éperon*, is the «same word» as the German *Spur*: or, in other words, trace, wake, indication, mark.[19]

Surround

Parages (surrounds) again: this noun seems to emerge all by itself—that is at least what it looks like—in order to record a certain economy of themes and senses, for example the undecidability of close and far, setting off [*appareil-lage*] in the mist, in sight of what does or doesn't arrive or moor itself to the vicinity of the coast, the impossible and necessary cartography of a littoral, an incalculable topology, the laws of movement of what cannot be governed.[20]

Parages: let us entrust in this single word what situates, near or far, the double movement of approach and distancing, often in the same step, singularly divided, older and younger than itself, always other, on the verge of the event, when it arrives *and* doesn't arrive, infinitely distant at the approach of the other shore.[21]

Margin

The surrounds "mark a margin" that philosophical discourse cannot "infinitely reappropriate."[22] To give the margin its due comes down to taking into account a labyrinthine structure, like that of the ear or its "tympan," "a partition in a delicate, differentiated structure whose orifices may always remain unfindable, and whose entry and exit may be barely passable."[23]

Where has the body of the text gone when the margin is no longer a secondary virginity but an inexhaustible reserve, the stereographic activity of an entirely other ear?

Overflows and cracks: that is, on the one hand compels us to count in its margin more and less than one believes is said or read, an unfolding due to the structure of the mark (which is the same word as *marche*, as limit, and as margin); and on the other hand, luxates the very body of statements in their pretension to univocal rigidity or regulated polysemia. A lock opened to a double understanding no longer forming a single system.

Which does not just amount to acknowledging that the margin maintains itself within *and* without. Philosophy says so too: *within* because philosophical discourse intends to know and to master its margin, to define the line, align the page, enveloping it in its volume. *Without* because the margin, *its* margin, *its* outside are empty, are outside: a negative about which there seems to be nothing to do, a negative without effect in the text *or* a negative working in the service of meaning, the margin *relevé* (*aufgehoben*) in the dialectics of the Book. Thus, one will have said nothing, or in any event done nothing, in declaring "against" philosophy or "about" philosophy that its margin is within or without, within and without, simultaneously the inequality of its internal spacing and the regularity of its borders. Simultaneously, by means of rigorous, philosophically *intransigent* analyses, *and* by means of the inscription of marks which no longer belong to philosophical space, not even to the neighborhood of its other, one would have to displace philosophy's alignment of its own types. To write otherwise. To delimit the space of a closure no longer analogous to what philosophy can represent for itself under this name, according to a straight or circular line enclosing a homogenous space. To determine, entirely against any philosopheme, the intransigence that prevents it from calculating its margin, by means of a *limitrophic* violence imprinted according to new *types*. To eat the margin in luxating the tympanum, the relationship to itself of the double membrane. So that philosophy can no longer reassure itself that it has always *maintained* its tympanum.[24]

[2]

15

The Prague Affair

The reprieve is incalculable. Who knows what can happen to the traveler, what inopportunity, what delay, what accident? Derrida could not, for example, have anticipated what was waiting for him in Prague, in 1981, as he was passing through customs at the airport, on his way back to France after giving a clandestine seminar with a group of students from the Jan Hus Association. How could he have foreseen that at that moment, when symbolically at least he was "with his own people," that drugs would be "found" in his luggage and that he would be sent to prison?[1] "The little Jew expelled from the Lycée Ben Aknoun" and "the purveyor of drugs incarcerated in Prague" are indeed the same person. From the time of the painful loss of his French citizenship in Algeria, Derrida was preparing for the worst: "Whether they expelled me from school or threw me into prison, I always thought the other must have good reason to accuse me."[2]

Q.: Last year, you went to Prague to meet some Czech intellectuals. At the airport, as you were leaving, the customs agents "found" drugs in your suitcase. You spent twenty-four hours in prison and were freed thanks to the intervention of the French government. What was, during those twenty-four hours, your experience of this dissociation?

J.D.: Perhaps a somewhat more ruthless insight, but also a sort of compassion. Despite everything, before my imprisonment, there was that eight-hour interrogation with some terrifying State officials whom one could also have pity for. The prosecutor, the police chief, the translator, and the lawyer assigned to me knew very well why this trap had been set, they knew that the others knew, were watching each other, and conducted the whole comedy with an unshakable complicity. They put on another play when the same ones came to liberate me, addressing me respectfully as "Monsieur le Professeur." Since I had often spoken of Kafka (at that time I was working on a little text on "Before the Law" which I had with me, and no doubt it was when I went to visit Kafka's grave that they took care of my valise in the hotel), the lawyer said to me in an aside: "You must have the impression of living in a Kafka story." And then later: "Don't take things too tragically; consider it a literary experience." I responded that I did take it tragically, but first of all for him—or for them, I don't know exactly. And then, as for me, the dissociations were different but just as indescribable in a few words. I knew the scenario and I did, I think, everything that *had* to be done. But how to describe all the archaic movements that are un-leashed below that surface, at the moment when the trap was sprung at customs, during the interrogation, during the first incarceration—the guards' yells and insults through the reinforced door and even in the soli-tary cell where one of them made a gesture to hit me because I asked for a French lawyer, and then the nudity, the photographs (I have never been more photographed in my life, from the airport to the prison, clothed or naked before putting on the prisoner's "uniform")? All of this is part of such a common experience, alas, that it would be indecent to tell it unless I could recapture some absolute singularity, which I cannot do while im-provising in front of a microphone. The very first time I spoke before a tel-evision camera, I had to be silent about what *my* experience was, which at that moment didn't hold any great interest. It was at night, in Germany, on the train that brought me back from Prague. It seemed to me that, at that moment, I ought to speak of what had just happened, to which I was the only one capable of testifying and which had some general interest. Still I had to be satisfied with broad stereotypes of the sort: "I-went-there-out-of-solidarity-with-those-who-are-struggling-for-the-respect-of-human-rights, etc." This was all true, and I wanted especially to salute those whom I had met there, both in and out of prison. But how can you expect me, in that situation, to say to someone from Channel 2 who puts a microphone in front of me: "You know, I am asking myself certain questions about the State, the foundations and the function of the discourse on human rights today"? Or else: "The essential then is what was said there in the outlawed seminar about the political question of the 'subject' and other related things"? Or else: "What I really lived through there would demand a completely different form of narration, another poetics than that of the evening news"? Or else: "There was someone in me who seemed, in spite of everything, to take pleasure in something about that prison, who seemed to be reliving some hallucination, who seemed to want it to last longer, and to regret bitterly the betrayal he felt at the moment of leaving the five kids who were with me in the second prison cell"?

Just imagine the look on the faces of the reporters and the TV viewers. But the difficulty I felt in the most acute way at that moment is permanent, and it is what paralyzes me every time I have to take the floor and speak in public. Even here, still, now.[3]

Ten years ago in Prague, just before being taken to prison and just after an eight-hour official interrogation, I asked the commissar in an aside, "Come on, just between us, tell me, do you really believe, deep down, that someone like me—an intellectual, a philosopher, an old prof—is going to amuse himself by coming to Czechoslovakia to undertake some drug trafficking?" (Production and traffic of drugs were the charges that had just been officially brought against me.) The commissar's response: "Yes, yes, exactly, we are used to it; it's people like you who do that, most often, well-known intellectuals, artists—look what happened to the Beatles in Japan. Listen, I tell you this to reassure you, they also were indulgent with them precisely because they are very well known.[4]

And I tell myself this morning in the mirror who are you talking to, I've missed you, you've missed me, there are still a few days to be spent here before passing from life to death, hers or mine, I have begun to enter old age and see my eyebrows turn white without having known the writing of conversion, that convent that the Ruzyne prison made me dream of for a few hours, in Prague, between Christmas and New Year 1982, when in a

terrified jubilation, before seeing the infernal cell, before that Czech offi-
cer had screamed and threatened me, hand raised, before putting on the
striped pajamas, I thought that at last, at last, I was going to be able to re-
hearse, and then write, write for years in pencil on a clean whitewood political prisoners' table, I see the film of my whole life, henceforth, ten years
after my birth, and for ten years now, framed by two sets of bars, two
heavy, metal interdictions, the expulsion and the incarceration, out of
school and into prison, that's what I return to every day, that's what I'm becoming, that's what I was, that's where I write, each time caught up again
by one and freed from the other, more locked up in one than in the other,
but which, each time from the feeling of an illegible accident, of a wound
as virtual, as unmemorable as it is undecipherable to the fortuitous victim
of the modern sacrifice which would give me space, to me, irreplaceably,
where they got me, where they will never get me, they masculine or feminine, the irreplaceable mission no longer leaving you, any more than
here, the choice between the aleatory and the calculable, myself where I
am, on this day, only by no longer trying to rediscover myself according to
some regular and geological relation between chance and necessity, up to
the other to invent me.[5]

[20]

16

Correspondences

Telegram

I did not like your sending me that telegram. I thought I felt something other than haste in it, even the opposite, an economical way of not writing to me, of saving your time, of "expediting." You expedite me in a way that I previously would have accepted from no one—but I no longer cry when you depart, I walk, I walk, on my head of course. You forgot perhaps that the first telegram danced (years ago). It came from the neighboring post office, you could have brought it yourself. I understood nothing except that it danced and while driving I held it on the steering wheel our telegraphic style, our post card love, our tele-orgasmization, our sublime stenography[1]

Stamp

Have still received nothing from you, it is long, I miss you. Yesterday already I took control of the place, as I do everywhere that I arrive. Translation: I am preparing the maximum of pickups for myself, counting them, very attentive especially to such and such a one, that I must not miss, for example Saturday afternoon or Sunday. This is the first appeasement, when I am without you, and in order really to feel what I am talking about, I mean about my body, you must recall what an American mailbox standing in the street is like, how one opens it, how the pickups are indicated, and the form and the weight of that oblique cover that you pull toward yourself at the last moment. And then I go over to the other end of the mall, the large, all-white post office, to buy a series of rare or recent stamps and how well you know that this becomes a rite, a slow ceremony for every letter. I choose, I calculate, I write to you on the envelope with all these *stamps* (every autumn I again find the lady who sells the stamps in bulk or for philatelists, she is enormous and has difficulty moving around in the glass booth where she is enclosed; she is very bossy and very lively nevertheless, I think she really understands me, she would like to take part in a great scene that she doesn't follow, she treats me a bit like a son who comes to make obscene confidences to her). It's new, the love of stamps, in me, it's not a collector's love but only a sender's love. And I want you to look at the envelope for a long time before you open me. Here I am not speaking of the word *"timbre,"* with which I have a very old liaison (along with the types, the tympans, *qual quelle*, etc.), but of the little rectangular sticker charged with captions and pictures. It is an allegory of all of history, our history, that I would like to recount to you interminably in the letter every time, as if I were boasting by lodging it there entirely. For example, suppose that one day a stamp of S. and p. is made. Well then, in advance those two would comprehend us. Using a certain art of classic composition, and of recomposition, one could tell everything about us with the traits of this scene. I bet that nothing is missing and that we are right there.[2]

Hanging up just now (as always, "hang up,"—"No, you hang up,"—"No, you,"—You hang up, you," "You hang up," "I'm hanging up," etc.), I was in seventh heaven, I was laughing softly over our learned conversation (we are completely crazy!) concerning the word "philately." Learned, finally, is saying a lot. For in the end, Diotima, they are somewhat lacking a dictionary in your country house. No, philately does not mean love of distance, of the term, of the *telos* or of the tele-, nor the love of letters, no, my very near one full of sun, it is a very recent word, it is only as old as stamps, that is of the State monopoly, and it treats of *ateleia* (the *facteur*, not the truth). *Ateleia* is franking, the exemption from taxes, whence the

"There is but that, this reproduction of a reproduction of which
I am dying and which forbids me" (*The Post Card*). (Erik Bullot)

stamp. It is true that it maintains therefore a relation with one of the senses of
telos: acquittal, exemption, payment, cost, expenditure, fee. From acquittal
one could go to gift, offering, and even, in Sophocles, marriage ceremony!
Phila-tely then is love *without*, with/without marriage, and the collection of
all stamps, the love of the stamp with or without stamped love. But along with
all the other senses of *telos* (particularly that of power, of absolute jurisdiction
or of full power, that of the pleasure principle, the PP that I talk about all the
time in *Legs*), you can see all that one might do. I will leave the thing to be
done all by itself, I always prefer. But I would really like to call the book *philately* in order to commemorate secretly our somewhat nutty phone call.[3]

Postcard

I will have sent you only cards. Even if they are letters and if I always put
more than one in the same envelope.[4]

I prefer cards, one hundred cards or reproductions in the same envelope rather than a single "true" letter.[5]

I write you the letters of a traveling salesman.[6]

You said it to me one day, I think, I always write *on* support, right on the support but also on the subject. Expected result, it deforms it, thereby I broach its destruction, all the while showing it, itself, in the course of *being* that which destroys itself, falls into pieces, a bit theatrical, and then incinerates itself beneath your eyes and there is no longer anything but your eyes. You understand that this is the insupportable partition of the support. It is within reason not to support it, and I understand this readily to the extent that I am reasonable, like you and like everyone, but precisely at stake there is reason. Okay.

For example I write *on* post cards, oh well I write on post cards. "I" begins again with a reprosuction (say, I just wrote reproSuction: have you noticed that I make more and more strange mistakes, is it fatigue or age, occasionally the spelling goes, phonetic writing comes back in force, as in elementary school where it did not happen to me moreover, only to others whom I confusedly looked down on—plus the *lapsus* or "*slips*" obviously). And by means of a reproduction itself reproduced serially, always the same picture on another support, but an identical support, differing only *numéro*. It dates from when, the post card, "properly speaking," do you know? Nineteenth century necessarily, with photography and the stamp, unless . . . Want to write and first to reassemble an enormous library on the *courrier*, postal institutions, techniques and mores of telecommunication, networks and epochs of telecommunication throughout history—but the "library" and the "history" themselves are precisely but "posts," sites of passage or relay among others, stases, moments or effects of *restance*, and also particular representations, narrower and narrower, shorter and shorter sequences, proportionally, of the Great Telematic Network, the *worldwide connection.*[7]

Again the card (S *et* p, this is the proposition made to us and if you get it, come to the rendez-vous). From the beginning of this trip I have had the impression—it is taking on a very "compulsive" aspect as they say (compulsion is a very beautiful word no longer understood, one no longer feels the assembling of the push [you, you are the push] and repetition compulsion is understood even less)—I have the impression that everything comes to resemble itself, and me first of all, in a post card, the post card—that I am, am following [*que je suis*]. There is but that, this reproduction of a reproduction of which I am dying and which forbids me, which makes of you, my living one, an interdiction

they have *intercepted* us

and I do not believe that one can properly call "post card" a unique or original image, if some such thing ever occurs, a painting or drawing destined to someone *in the guise* of a post card and abandoned to an anonymous third party, to a neutral machinery that supposedly leads the message to its destination, or at least that would have its support make its way, for if the post card is a kind of open letter (like all letters), one can always, in time of peace and under certain regimes, attempt to make it indecipherable without compromising its making its way. Indecipherable, my unique one, even for the addressee. And yet there are but post cards, it's terrifying.[8]

Telephone

3 June 1977.

and when I call you my love, my love, is it you I am calling or my love? You, my love, is it you I thereby name, is it to you that I address myself? I don't know if the question is well put, it frightens me. But I am sure that the answer, if it gets to me one day, will have come to me from you. You alone, my love, you alone will have known it.

we have asked each other the impossible, as the impossible, both of us.

"*Ein jeder Engel ist schrecklich,*" beloved.

when I call you my love, is it that I am calling you, yourself, or is it that I am telling you my love? and when I tell you my love is it that I am declaring my love to you or indeed that I am telling *you*, yourself, my love, and that you are my love. I want so much to tell you.[9]

Your voice just now again (small, red, paned booth in the street, under a tree, a drunk was watching me the whole time and wanted to speak to me; he circled around the glass cage, stopped from time to time, a bit frightening, with a solemn air, as if to pronounce judgment), your voice closer than ever. The chance of the telephone—never lose an opportunity—it gives back our voice certain evenings, at night especially, even more so when it is all there is and the device blinds us to everything (I don't know if I ever told you that, additionally, I often close my eyes while talking to you), when the line is clear and the *timbre* refinds a kind of "filtered" purity (it is a bit in this element that I imagine the return of revenants, by means of the effect or the grace of a subtle and sublime, essential, sorting—through the static [*parasites*], for there is nothing but parasites, as well you know, and therefore the revenants have no chance, unless there have only ever, from the first "come" [*viens*], been revenants. The other day, in the course of a small task, I noticed that the word "parasite" had regularly imposed itself upon me an incalculable number of times, for years, from "chapter" to "chapter." Now, parasites, here it is, can love each other [*s'aimer*]. We[10]

10 June 1977.

I am arriving now

Forgot again just now the time difference [*décalage horaire*], doubtless because I knew that you would not be alone. You can imagine (I would like us to read it together, losing ourselves in it) the immense *carte* of the communications called "immediate" (the telephone, etc., call it telepathy) across the distance and network of "time differences" (all the red points that light up at the same time on our map of Europe). We would have arranged things, this fine morning, first gear passed, in order to speak to each other *all the time*, write to each other, see, touch, eat, drink, send, destine this or that, you or me, permanently, without the slightest interruption, without half-time, simply by banking on relativity, calculating with the universal time difference [*décalage*] (pulling out the stops [*cales*] or multiplying them?). *Moreover, this is what does happen.* Between writing with a pen or speaking on the telephone, what a difference. That is the word. How well I know the system of objections, but they do not hold, in sum do not go far enough. You can see clearly that S. is telephoning and behind the other one is whispering.[11]

Plane from Heathrow tonight. I will have tried to call you back again (*collect*) from now till then, if the line is free. If ever I should no longer arrive, you know what will have been my last, my last what in fact? Certainly not will. My last image at the back of my eyes, my last word, the name, all of this together, and I will not have kept my belt buckled, one strophe more, the orgasm and final compulsion, I will swim in your name without turning back, but you will never be your name, you never have been, even when, and especially when you have answered to it. The name is made to do without the life of the bearer, and is therefore always somewhat the name of someone dead. One could not live, be there, except by protesting against one's name, by protesting one's non-identity with one's proper name. When I called you, at the wheel, you were dead. *As soon as* I named you, as soon as I recalled your first name. And you came right out and said so on the phone, before the first rendez-vous, timorously invoking, with what lucidity, your "instinct of conservation." By blackmailing your higher feelings ("you say instinct of conservation? don't you find that this lacks a little . . . ?") I made you give it up for a time, but according to your criteria, which will never be mine, conservation seems to have gotten the upper hand again. In order to conserve what, the calculation is impossible. I hope I can spot you when I land[.][12]

Fax

Once unfolded, the title itself, *faxitexture*, would play among Greek, Latin, and English idioms: *architecture, fac, tele-fax*, that is to say, *tele-fac-simile, fact* and *fake, false, faux, fausse-facture, fausse préface*, etc.[13]

I insist on the Fax: it already signals something of speed and the televisual mode of communication that links, although still on a paper support, any point in space with any other (from anywhere to anywhere), thus conditioning in a certain way the production, the construction, but also, perhaps, the de-construction of places, localization and delocalization, occupation or habitation of territories, their centering, their assembling, but also their decentering and their dissemination, their placement and their replacement, affecting also both reflection and decision in these domains that are no longer exactly *domains*.[14]

Telepathy

Always difficult to imagine that one can think something to oneself [*a part soi*], deep down inside, without being surprised by the other, without the other being immediately informed, as easily as if it had a giant screen in it, at the time of the talkies, with remote control [*télécommande*] for changing channels and fiddling with the colours, the speech dubbed with large letters in order to avoid any misunderstanding.[15]

For here is my final paradox, which you alone will understand clearly: it is because there would be telepathy that a postcard can not arrive at its destination. The ultimate naivety would be to allow oneself to think that Telepathy guarantees a destination which "posts and telecommunications" fail to provide. On the contrary, everything I said about the postcard-structure [*la structure cartepostalée*] of the mark (interference, parasiting, divisibility, iterability, *and so on*) is found in the network. This goes for any tele-system—whatever its content, form, or medium of support.[16]

[19]

"The Oxford Scene"

The Event That Reverses

"The space of reversibility" could be another name for *The Post Card* for it explores such a space in every sense and direction. Indeed, what is a postcard if not reversibility itself, a message that gets turned around, image and text, a brief message sent while one is traveling, legible to all along the way, although reserved for one addressee in particular, delivering its secret to whichever postman comes along?

Derrida has "a whole supply"[1] of postcards and he disseminates them throughout the itinerant text of "Envois," between Europe and the United States, from Oxford to Paris by way of Reading, Antwerp, Geneva, Strasbourg, or Italy, and from New York to Irvine by way of Yale or Washington. A whole supply of one and the same card, the one discovered in Oxford, whose image is precisely the revelation of reversibility itself: Socrates writing while Plato dictates, providing a graphic inversion of the traditional order of derivation obtaining between speaking and writing. This about-face, explicitly called "the initial catastrophe,"[2] motivates all the voyages undertaken by the card's sender. The reversal represented on the card emblematizes a certain path of thinking and of the letter whose convolutions are revealed while Derrida travels abroad. "Envois" stages the startling collision between "lived" and "theoretical" voyage, a collision that makes the sense of *destination* vacillate and, against this epistolary background, upsets derivative logic, that of a continuous passage from one shore to another, from one country or continent to another, from a sender to an addressee.

Accident–Apocalypse

In a way "the Oxford scene"[3] (Derrida discovers the Socrates–Plato postcard in the Bodleian Library) repeats "the Writing Lesson" by reversing it. The encounter with the card is indeed an accident, a *revealing* incident, and once again it provokes a catastrophe by unveiling it. The discovery of this card takes place thanks to the "machinations" of two of Derrida's friends, Jonathan and Cynthia, who are guiding him in a labyrinthine circuit through the town and through the different colleges comprising Oxford University.

Coming back to Plato and Socrates. Yesterday, then, Jonathan and Cynthia are guiding me through the city. I like them, he is working on a poetics of the apostrophe. While we walk, she tells me about her work projects (18th century correspondence and libertine literature, Sade, a whole plot of writings that I cannot summarize, and then Daniel Deronda, by G. Eliot, a story of circumcision and of double-reading) and we turn into the labyrinth between the colleges. I suspect them of having had a plan. They themselves know the *carte*. No, not the map of the city, but the one that I am sending you, this incredible representation of Socrates (if indeed it is him) turning his back to Plato in order to write. They had already seen it, and could easily foresee the impression it would make on me. The program was in place and working.[4]

Jonathan and Cynthia were standing near me next to the glass case, the table rather, where laid out, under glass, in a transparent case, among the hundreds of reproductions displayed there, this card had to jump out at me. I saw nothing else, but that did not prevent me from feeling that right near me Jonathan and Cynthia were observing me obliquely, watching me look. As if they were spying on me in order to finish the effects of a spectacle they had staged (they have just married more or less)

I no longer knew what to do with myself. How to see to the bottom of all those rectangles between Socrates' legs, if it is Socrates? I still do not know how to see what there is to see. It gives the impression (look at it from the other side, turn the card over) that Plato, if it is Plato, does not see either, perhaps does not even want to know, looking elsewhere and further off over the shoulder of the other, what S. is in the middle, in train, yes, *en train*, of writing or scratching on a last little rectangle, a last little one in the middle of all others (count them, there are at least 23). This last little one is the most "interior" of all of them, it appears untouched. It is Socrates' writing surface, and you can imagine the missive or the rectangular chart, Socrates' post card. To whom do you think he is writing? For me it is always more important to know that than to know what is being written; moreover I think it amounts to the same, to the other finally. And plato, distinctly smaller, hitches himself up behind Socrates, with one foot in the air as if he wanted to come up to the same height or if he were running in order to catch a moving train (which is what he did anyhow, no?).[5]

The image of the postcard (reproduction from an illuminated manuscript) is itself in a certain sense accidental. Normally it would be Socrates who speaks and Plato who writes, not the reverse. The author of the illumination, Matthew Paris, illustrator of a fortune-telling book, book of fate, divination, good fortune, adventure, or chance, must have made a mistake, gotten distracted or diverted. An error of fate, therefore, perhaps, but also, and at the same time, a sign of destiny. In fact, this gross mistake, this inversion, this illustrative catastrophe comes to attest—without our being able to understand its provenance or origin—to the very failure of provenance and the absence of origin, the inversion or initial fault elaborated by Derrida well before his encounter with the card. There again, as in Lévi-Strauss's account, the card-accident seems to confirm a structural law, but in reverse: Plato behind Socrates, writing before speaking.

Have you seen this card, the image on the back [*dos*] of this card? I stumbled across it yesterday, in the Bodleian (the famous Oxford library), I'll tell you about it. I stopped dead, with a feeling of hallucination (is he crazy or what? he has the names mixed up!) and of revelation at the same time, an apocalyptic revelation: Socrates writing, writing in front of Plato, I always knew it, it had remained like the negative of a photograph

Bodleian Library, Oxford ("The Duke Humphrey Room, in the *Old Library*... sanctuary of the most precious manuscripts" [*The Post Card*]). (Jean-Michel Voge)

waiting to be developed for twenty-five centuries—in me of course. It just needed to be written in broad daylight. The developer [*révélateur*] is there, unless I still can't decipher anything in this picture, which is what is most probable in fact. Socrates, the one who writes—seated, bent over, as scribe or docile copyist, Plato's secretary, no? He is in front of Plato, no, Plato is *behind* him, smaller (why smaller?), but standing up. With his outstretched finger he looks like he is indicating something, designating, showing the way or giving an order—or dictating, authoritarian, masterly, imperious. Almost wicked, don't you think, and intentionally so. I bought a whole supply of them.[6]

I have not yet recovered from this revelatory catastrophe: Plato behind Socrates. Behind he has always been, as it is thought, but not like that. Me, I always knew it, and they did too, those two, I mean. What a couple. Socrates turns his *back* to plato, who has made him write whatever he wanted while pretending to receive it from him. This reproduction is sold here as a *post card*, you have noticed, with *greetings* and *address*. Socrates writing, do you realize, and on a post card. I know nothing more about it than what the caption says (it has been taken from a fortune-telling book, an astrological book: prediction, the book of destinies, fate, sort, encounter, chance, I don't know, I'll have to see, but I like this idea), I wanted to address it to you right away, like a piece of news, an adventure, a chance simultaneously anodine, anecdotal, and overwhelming, the most ancient and the last.[7]

What I admired the most, then, is rather the overturning [*renversement*], or say, rather, the final *reversement*, for it might indeed be a question of that, and the English word ("reversed") puts us on the track of the French *reverser* better, even if it primarily means overturned or inverted, permuted.[8]

Seen from the Back: "Reversibility Goes Mad"

This is what makes all the difference with respect to the "Writing Lesson": accident and discovery intervene not in order to affect or harm a state of affairs, but in order to confirm a generalized accidentality, as if in passing, between chance and necessity. This is a truth that cannot be looked at face on because, in its very evidence, it turns its back and removes itself from sight: *it does not present itself.* Writing pushes speaking in the back, and everything happens as if the postcard were sent even before the voyage took place, preceding it always, from the start. Moreover, no voyage is possible without this priority, and it destines every messenger, every speaking or writing subject, to run without respite, to receive the baton without ever being able to catch up with the starting point of the first archive. This relay race is another name for the history of philosophy. A mad reversibility that opens up thinking to its *project.*

What I prefer, about post cards, is that one does not know what is in front or what is in back, here or there, near or far, the Plato or the Socrates, recto or verso. Nor what is the most important, the picture or the text, and in the text, the message or the caption, or the address. Here, in my post card apocalypse, there are proper names, S. and p., above the picture, and reversibility unleashes itself, goes mad.[9]

9 June 1977.

Plato wants to emit. Seed, artificially, technically. The devil of a *Socrates* holds the syringe. To sow the entire earth, to send the same fertile card to *everyone*. A *pancarte*, a pan-card, a billboard that we have on our backs although we can never really turn our back on it or turn it around. For example, poor Freud, Plato, via Socrates, via all the addressees who are found on the Western way, the relays, the porters, the readers, the copyists, the archivists, the guardians, the professors, the writers, the *facteurs*, right?, Plato sticks him with his *pancarte* and Freud has it on his back, can no longer get rid of it. Result, result, for it is not so simple and as-I-show-in-my-book it is then Plato who is the inheritor, for Freud. Who pulls the same trick, somewhat, on Plato that Plato pulls on Socrates. This is what I call a catastrophe.[10]

Interminable lineage: all the philosophers push in each other's back, repeating without knowing it the initial catastrophe, involving it in the adventure of history and of filiation: "The first catastrophe is the ignoble archive which rots everything, the descent [*descendance*] into which everything tumbles."[11]

The fantasy of a whole metaphysics consists in wanting—without even knowing it—to counter the travel drive (the *ec-static* structure of the postcard that leaves ahead of every departure), to bring order to the race: knowing from whence one has left, whither one is going, writing after having spoken, seen, traversed, explored; just as the father precedes his son in time, *de facto* and *de jure*, so the voyage should precede, *de facto* and *de jure*, its own archivation, so the origin should precede its consequence, and indigenous innocence every technical procedure. This would be, precisely, the reassuring and methodical order of derivation: lineage, filiation, genealogy. But what becomes of lineage, filiation, and genealogy once the photograph of the origin has been developed, once there is revealed this cliché that reverses, that of a father smaller than his son?

You are going to think that I venerate this catastrophic scene (my new fetishes, the "hit" of the summer): Plato, teacher, in erection behind Socrates, student, for example, and in saying "catastrophic," I am thinking, of course, of the overturning and inversion of relations, but also, suddenly, of the apotrope and the apostrophic: p. a father smaller than his son or disciple, it happens, p., unless it is S., whom he resembles, devilishly, shows him (to others) and at the same time shows him the way, sends him, and at the same time apostrophizes him, which always amounts to saying "go" or "come," *fort, da. Fort/da* of S. and p., this is what it is, the entire post card ontology. What it leaves strangely unexplained, is that himself he addresses himself to S. or to others beyond S. But does one ever know.[12]

The paradigm of derivation (genealogy, order of sense) is ruined from the start. "What does it mean 'to have behind oneself'"?[13] Derrida asks, what does it mean to inherit or receive a legacy when this "behind oneself" precedes all lineage, obliterates every origin in advance? "You kill me in advance,"[14] he tells his addressee a little later. One cannot even count on a situational reversal, or hope that the advance of writing founds a backwards drift. Let us, however, risk this question: what if, at bottom, by means of this fabulous windfall that is the postcard, difference were thereby to find itself transformed into an Odyssey? That would perhaps be the apocalypse: everything ending up by returning to the sender, in an economic loop of sense, *QED*, without wandering, without the possibility of chance, the discovery being nothing more than one of the most subtle masks of an eschatology. And if at bottom everything were to finish by returning to the derivative schema? Well, after all, speech does in fact derive from writing. That's it. Nothing more to do or see. Happy is he who is Ulysses. The absence of a confirmed origin, that is to say an origin attested to by this reproduction as reproduction. Proof and end of journey. Like Penelope, this photo waiting so long for its developer. What else would still be able to arrive or happen? What would remain to be discovered? What country? What landscape?

The text of "Envois" causes these questions to constantly tremble in the vertigo of their displacement, proving nevertheless, by its very trajectory, that this Odyssey in reverse is precisely impossible. If the post is primary, whatever is sent can never return to itself, it cannot let itself be deduced or demonstrated, the circle can never be closed, instead being repeated, diffused in its very impossibility; what can happen or arrive is situated in the irreducible opening [*écart*] that at once separates and unites what can be guessed or foreseen.

1 September 1977.

S. is P., Socrates is Plato, his father and his son, therefore the father of his father, his own grandfather and his own grandson. When the stroller overturns after having "bumped" against the threshold is the first true event in *La folie du jour,* after which the day "hastens to its end." Already a kind of primal, and repeated, scene. Divine, who can guess what is going to happen to us. Whatever happens, I can do no more about it. I await everything from an event that I am incapable of anticipating. No matter how far my knowledge goes and however interminable my calculations, I see no way out that is not catastrophic. The deal is implacable, we are losers at every turn. We must have been looking for it.[15]

It now resembles a rebroadcast, a sinister *play-back* (but give ear closely, come near to my lips), and while writing you I henceforth know what I am sending to the fire, what I am letting appear and that you give me back even before receiving it. *Back* could have orchestrated all of this starting from the title: the *back* [dos] of Socrates and of the card, all the *dossiers* that I have bound, the *feed-back,* the *play-back,* the returns to sender, etc., our tape-recorders our phantom-cassettes.[16]

One can never be sure that something has reached its end. The catastrophic revelation, the postcard, the apocalypse of a library are not the ruses of some teleology. On the contrary, there is an incessant differing of the end, an irreducibility of the bad infinite. The *envoi* always misses its aim. Not even God can guarantee that it will be otherwise.

P.S. I forgot, you are completely right: one of the paradoxes of destination is that if you wanted to *demonstrate,* for someone, that something never arrives at its destination, it's all over. The demonstration, once it had reached its end, would have proved what was needing not to be demonstrated. But that is why, dear friend, I always say "a letter *can* always *not* arrive at its destination, etc." It's a chance.*

*P.S. Finally a chance, if you will, if you yourself can, and if you have it, the chance (*tukhē,* fortune, this is what I mean, food fortune, good fate: us). The mischance (the mis-address) of this chance is that in order *to be able* not to arrive, it must bear within itself a force and a structure, a drift of destination, such that it *must* all the same also not arrive. Even in arriving (always to some "subject"), the letter takes itself away *from the arrival at arrival*. It arrives elsewhere, always several times. You can no longer take hold of it. It is the structure of the letter (as post card, in other words the fatal partition that it must support) which demands this, I have said it elsewhere, delivered to a *facteur* subject to the same law. The letter demands this, right here, and you, too, you demand it.[17]

> For the day that there will be a reading of the Oxford card, the one and true reading, will be the end of history. Or the becoming-prose of our love.[18]

A letter, at the very instant when it takes place (and I am not only speaking of consciousness), divides itself into pieces, falls into a post card. Well yes, this is our tragic lot, my sweet love, the atrocious lottery, but I begin to love you on the basis of this impossibility; the impasse devoted to fate cannot leave us to await anything from a chance to see it open itself one day. We know that this is unthinkable, and that God himself could not provide for the aleatory in this form (yes, God would be impotent to make possible today what you know remains forbidden to us, God himself, which should give you the measure of the thing), but the chance of the impasse devoted to fate can be the impasse itself, and what comes to pass in it for being unable to pass. This chance (affirmation without exit) can only come to us from you, understand?[19]

Destinerrance

If the letter precedes every addressee, it can always not arrive (reach its shore), and is thus involved in a *destinerrance* or indeed an *adestinerrance* without end, an irremediable delay [*souffrance*] of destination.

There is there a *souffrance de la destination* (no, not a fate neurosis, although . . .) in which I have every right to recognize myself. I am suffering (but like everyone, no? me, I know it) from a real pathology of destination: I am always addressing myself to someone else (no, to someone else still!), but to whom? I absolve myself by remarking that this is due, before me, to the

power, of no matter what sign, the "first" trait, the "first" mark, to be re-
marked, precisely, to be repeated, and therefore divided, turned away from
whatever singular destination, and this by virtue of its very possibility, its very
address. It is its address that makes it into a post card that multiplies, to the
point of a crowd, my addressee, female. And by the same token, of course,
my addressee, male. A normal pathology, of course, but for me this is the only
one that kills [*meurtrière*]: one kills someone by addressing a letter to him that
is not destined to him, and thereby declaring one's love or even one's hatred.
And I kill you at every moment, but I love you. And you can no longer doubt
it, even if I destroy everything with the most amorous patience (as do you,
moreover), beginning with myself. *I'm destroying my own life,* I said to him
[*lui*] in English in the car. If I address (myself, as one says in French), always
to someone else, and otherwise (right here, again), I can no longer address
myself by myself. Only to myself, you will say, finally sending me all those
cards, sending me *Socrates* and *Plato* just as they send themselves to each
other. No, not even, no return, it does not come back to me. I even lose the
identity of the, as they say, sender, the emitter. And yet no one better than I
will have known how, or rather will have loved to destine uniquely. This is
the disaster on the basis of which I love you, uniquely. You, toward whom at
this very moment, forgetting even your name I address myself.[20]

. . . the proof, the living proof precisely, that a letter can always not arrive at
its destination, and that therefore it never arrives. And this is really how it is,
it is not a misfortune, that's life, living life, beaten down, tragedy, by the still
surviving life. For this, for life I must lose you, for life, and make myself illegible for you. *J'accepte.*[21]

Destinerrance is the other name for the "postal principle," according to
which "one cannot say of the addressee that s/he exists before the letter
[*avant la lettre*]."[22]

Would like to address myself, in a straight line, directly, without *courrier*, only
to you, but I can't manage to arrive, and that is the worst of it. A tragedy, my
love, of destination. Everything becomes a post card once more, legible for
the other, even if he understands nothing about it. And if he understands
nothing, certain for the moment of the contrary, it might always happen to

you, arrive for you, too, and happen that you, too, understand nothing, and therefore me also, and therefore fail to arrive, I mean at the destination. I would like to happen to you, to arrive right up to you, my unique density, and I run I run and I fall all the time, from one stride to the next.[23]

The stereotypical character of correspondence echoes that of the world that is these days made available to the eyes and footsteps of the traveler, as a reproducible space, where nothing really remains impenetrable, whose every region is reproduced or reproducible as a postcard, dispossessed of its secrets, as if dead. For Derrida, legibility is death. To give something to be read is to rush headlong toward death, to kill, to consign to the flames.

Think of everything I have been able to destroy in the shape of letters in this short life (how short life will have been!). One day especially (it lasted one entire day, I don't think we knew each other yet), I'll tell you about it, one of the most comic and sinister, most unspeakable, scenes of my existence. It was like an interminable murder. Technically, materially I could not get to the end of it, because what with my rush and my absurd fear of being surprised I chose the worst means. Everything went into it and in different places, I got there by car (almost looking in the rearview mirror to make sure no one was following me). The most beautiful letters in the world, more beautiful than all literatures, I began by tearing them up on the banks of the Seine, but it would have taken twenty-four hours and the people passing and the fragments that could have been put back together, all those cops always on my path as if obsessed about my private life of which they know nothing, all that. I packed it all back into the car and in a suburb that I did not know, where I chose to wind up, I burned everything, slowly, at the side of a road. I told myself that I would never start again

very banal today the idea that one is killing by burning a letter or a sign, a metro ticket that the other has held in his hand, a movie ticket, the wrapper of a sugar cube. . . . Murder is everywhere, my unique and immense one. We are the worst criminals in history. And, right here I kill you, save, save, you, save you run away [sauve-toi], the unique, the living one over there whom I love. Understand me, when I write, right here, on these innumerable post cards, I annihilate not only what I am saying but also the unique addressee that I constitute, and therefore every possible addressee, and every destination. I kill you, I annul you at my fingertips, wrapped around my finger. To do it suffices only that I be legible—and I become illegible to you, you are dead. If I say that I write for dead addressees, not dead in the future but already dead at the moment when I get to the end of a sentence, it is not in order to play. Genet said that his theater was addressed to the dead and I mean the same thing for the train in which I am going writing you without end. The addressees are dead, destination is death: no, not in the sense of S. or p.'s predication, according to which we would be destined to die, no, not in the sense in which to arrive at our destination, for us mortals, is to end by dying. No, the very idea of destination includes analytically the idea of death, like a predicate (p) included in the subject (S) of destination, the addressee or the addressor. And you are, my love, unique.[24]

Voyage and Paralysis

The catastrophe or dangerous reversal results from a collision—which is at the same time by chance and of necessity—between the desire for an absolute intimacy with the other and the very impossibility of every joining-together. The other can be the loved one, the foreigner, the far-off land, a language, an island or a city. "Envois" expresses the shock of this collision between desire and the impossible by multiplying places, means of transport, and correspondence, by sowing doubt on the gender and identity of the addressee or addressees. Such an excess of exteriority (the constant running is indeed impressive: airports, streets, universities, telephone calls, telegrams, letters, trains, planes, cars, perpetual separation and distance, etc.) is matched by the fantasy of a total immobility, of a place where one can wall oneself in, never leaving or moving.

9 June 1977.

distance myself *in order* to write you. If now I am still sending you the same card, it is because I would be willing to die, to enclose myself finally in a single place that is a place, and bordered, a single word, a single name. The unique image then would carry off my immobile, extended body, then slowly what you will

have sent me back

you know now on the basis of what catastrophe, what disaster, this mortal desire to wall myself up in the repercussions of a name, to let me beat my head to the song of a name, the only one. And of an image. The image and the name are the same. You have given me this but I would like you to catch me at it and take me without

The return frightens me and I am even frightened to call. And if you were not there without having been able to warn me? During trips, at those moments when I am inaccessible, between two "addresses," when no wire or wireless links me to anything, to you, I die of anxiety and then doubtless you give me (and pardon me too) the pleasure which is not far from cresting, as near as possible, without measure finally, beyond everything, that which we, according to the said ecstasy

airplanes

[avions]-two wings [deux ailes], that is what I need

without which, crash, falls from the nest

like a bad card, the losing one, the underside of which must be shown, not only to the other, but to oneself. When I will know what game I am playing with myself, my love. But when I fly with you why doesn't the anxiety disappear? You yourself are very tranquil, you are turned toward the scenery and you take pleasure in the outside as if you had just been born. I ask myself occasionally quite simply if you exist and if you have the slightest notion of it.[25]

The anxiety of being outside within the nest itself, of losing the other within the very heart of love, in the anonymity of all the interchanges, works on the traveler's *body*, subjecting it to the contradictory pressures of *speeding* and *paralysis*. This double constraint also goes by the names of time difference and jetlag.

22 September 1977.

between us the song was anachronistic, and ecstasy itself. One day I was talking to you about it—as I do too often—and you pronounced across the static [parasites] (for we were telephoning each other) "god of the time difference." I still keep the two watches on my arm, on the left I am six hours ahead of everything that I appear to live at Trumbull. I simulate everything, that you are simultaneous for me, my love, and that at the moment when I call you, by your name, light and the rhythms of bodies, sun and sleep, no longer make a screen. And it's not so illusory. I woke up at about the same time as you this morning (but it's only the first day, yes) and very soon you are going to "ring," I am going to count the times. Yesterday at Kennedy, same scenario as the preceding years, I had the impression it was yesterday: Paul and Hillis waiting for me, come down from Yale (how is an appointment possible, despite all the intervals and transcontinental differences, and the fidelity on which I live, and this miracle before which I will always remain a child?). After saying hello, I made them wait (again), as always, in order to call you from the public booth, the only one that I know here along with the one in Grand Central or Penn Station, the only one from which one is not obliged to call "collect" at the expense of the addressee. In a second I had you in the night, you were going to bed with me in the big bed, and I came out of the airport crushed by the sun (the New York heat in August which never goes away), serene and desperate, amiable with my friends and incapable of re-membering myself. I less and less know where my body is—and all these phantoms, here or there, and at what time. Keep me, keep us, give me time.

Like him (M.B.), I like the word "disaster," to name thus the bottomless misfortune to which the first morning, the first sleepless night had destined us. Despite the time that will until the end of time forbid us to reach [*joindre*] (what a word, don't you think?) each other—(you have just called, you have just entered the room), disaster brings us together. I love all the words, all the letters, in the word disaster [*désastre*], its entire teeming constellation, all the fates cast in it, and even that it sublimates us a bit.

The time difference [*décalage horaire*] is in me, it is me. It blocks, inhibits, dissociates, arrests—but it also releases, makes me fly, I never forbid myself anything, you know, finally not me, and it is toward you, it is to you that I fly. Uniquely. At this very second.[26]

I myself am in mourning. For you, by you, smeared with death, and para-lyzed. Paralyzed: paralysis does not mean that one can no longer move or walk, but, in Greek if you please, that there is no more tie, that every bind, every liaison has been unknotted [*dénouée*] (in other words, of course, analyzed) and that because of this, because one is "exempt," "acquitted" of everything, nothing works any more, nothing holds together any more, nothing advances any more. The bind and the knot are necessary in order to take a step.[27]

The Dénouement

Paralysis relates to catastrophe inasmuch as it signals an unknotting or *dénouement.* When derivation is doubled and overtaken by the speed of the postal principle, the event is freed, dissociated in its possibility from every methodical anticipation, from every order of arrival. The voyage takes place on the basis of this unlinking, destining the traveler to confront both punishment and fortune, which is always the case in terms of fate or the lottery. Is it by chance that later, in 1990, Derrida was stricken with a case of facial paralysis caused by a virus? In "Circumfession" he asks whether this paralysis is not precisely the price to be paid for developing the print of the initial catastrophe and for robbing the voyage of its origin:

I seem to have seen myself near to losing my face, incapable of looking in the mirror at the fright of truth, the dissymmetry of a life in caricature, left eye no longer blinking and stares at you, insensitive, without the respite of *Augenblick*, the mouth speaks the truth sideways, defying the diagnostics or prognostics, the disfiguration reminds you that you do not inhabit your face because you have too many places, you take place in more places than you should, and transgression itself always violates a place, an uncrossable line, it seizes itself, punishes, paralyzes immediately, topology here both being and not being a figure, and if it is a disfiguration, that's the trope I've just been hit right in the face with for having violated the places, all of them, the sacred places, the places of worship, the places of the dead, the places of rhetoric, the places of habitation, everything I venerate.[28]

Violating all the places, reversing or overturning the orders, no doubt calls down punishment. But this fault also opens the space of a new chance, the chance that something other than the voyage can happen or arrive within the voyage.

Now, my post card, this morning when I am raving about it or delivering it [*quand je la délire ou la délivre*] in the state of jealousy that has always terrified me, my post card naively overturns everything. In any event, it allegorizes the catastrophic unknown of the order. Finally one begins no longer to understand what to come [*venir*], to come before, to come after, to foresee [*prévenir*], to come back [*revenir*] all mean—along with the difference of the generations, and then to inherit, to write one's will, to dictate, to speak, to take dictation, etc. We will finally be able to love one another.[29]

We'll follow up on this.

[16]

London–Brighton, 29 November–1 December 1997

. . . ICA: lots of friends. Improvising in the end on "The Politics of Friendship," recounting an amazing dream I had the night before in the Hotel Russell (one day I'll tell you my long history in this dearly loved hotel . . . once before I invented a fiction around it that got published, a hoax that passed unnoticed, like clockwork [*comme une lettre à la poste*], on the occasion of a polemic with some young bloodhounds concerning my text on apartheid and Mandela).[18] The dream, then: I am diving from a balcony and land then bounce back immediately off the naked backs of some young Asians lying face down, then I jump from back to back, something like that, I have forgotten it since, but I'm told that already the narrative of this dream is doing the rounds with all the necessary details on "my" internet page—to which I myself don't have access. At Brighton, where I also love to come back to see Geoff, I improvised again. Responding to English Marxists, you know how they are . . .

[18] [See "But, beyond . . . (Open Letter to Anne McClintock and Rob Nixon)." (C.M.)]

18

The Last Voyage

And if this voyage were to be the last? The haunting fear of an accident, of not coming back, a feeling of imminent peril accompanies Derrida everywhere he goes, puncturing his writing, darkening the landscape. From what cape, from what Land of Fire, will death come?

The Cape

A cape is a piece of land jutting into the sea, from which one can scan the horizon. It allows one to see what is coming, to wait or to anticipate. It tends entirely toward the "imminence" of the event, toward "that which *comes* [vient], which comes perhaps and perhaps comes from a completely other shore,"[1] the future itself. Whether it refer to a "tremor [*séisme*]"[2] or a "danger,"[3] to a surprise or to death, the event is "something that does not yet have a face."[4]

While on Cape Sounion, near Athens, Derrida cannot help thinking of Socrates and his impending death, something the latter thought he saw coming from that precise place, from that cape:

> *Socrates*: Why, what is this news? Has the boat come in from Delos—the boat which ends my reprieve when it arrives?
>
> *Crito*: It hasn't actually come in yet, but I expect it will be here today, judg-

ing from the report of some people who have just arrived from Sunium and left it there. It is quite clear from their account that it will be here today, and so by tomorrow, Socrates, you will have to . . . end your life.

Socrates: Well, Crito, I hope that it may be for the best. If the gods will it so, so be it. All the same, I don't think it will arrive today.

Crito: What makes you think that?

Socrates: I will try to explain. I think I am right in saying that I have to die on the day after the boat arrives?

Crito: That's what the authorities say at any rate.

Socrates: Then I don't think that it will arrive on this day that is just beginning, but on the day after. I am going by a dream that I had in the night, only a little while ago. It looks as though you were right not to wake me up.

Crito: Why, what was the dream about?

Socrates: I thought I saw a gloriously beautiful woman dressed in white robes, who came up to me and addressed me in these words: Socrates, "To the pleasant land of Phtia on the third day thou shalt come."[5]

Socrates waits for his death, its coming to be announced by the return of the boat, sighted from Cape Sounion. Athens had made a vow to Apollo that it would organize a pilgrimage to Delos every year and the law decreed a reprieve during the period of the pilgrimage: "the city must be kept pure, and no public executions may take place until the ship has reached Delos and returned again."[6] Socrates will therefore die only once the boat returns. In one sense, that return cannot be anticipated, it depends on the seas and the strength of the winds. However, Socrates claims "to see in advance, to foresee and to not allow himself to be surprised by the delay in his death."[7] His resolution is set in train, and once he has decided not to escape he prepares himself, forces upon himself the discipline of dying (*epimeleia thanatou*) and of the last voyage. He "awaits the arrival," which means that he "arrives at the departure."[8] He "owes himself to death." But what is the precise sense of the statement "We are owed to death" [*Nous nous devons à la mort*]?

We are owed to death. Once for all time. The sentence surprised me . . . but I immediately knew that it had to have been waiting for me for centuries, crouching in the shadows, knowing ahead of time where to find me (where to *find* me? what does that mean?). However, I would be ready to swear it, that sentence only ever appears once. It is never given over to commentary, it never makes its modality explicit. Is this a statement or a piece of advice: "we are owed to death"? Does it declare the law of what *is* or the law that prescribes what *should be*? Is it to be understood that we owe ourselves to death in fact or in truth? or else that we must [*devons*] or should [*devrions*] owe [*devoir*] ourselves to death? For, in a manner of speaking, it has only ever come to me once, the oracular thing, this one, once only, at the same time the first and the last, on such and such a day in July at such and such a moment, and every time I make it come back, each time, rather, that I let it reappear, it is *one time for all* . . . like death. . . . What does this duty, this owing, this first indebtedness have to do with the verb of this inappropriable declaration "we are *owed* to death"? With what it seems to mean? Neither "we are owed until death [*à mort*]," nor "we owe ourselves death," but "we are owed to death."

Who is this, death? (Where is it to be found? as in the curious French expression *trouver la mort*, to find death, meaning, to die).[9]

The Verdict

"*Nous nous devons à la mort.*" This duty or obligation, with its dissociation of the subject and reflexive pronouns "*nous,*" does not however refer completely to the Socratic discipline of dying. The event is such that it remains forever impossible to prepare for it. One cannot, by anticipating it, lessen its surprise. Imminence knows no end, what is coming doesn't accomplish it. Its verdict is therefore without truth, retaining itself without standing still in a strange space, a strange situation, like a plane in the process of landing.

It is, indeed, in an airplane, "in sight of Tierra del Fuego, in the Magellan strait, in memory of the caravels,"[10] in the course of a flight to Buenos Aires, that Derrida waits for a verdict, but a verdict that isn't presented, doesn't unveil anything, like a decree or a threat suspended in the air:

—Who knows? Perhaps we have to dare, indeed. As for the verdict thus suspended, what we ought to risk will always depend on a "perhaps." The fulgurating newness of this day depends, or tends. Toward whom or what I know not yet. But it tends and depends on what no doubt I knew without

At the home of Jorge Luis Borges, Buenos Aires, 20 October 1985.
(Lisa Block de Behar)

knowing. I was expecting it without knowing: so without expecting, some will say. Yes, a bit like in the strait-time that separates me from this verdict, the expected, feared, hoped-for verdict at the end of the trip to Latin America, on my return from Buenos Aires, Santiago de Chile, and São Paulo. Where one knows nothing of the future of what is coming, before the throw of the dice or rather the shot fired at the temple in Russian roulette. So, what? Who does this re-commencement without precedent look like if still it expects a return? But "resurrection" is not the right word. Neither the first nor the second res-urrection Saints Paul and Augustine talk to me about.

——>**Too obvious, that's my age, true enough**: know enough, more than enough, it's obvious, about the truth you're so attached to, the truth as a his-tory of veils. What fatigue. Exhaustion. Proofs tire truth, as Braque said, more or less. That's why I've gone so far to wait for the verdict, to the tropics. From Saint James [Santiago] to Saint Paul [São Paulo]. Maybe with a view not to return. But "fatigue" still doesn't mean anything in this case. . . . You still don't know the "fatigue" I'm talking about. The exhaustion of this fatigue will gain its meaning, tomorrow, perhaps, from the truth that engenders it and when one has understood what it means, for someone like me, at the moment when he is dreaming of writing it in Spanish, one of his forgotten ancestral languages, from the bottom of the map of the world, what **to be fatigued, yes, fatigued of the truth** . . . [11]

The Accident

Derrida has always been haunted by a "compulsion to overtake [*doubler*] each second, like one car overtaking another," a "photographic" compulsion that introduces the testamentary lining of an archive under the living present of life: "The racing of a car is filmed or photographed, always on the verge of having an accident, from one end of J.D.'s work to the other."[12]

"I want to kill myself" speaks less the desire to put an end to my life than a sort of compulsion to overtake each second, like one car overtaking another, doubling it rather, overprinting it with the negative of a photograph already taken with a "delay" mechanism.[13]

I was risking accidents in the car, writing on the wheel or on the seat next to me, except, as you well know, when you accompany me. And I added that in fact I never write, and that what I note in the car or even while running are neither "ideas," of which I have none, nor sentences, but just words that come, a bit luckier, little precipitates of language.[14]

I decided to stop here because I almost had an accident just as I was jotting down this last sentence, when, on leaving the airport, I was driving home after the trip to Tokyo.[15]

"You'll End Up in Imminence"

The verdict reveals nothing, bares nothing. The event it promises is "neither known nor unknown, too well known but a stranger from head to foot, yet to be born."[16]

At the other end of the world, in the shaded area of my life, this is where I am already, there, in the west, and I await you, there where we are not yet either one or the other.[17]

I am not well this morning. There will never be any possible consolation, the disaster is ineffaceable. And yet, at this very moment when the ineffaceable appears to me as the self-evident itself, the opposite conviction is just as strong. The entire misfortune, this unlivable suffering that you know always will be capable of dissipating itself at this very second, was in sum due only to a bad chance, a stroke of fate, an instant that we are no longer even sure had the slightest consistency, the slightest thickness of life. Disaster—we have dreamed of it, no? One day will suffice—[18]

Too late, you are less, you, less than yourself, you have spent your life inviting calling promising, hoping sighing dreaming, convoking invoking provoking, constituting engendering producing, naming assigning demanding, prescribing commanding sacrificing, what, the witness, you my counterpart, only so that he will attest this secret truth i.e. weaned from the truth, i.e. that you will never have had any witness, *ergo es*, in this very place, you alone whose life will have been so short, the voyage short, scarcely organized, by you with no lighthouse and no book, you the floating toy at high tide and under the moon, you the crossing between these two phantoms of witnesses who will never come down to the same.[19]

There's no chance of that ever happening, of belonging to oneself enough (in some *s'avoir*, if you want to play) and of succeeding in turning such a gesture toward oneself. You'll end up in imminence.[20]

[23]

19

The "Metaphoric Catastrophe"
(Heliopolis)

Paralyzed, therefore, disfigured, as he says, punished by a virus, a trope taken right on the kisser. Chastised by metaphor, a figure full in the face [*figure*]. For having violated all the places, as he puts it, for having provoked disorder and catastrophe in the tropics, under the tropics in fact, reversing them the better (not) to see them from the back. As he declares in *The Post Card*, this is "what-I-call, citation, 'the metaphoric catastrophe.'"[1]

A trope (Gk. *tropos*, turn, direction, and *trepein*, to turn) is a figure of speech by means of which a word or expression is diverted, turned away from its proper sense. Rhetoric as a whole presents itself in this way as a theory of travel:

No less than architecture, as much as urbanism, rhetoric presents itself as a theory of places: topology and tropology. Tropes are tours, changes of place, from somewhere to somewhere else: displacement, voyage, transfer or transposition, metonymy or metaphor, translation or transhumance.[2]

Metaphor is the most familiar tropic instance, inscribing detour and transport within its very name (in fact, in Greek, "metaphor" literally means "transport"), and inaugurating the condition of travel within language, at the level of language.

[Metaphor] is a very old subject. It occupies the West, inhabits or lets itself be inhabited: representing itself there as an enormous library in which we would move about without perceiving its limits, proceeding from station to station, going on foot, step by step, or in a bus (we are already commuting with the "bus" that I have just named, in translation and, according to the principle of translation, between *Übertragung* and *Übersetzung, metaphorikos* still designating today, in what one calls "modern" Greek, that which concerns means of transportation). *Metaphora* circulates in the city, it conveys us like its inhabitants, along all sorts of trajectories, with intersections, red lights, one-way streets, crossroads or crossings, patrolled zones and speed limits. We are in a certain way—metaphorically of course, and as concerns the mode of habitation—the content and the tenor of this vehicle: passengers, comprehended and displaced by metaphor.[3]

We are therefore passengers, not drivers, of the metaphoric vehicle. This statement inverses the order of priority that normally governs the relation between literal and metaphorical sense, where the latter is a simple derivation of the former. The reversal of this relation is indeed a "metaphoric catastrophe," in all senses of the term. If metaphoricity is originary, it becomes precisely impossible to "master completely," without remainder, the metaphoric "drift," to give it back to literal sense, to bring to a halt its infinite voyage.

A strange utterance to start off—you might say. Strange at least to imply that we might know what *inhabit* means, and *circulate*, and *to transport oneself*, to *have* or *let* oneself be transported. In general and in this case. Strange too because it is not only metaphoric to say that we inhabit metaphor and that we circulate in it as in a sort of vehicle, an automobile. It is not simply metaphoric. Nor anymore proper, literal or usual, notions that I do not confound in bringing them together, it being better to specify this immediately. Neither metaphoric nor a-metaphoric, this "figure" consists singularly in changing the places and the functions: it constitutes the so-called subject of utterances [*sujet des énoncés*] (the speaker [*locuteur*] or the writer [*scripteur*] that we say we are, or anyone who would believe himself to be *making use* of metaphors and speaking *more metaphorico*) as *content* or *tenor* (still partially, and always already "embarked," "aboard") of a vehicle that comprehends the subject, carries him away, displaces him at the very moment when this subject believes he is designating it, saying it, orienting it, driving it, governing or steering it, "like a pilot in his ship."

Like a pilot in his ship.

I have just changed the principle and means of transport. We are not in metaphor like a pilot in his ship. With this proposition, I (drift). The figure of the vessel or of the boat, which was so often the exemplary vehicle of rhetorical pedagogy, of discourse teaching rhetoric, makes me (drift) toward a quotation of Descartes whose displacement in turn would draw me much further away than I can allow at this moment.

Therefore I ought to decisively interrupt the (drifting) or skidding. I would do it if it were possible. But what have I just been doing? I skid and I (drift) irresistibly. I am trying to speak *about* metaphor, to say something proper or literal on the subject, to *treat* it as my subject, but through metaphor (if one may say so) I am obliged to speak of it *more metaphorico*, in its own manner. I cannot *treat it* [*en traiter*] without *dealing with it* [*sans traiter avec elle*], without negotiating with it the loan I take from it in order to speak of it. I do not succeed in producing a *treatise* [*un traité*] on metaphor which is not *treated with* [*traité avec*] metaphor which suddenly appears *intractable* [*intraitable*].

That is why just now I have been moving from digression to digression [*d'écart en écart*], from one vehicle to another without being able to brake or stop the autobus, its automaticity or its automobility. At least, I can brake only by skidding, in other words, letting my control over the steering slip up to a certain point. I can no longer stop the vehicle or anchor the ship, master completely [*sans reste*] the (drifting) or skidding (I had recalled somewhere that the word "skid" [*dérapage*], before its greatest metaphoric skidding, had to do with a certain play of the anchor in nautical language, or rather the language of the fleet and of waterways [*parages*]). At least, I can only stop the engines of this floating vehicle which is here my discourse, which would still be the best means of abandoning it to its most unforeseeable (drifting). The drama, for this is a drama, is that even if I had decided *to no longer speak* metaphorically about metaphor, I would not achieve it, it would continue to go on without me in order to make me speak, to ventriloquize me, to *metaphorize* me. How not to speak? Other ways of saying, other ways of responding, rather, to my first questions. What is happening *with* metaphor? Well, every-

Signing, with the Mayor of Porto (*left*) and the Portuguese Minister of Culture, on behalf of the International Parliament of Writers, of the convention establishing Porto as City of Asylum, December 1997. (Jacques Derrida Archives)

Porto, 4–5 December 1997

Before a conference last night, official ceremony, international diplomacy style: I signed an agreement between Porto, which is becoming a City of Asylum, and the International Parliament of Writers. In the presence of the Portuguese Minister of Culture, a friend, my host in Lisbon in 1984, when I was lecturing at the University, and who had to take me to the hospital at three in the morning. I had phoned him in an awful state, it happened often that year, before I had my gallstone and bladder removed. Yes, Catherine, like my ancestor on the side of the Portuguese Jewish women, precisely, a certain Antoinette de Loupes, I have suffered from similar attacks of colic, and, like her, I am led to believe "that I owe this stony propensity to my father."[19] 1984, the year of the stone [*calcul*], is, however, the year in which I traveled and wrote the most in my life, although I hardly dare admit it: in barely a few months there was Yale, New York, Berkeley, Irvine, Cornell, Oxford (Ohio), Tokyo, Frankfurt, Toronto, Bologna, Urbino, Rome, Seattle, Lisbon, *Memoires: for Paul de Man*—who had just died, in December 83, and who therefore never again came to meet me at JFK with Hillis,

[19] Montaigne, *Essays* II:37 (*Complete Works*, 578).

thing: there is nothing that does not happen with metaphor and by metaphor. Any utterance concerning anything that happens, metaphor included, will be produced *not without* metaphor. There will not have been a metaphorics consistent enough to dominate all its utterances.[4]

It is the figure of drifting [*dérive*] as skidding—one cannot put the brakes on the metaphoric vehicle—that here allows Derrida to affirm the impossibility of inscribing metaphor within a derivative structure. The impossibility of mastering metaphoric drift means that metaphor is impossible to derive, that is to say for the vehicle to be driven back to the garage of literal sense, for it to be moored to the shore of a circular Odyssey. The metaphoric catastrophe is precisely that, the failure of any anchor.

The Odyssey of Metaphor

The Transport Company

What type of anchor in particular are we talking about? One normally supposes the tropic circulation of sense to be merely secondary and temporary—it would last only the time of a detour—with respect to the literal sense considered as veritable mooring place and origin. Thus, metaphor is traditionally defined as a substitutive voyage of signs, displacement of one sign onto another and of a signified onto a signifier. In one of his great texts dedicated to metaphor, "White Mythology," Derrida declares: "Metaphor has always been defined as the trope of resemblance, not simply as the resemblance between a signifier and a signified but as the resemblance between two signs, one of which designates the other."[5]

Metaphor thus transports by substitution and displacement. In his *Traité des tropes*, the rhetorician Du Marsais defines it, following Aristotle, as "a figure by means of which the proper, literal meaning of a noun is transported."[6] His famous example, borrowed from the *Poetics*, is "old age is the evening of life." The sense of a noun is exported toward something else rather than designating the thing it is supposed to designate: "Habitually, usually, a metaphor claims to procure access to the unknown and to the indeterminate through the detour of something recognizably familiar."[7] In

as he always had, *Psyché* (the lecture), "No Apocalypse, Not Now," *Ulysse Gramophone, Schibboleth*, reading of *Droit de regards* [Right of Inspection], the text for Lyotard's *Les Immatériaux*, etc. And so Porto: from the perspective of this Parliament, what I am trying to have understood concerning a "beyond cosmopolitanism" ("Cosmopolitans of every country, yet another effort")[20] is also based on this critical experience of travel in the era of (what they want to make us swallow from the menu of) globalization. But how does a postcard measure up against all that? . . .

20 [The French title of Derrida's address *(Cosmopolites de tous les pays, encore un effort)*, echoing Danton's rallying cry to Republicans, which is published in English as "On Cosmopolitanism." (D.W.)]

"old age is the evening of life," evening is the vehicle of metaphor. Diverted from its familiar and current sense, it displaces its crepuscular value, effacing itself for an instant before the phenomenon it sheds light on, namely old age. The signs are exchanged and the literal sense of the thing is thereby taken over, for the term of a detour, by something foreign:

The sense of a noun, instead of designating the thing which the noun habitually must designate, carries itself elsewhere. If I say that evening is the old age of the day, or that old age is the evening of life, "the evening," although having the same sense, will no longer designate the same things. By virtue of its power of metaphoric displacement, signification will be in a kind of state of availability, between the nonmeaning preceding language (it has a meaning) and the truth of language which would say the thing such as it is in itself, in act, properly.[8]

Metaphor thus appears as a transport company that has sense travel with itself, using interchanges and organizing stopovers in various "borrowed dwellings." Indeed, according to Du Marsais: "Metaphor is therefore a species of Trope; the word which one uses in the metaphor is taken in an other than the literal, proper sense: *it is*, so to speak, *in a borrowed dwelling*, as one of the ancients says; which is common to and essential for all Tropes."[9] According to this conception of metaphor the vacation or detour through foreignness will not affect the circulation of sense. The latter will always be capable of returning home intact. Tropes would thereby navigate as if in the current of a derivative logic which would have no negative effect on what it touches and displaces and which would permit the transfer and translation of an ideal sense, "transport of an intact signified in the vehicle of another language"[10] (without any gash or slit, cut or slice).

The "Continuist Presupposition"

In the course of their voyage across meaning, the transferred entities would be displaced without any rupture, they would remain identifiable and recognizable as such, essences indifferent to their means of transport. Derrida shows that two metaphoric paradigms traditionally serve as figures for this derivation: usury/wear and tear [*usure*] and the turning of the sun.

USURE

[The value of *usure*] seems to have a systemic tie to the metaphorical perspective. It will be rediscovered wherever the theme of metaphor is privileged. And it is also a metaphor that implies a *continuist presupposition*: the history of a metaphor appears essentially not as a displacement with breaks, reinscriptions in a heterogeneous system, mutations, separations without origin, but rather as a progressive erosion, a regular semantic loss, an uninterrupted exhausting of the primitive meaning: an empirical abstraction without extraction from its own native soil. . . . This characteristic—the concept of *usure*—belongs not to a narrow historico-theoretical configuration, but more surely to the concept of metaphor itself, and to the long metaphysical sequence that it determines or that determines it. . . . In signifying the metaphorical process, the paradigms of coin, of metal, silver and gold, have imposed themselves with remarkable insistence. Before metaphor—an effect of language—could find its metaphor in an economic effect, a more general analogy had to organize the exchanges between the two "regions." The analogy within language finds itself represented by an analogy between language and something other than itself. But here, that which seems to "represent," to figure, is also that which opens the wider space of a discourse on figuration, and can no longer be contained within a regional or determined science, linguistics or philology.

Inscription on coinage is most often the intersection, the scene of the exchange between the linguistic and the economic.[11]

"Progressive erosion, a regular semantic loss, an uninterrupted exhausting of the primitive meaning," such are the dominant traits characterizing *usure* in the derivative schema, allowing tropic movement to be conceived of as an "economic" circulation within a dwelling that keeps and saves the literal in the course of its figurative trajectory (let us remember that *oikos* means "house, room, tomb, crypt").[12]

METAPHOR AND HELIOTROPE

The "continuist presupposition" conveyed by such a rhetorico-philosophical conception of metaphor implies a hierarchical derivation not only between literal and metaphoric sense but also between metaphor and concept. It is generally admitted that philosophical concepts such as the absolute, God, system, speculation, were originarily metaphors, that is to say material and sensible figures. The chronological anteriority of the primitive-sensible with respect to literal-conceptual would thus have ended up by being reversed, under the effect once again of *usure*. These metaphors would have worn themselves out to the point of effacing themselves and becoming transparent: "Simultaneously the first meaning and the first displacement are then forgotten. The metaphor is no longer noticed, and it is taken for the proper meaning."[13]

Worn-out metaphors work, therefore, like whitewashed myths, myths that have been subdued, colonized. That explains why metaphor finds its explanatory metaphor in coinage. There would reside at the origin of these conceptual metaphors a forgotten primitive inscription. As for "live metaphors," they would survive by coming into relief against this worn-out background (that of "dead metaphors"). Unusual, unexpected metaphors, "effects of style," would thus be like foreigners in transit, without working papers, discursive tourists rubbing shoulders in language with naturalized, properly used (and worn-out) foreign figures.

The opposition between actual, effective metaphors and inactive, effaced metaphors corresponds to the value of *usure* (*Abnützung*), whose implications we have already discussed. This is an almost constant characteristic in discourse on philosophical metaphor: there are said to be inactive metaphors, which have no interest at all since their author *did not think of them*, and since metaphorical effect is analyzed within the field of consciousness. The traditional opposition between living and dead metaphors corresponds to the difference between effective and extinct metaphors. Above all, the movement of metaphorization (origin and then erasure of the metaphor, transition from the proper sensory meaning to the proper spiritual meaning by means of the detour of figures) is nothing other than the movement of idealization.[14]

These "layers" of *usure* constitute a veritable philosophical geography. They correspond to degrees of truth and light that are distributed unevenly in space, from East to West. This explains the frequent recourse had by philosophers to the metaphor of the movement of the sun in order to signify the progress of thinking: "the turning of the sun always will have been the trajectory of metaphor. . . . Metaphor means heliotrope, both a movement toward the sun and the turning movement of the sun."[15] In philosophy—notably in Plato—the sun has always been the sensible signifier of the intelligible, the privileged figure of good or of truth. Philosophical discourse turns around the sun; it makes use of the sun as figure in order to orient itself toward the proper sense, as figure of "philosophical metaphor as a detour within (or in sight of) reappropriation, *parousia*, the self-presence of the idea in its own light. The metaphorical trajectory from the Platonic *eidos* to the Hegelian idea."[16] Such a trajectory describes "the history of 'proper' meaning . . . whose detour and return are to be followed."[17] From Orient to Occident, between rising and setting of the sun, wakening and decline of revelation, the movement of sense is accomplished metaphorically.[18] The sun thus "structures the metaphorical space of philosophy."[19]

The point of emergence of light, inscribed by metaphor, is the point of departure of a metaphysical Odyssey within which "literal sense" always ends by arriving, by returning to itself at the conclusion of its driftings. From dwelling to dwelling, from primitive inscription to conceptual transparence, from clandestine immigration to process of naturalization, tropes always finish by arriving, turning themselves in.

Metaphor, therefore, is determined by philosophy as a provisional loss of meaning, an economy of the proper without irreparable damage, a certainly inevitable detour, but also a history with its sights set on, and within the horizon of, circular reappropriation of literal, proper meaning. This is why the philosophical evaluation of metaphor always has been ambiguous: metaphor is dangerous and foreign as concerns *intuition* (vision or contact), *concept* (the grasping or proper presence of the signified), and *consciousness* (proximity of self-presence); but it is in complicity with what it endangers, is necessary to it in the extent to which the de-tour is a re-turn guided by the function of resemblance (*mimesis* or *homoiosis*), under the law of the same.[20]

"We Are Not in Metaphor Like a Pilot in His Ship"

In order to draw a definite borderline between literal sense and its tropic excursions, it would be necessary—as derivative logic presupposes—to be able to situate oneself outside of metaphorical play. But that is purely and simply impossible. Let us remember that "even if I had decided *to no longer speak* metaphorically about metaphor, I would not achieve it." That is the catastrophe, "the drama, for this is a drama": literal sense is always already transported, diverted from itself. A metaphor is always pushing in the back of another, without there being any possibility of following back to the origin of the sequence. One has to accept it: "Our great tropics: to turn the *"dos"* in every sense, on all sides."[21]

"What Is 'Inside' and What is 'Outside'?"[22]

The project that upholds metaphysical rhetoric and that involves dominating the entire mass of the philosophical corpus, or even of language, in order to be assured, over and against them, of an impregnable vantage point, is thus doomed in advance: "Classical rhetoric, then, cannot dominate, being enmeshed within it, the mass out of which the philosophical text takes shape. Metaphor is less in the philosophical text (and in the rhetorical text coordinated with it) than the philosophical text is within metaphor."[23] It is therefore impossible to assign strict limits to the tropics, to discriminate between primitive inscriptions and worn-out truths, like an owner doing the rounds of the property of language: "the detour does not overtake the road, but constitutes it, breaks open the path."[24]

The Place of Language

The "graphics of this *différant* detour"[25] is what opens language to it-self and gets inscribed in it as originary spatiality. The text entitled "Violence and Metaphysics" describes this in an exemplary way, pointing to the metaphorical condition, what sends language on its way, as the "wound and finitude of birth" of language:

Before being a rhetorical procedure within language, metaphor would be the emergence of language itself. And philosophy is only this language; in the best of cases, and in an unaccustomed sense of the expression, philosophy can only *speak it*, state the metaphor *itself*, which amounts to *thinking* metaphor within the silent horizon of nonmetaphor: Being. Space being the wound and originary finitude (the finitude of birth) without which one could not even open language, one would not even have a true or false exteriority to speak of. Therefore, one can, by using them, *use up* tradition's words, rub them like a rusty and devalued old coin; one can say that true exteriority is nonexteriority without being interiority, and one can write by crossing out, by crossing out what already has been crossed out: for crossing out writes, still draws in space. The syntax of the Site whose archaic description is not legible *on* the metal of language cannot be erased: it is this metal itself, its too somber solidity and its too shining brilliance. Language, son of earth and sun: writing. One would attempt in vain, in order to wean language from exteriority and interiority, in order to wean language from weaning, to forget the words "inside," "outside," "exterior," "interior," etc., and to banish them by decree; for one would never come across a language without the rupture of space, an aerial or aquatic language in which, moreover, alterity would be lost more surely than ever. For the meanings which radiate from Inside-Outside, from Light-Night, etc., do not only inhabit the proscribed words; they are embedded, in person or vicariously, at the very heart of conceptuality itself. This is because they do not signify an immersion *in* space. The structure Inside-Outside or Day-Night has no meaning *in* a pure space given over to itself and dis-oriented. It emerges on the basis of an *included* origin, an *inscribed* orient which is neither within nor without space. This text of the gaze is *also* the text of speech. . . . No philosophical language will ever be able to reduce the naturality of a spatial praxis in a language.[26]

Metatelerhetoric

If the delocalization of sense—what Derrida calls writing—is originary, if there is an irreducible spatiality to language such that meaning is always placed outside of itself, then metaphor loses the status of an accident occurring to literality. The metaphoric catastrophe is also an accident that doesn't occur, or, which is the same thing, occurs originarily. It is therefore important to "explode the reassuring opposition of the metaphoric and the proper,"[27] which amounts to situating tropic movement beyond the effects of property or non-property. Another rhetoric would then become possible, a rhetoric of contamination, of the virus, and the voyage conceived of as derivation would come up against the figure of a displacement by contagion. Derrida calls this a "telerhetoric," or even "metatelerhetoric."

I propose the word *telerhetoric* or *metatelerhetoric* to designate that in general and more than general space in which these matters would be treated. For example: in the case of computers, is the use of the word "virus" simply a metaphor? And we might pose the same question for the use of the word "parasite." The *prerequisite* to this sort of problematic would have to concern rhetoric itself, as a parasitic or viral structure: originarily and in general. Whether viewed from up close or from far away, does not everything that comes to affect the proper or the literal have the form of a parasite or virus (neither alive nor dead, neither human nor "reappropriable by the proper of man," nor generally subjectivable)? And doesn't rhetoric always obey a logic of parasitism? Or rather, doesn't the parasite logically and normally disrupt logic? If rhetoric is viral or parasitic (without being the AIDS of language it at least opens up the possibility of such an affection) how could we wonder about the rhetorical (drift) of words like "virus," "parasite," and so forth? And furthermore, the computer virus, just like its "literal" counterpart, attacks, in this case telephonically, something like the "genetic code" of the computer (cf. Fabien Gruhier, "Votre ordinateur a la vérole" [Your Computer Has the Pox], *Le Nouvel Observateur*, November 18–24, 1988. The author notes that computer viruses are "contagious" and "travel through telephone lines at the speed of an electron. . . . One need only be equipped with a modem to be contaminated by a virus from Asia, America, or a nearby suburb"). Even now "software vaccines" are being developed. Once again we have the question of the *pharmakon* as the familial scene and the question of paternity: last year it was a student at Cornell, the son of an official responsible for electronic security, who sent this virus "guilty" of spreading this "infection" (and will we put quotation marks everywhere, these speech act condoms, to protect our language from contamination?).[28]

And what goes for the word "virus" also counts, of course, for the word "voyage" itself:

. . . everything that concerns the *voie*, viability, crossroads, walking, feet and legs, back-and-forth, the *fort/da*, proximity and distancing. Of course it will be difficult to decide, to sort out, to separate on the one hand and the other: when is it a question of all this directly, or "literally"? And when by means of a detour, a figure or presupposition? Have confidence in me for once.[29]

Context becomes a question of confidence.

[9]

20

Deconstruction Is America?

No-one knows, therefore, what can occur in the course of a voyage. The event, chance, or disaster, cannot be anticipated. Anything can happen or arrive; yet nothing can derive from the originary derivation that constitutes the first exile. Deconstruction is *"what happens or comes to pass,"*[1] says Derrida, reformulating thus the only definition he consents to give to it, namely "more than one language."[2] To arrive without deriving means renouncing the idea of leading the event back to a unique cause. Every event also speaks several languages.

"Deconstruction is what happens," "more than one language": it is often on the basis of an American perspective, concerning the United States and the American destiny of deconstruction, that Derrida analyzes these two statements. In *Monolingualism of the Other* he evokes his childlike desire to make something happen to the French language: "the dream, which must have started to be dreamt, at the time, was perhaps to make something happen to this language . . . , forcing the language then to speak itself by itself, in another way, in his language."[3] Indeed, is not one of the most spectacular elements of what has happened to that language to be found in the sort of voyage or fortune relating to the word "deconstruction," a word which, although of French origin, seems to be in many respects an American appellation?

As Umberto Eco noted in an interview in the newspaper *Libération* (August 20–21, 1983), deconstruction in Europe is a sort of hybrid growth and is generally perceived as an American label for certain theorems, a discourse, or a school. And this can be verified, especially in England, Germany, and Italy.[4]

Many will go so far as to identify deconstruction with America itself, proclaiming "Deconstruction is America!" Derrida never stops questioning the legitimacy of such an identification. If, indeed, there is an American phenomenon of deconstruction, it cannot claim to dominate or erase other forms of it.

But is there a proper place, is there a proper story for this thing [deconstruction]? I think it consists only of transference, and of a thinking through of transference, in all the senses that this word acquires in more than one language, and first of all that of the transference between languages.[5]

Three fundamental texts allow us to sketch out the history of the impossible possibility of the formula "deconstruction is America." First, *Memoires: for Paul de Man*, which brings together three lectures given in 1984, in French first of all—at Yale University—then in English several weeks later at the University of California at Irvine, in the context of the René Wellek Library Lectures;[6] second, "Some Statements and Truisms . . . ," the conference paper given at Irvine in 1987; and third, "The Time Is Out of Joint," the text of a lecture given in New York in 1993 during a conference with the evocative title "Deconstruction is/in America."

East and West: Biographical
Reference Points

These three lectures, which deal in different ways with the same question, were delivered on the two sides, the two coasts, of the United States. Before exploring them further, it should be recalled that for many years now Derrida has been teaching on a regular basis on the East and West Coasts, and has given a large number of lectures throughout the country. Several dates and places mark his American history more than others, and emerge in his work. The first important trip was made in 1966 for the con-

Johns Hopkins University, Baltimore, 1996.
(Jacques Derrida Archives)

ference organized by René Girard at the Johns Hopkins University in Baltimore, where Derrida gave the lecture entitled "Structure, Sign, and Play in the Discourse of the Human Sciences," an event that sealed his success in the United States.[7] In 1975 he began teaching for several weeks each year at Yale, alongside Hillis Miller and Paul de Man. In 1982 he was named Andrew D. White Professor-at-Large at Cornell University. In his inaugural lecture, he commented on the expression "at-large":

I wondered whether a professor at large, not belonging to any department, nor even to the university, wasn't rather like the person who in the old days was called *un ubiquiste*, a "ubiquitist," if you will, in the University of Paris. A ubiquitist was a doctor of theology not attached to any particular college. Outside that context, in French, an *ubiquiste* is someone who travels a lot and travels fast, giving the illusion of being everywhere at once. Perhaps a professor at large, while not exactly an ubiquitist, is also someone who, having spent a long time on the high seas, "*au large*" (in French, more than in English, this refers especially to marine codes), occasionally comes ashore, after an absence which has cut him off from everything. He is unaware of the context, the proper rituals, and the changed environment. He is given leave to consider matters loftily, from afar. People indulgently close their eyes to the schematic, drastically selective views he has to express in the rhetoric proper to an academic lecture about the academy.[8]

In 1987 Derrida began teaching regularly at Irvine and in 1986 in New York (consortium of the City University of New York, New York University, New School for Social Research, and Cardozo Law School).

More than One Deconstruction

I have never claimed to identify myself with what may be designated by th[e] name [of deconstruction]. It has always seemed strange to me, it has always left me cold. Moreover, I have never stopped having doubts about the very identity of what is referred to by such a nickname.[9]

This declaration or "statement" might serve as the epigraph for any analysis of the relation between America and deconstruction. In *Memoires: for Paul de Man*, Derrida outlines the four reasons why he believes it is necessary to renounce the idea of speaking thematically about "Deconstruction in America":

Can we speak of "deconstruction in America"? Does it take place in the United States? First in Europe, and then in America—as some too quickly conclude. . . . Do we know first of all what deconstruction represents in Europe? We cannot know without drawing out all the threads of a knot where we see tangled with each other the history of philosophies, the histories of "Philosophy," of literatures, of sciences, of technologies, of cultural and university institutions, and of socio-political history and the structure of a multitude of linguistic or so-called personal idioms. These entanglements are multiple; they meet nowhere, neither in a point nor in a memory. There is no singular memory. Furthermore, contrary to what is so often thought, deconstruction is not exported from Europe to the United States. Deconstruction has several original configurations in this country, which in turn—and there are many signs of this—produce singular effects in Europe and elsewhere in the world. . . .

The second reason why I decided not to talk about "deconstruction in America," disregarding the advice of Suzanne Gearhart and David Carroll, is that one cannot and should not attempt to survey or totalize the meaning of an ongoing process, especially when its structure is one of transference. To do so would be to assign limits which are not its own; to weaken it, to date it, to slow it down. For the moment, I do not care to do this. To make "deconstruction in America" a theme or the object of an exhaustive definition is precisely, by definition, what defines the enemy of deconstruction—someone who (at the very least out of ambivalence) would like to wear deconstruction out, exhaust it, turn the page. You can well understand that in this matter I am not the one in the greatest hurry.

The third reason: I will only state its form. . . . There is no sense in speaking of *a* deconstruction or *simply* deconstruction as if there were only one, and especially as if the word had a (single) meaning outside the sentences which inscribe it and carry it within themselves.

The fourth reason is that of a singular circle, one which is "logical" or "vicious" in appearance only. In order to speak of "deconstruction in America," one would have to claim to know what one is talking about, and first of all what is meant or defined by the word "America." Just what is America in this context? Were I not so frequently associated with this adventure of deconstruction, I would risk, with a smile, the following hypothesis: America *is* deconstruction (*l'Amerique, mais* c'est *la deconstruction*). *In this hypothesis*, America would be the proper name of deconstruction in progress, its family name, its toponymy, its language and its place, its principal residence. And how could we define the United States *today* without integrating the following into the description: it is that historical space which today, in all its dimensions and through all its power plays, reveals itself as being undeniably the most sensitive, receptive, or reactive space of all to the themes and effects of deconstruction? Since such a space represents and stages, in this respect, the greatest concentration *in the world*, one could not define it without at least including this symptom (if we can even speak of symptoms) in its definition. In the war that rages over the subject of deconstruction, there is no front; there are no fronts. But if there were, they would all pass through the United States. They would define the lot, and, in truth, the partition of America. But we have learned from "Deconstruction" to suspend these always hasty attributions of proper names. My *hypothesis* must thus be abandoned. No, "deconstruction" is not a proper name, nor is America the proper name of deconstruction. Let us say instead: deconstruction and America are two open sets which intersect partially according to an allegorico-metonymic figure. In this fiction of truth, "America" would be the title of a new novel on the history of deconstruction and the deconstruction of history.[10]

The Deconstruction Jetty and Its Resistance to Theory

The text "Some Statements and Truisms . . . " again takes up this set of reasons. The word "theory," Derrida says, is "a purely North American *artifact*,"[11] which refers to disciplines taught in certain American university departments of "literature." He groups together a set of "-isms": "New Criticism, structuralism, poststructuralism, postmodernism, post-Marxism, new historicism, and so on,"[12] as well as "deconstruction" and "deconstructionism."[13] From that point of view, the general title of the colloquium he is addressing, "The States of 'Theory,'" can have real meaning only in the United States. What is at stake here is not, as one might understand from a European perspective, scientific (physics or mathematics), epistemological, or even philosophical theory. "Theory" corresponds to "the opening of a space, the emergence of an element in which a certain number of phenomena usually associated with literature will call for trans-, inter-, and above all ultra-disciplinary approaches"[14] such as linguistics, psychoanalysis, feminist studies, structuralism, or deconstruction.

These disciplinary fields act as forces. In order to characterize them, Derrida convokes the figure of the "jetty," a word that should be understood in two senses: in the first place, the jetty designates a movement (one can hear in it the French verb *jeter*, "to throw"). Derrida calls this "first" jetty a "destabilizing"[15] one:

By the word "jetty" I will refer from now on to the *force* of the movement—which is not yet *sub-ject*, *pro-ject*, or *ob-ject*, not even rejection . . . that finds its possibility in the jetty, whether such a production or determination be related to the subject, the object, the project, or the rejection.[16]

Each theoretical jetty has an antagonistic relation to the other. Whereas it could not simply be part of a whole, it nevertheless projects itself as a whole. It cannot comprise itself without attempting to include and en-globe all the other parts, without trying to account for them. For example, what, in the field of "literary theory" in the United States is these days called "Marxism" appropriates to itself fundamental concepts borrowed from psychoanalysis, from structuralism, and from poststructuralism. By means of this operation the jetty at the same time stabilizes what it names and transforms it into a "state":

Each theoretical jetty is the institution of a new statement about the whole state and of a new establishment aiming at state hegemony. Each jetty has a hegemonic aim, which isn't meant to subjugate or control the other jetties from the outside, but which is meant to incorporate them in order to be in-corporated into them.[17]

The second sense of the word "jetty" then comes into view, that of the "stabilizing jetty," which, like the construction in a harbor that is designed to protect ships anchored at low tide, fixes a set of axioms. In the order of theory, the stabilizing jetty

proceeds by predicative clauses, reassures with assertory statements, with as-sertions, with statements such as "this is that": for example, deconstruction is this or that.

For instance, one assertion, one statement, a true one, would be, and I would subscribe to it: Deconstruction is neither a theory nor a philosophy. It is neither a school nor a method. It is not even a discourse, nor an act, nor a practice. It is what happens, what is happening today in what they call soci-ety, politics, diplomacy, economics, historical reality, and so on and so forth. Deconstruction is the case. I say this not only because I think it is true and be-cause I could demonstrate it if we had time, but also to give an example of a *statement* in the *static* form of the jetty.[18]

Since it is clearly possible to formulate assertions on the subject of decon-struction, it remains subject, like every other theory, to the law of the sta-bilizing jetty. In other words, it is capable of being transformed into "de-constructionism," the formalization and systematization of technical rules, of teachable methodological procedures, into the codification of a discourse, etc.

There is *deconstructionism* in general each time that the destabilizing jetty closes and stabilizes itself in a teachable set of theorems, each time that there is self-presentation of *a*, or more problematically, of *the* theory.[19]

Yet, to the very extent that the statements or assertions that deconstruction gives rise to fundamentally oppose or resist "theory," it remains a destabilizing jetty even within its rationalizing and controlling structure. Because it destabilizes the conditions of possibility of objectivity, of the relation to the object, of everything that constitutes an assured subjectivity in the form of the *cogito*, the certainty of self-consciousness, etc., deconstruction proves the impossibility of closure, of totality, of a system or discourse of or on method. Deconstruction is not a theory of theory. And California, the seismic state of theory, is not its only homeland.

Deconstruction is/in America:
The Time of Mourning

Derrida returns to this point in "The Time Is Out of Joint":

I have often had occasion to define deconstruction as that which is—far from a theory, a school, a method, even a discourse, still less a technique that can be appropriated—at bottom *what happens or comes to pass* [ce qui arrive]. It remains then to situate, localize, determine what happens with what happens, *when* it happens. To date it. Has deconstruction happened? Has it arrived?[20]

Is it born? Dead? Still-born? Referring to those who delight in proclaiming the death of deconstruction, Derrida asks how it is possible to mourn something that, in a sense, does not exist. At what moment could its demise be dated? The questions of mourning and of dates are determinant ones. They are what allows the sentence uttered by Hamlet—"The time is out of joint"—to be brought into relation with the title of the colloquium, "Deconstruction is/in America." Derrida calls for an interrogation of the proximity in which "is" is found in the two cases: "Does this 'is' have the same meaning? Does it perform the same function, or rather the same dysfunctioning, in both propositions?"[21]

Hamlet utters his sentence in reference to mourning for his father, at the time of mourning for his father. Hamlet's memory "is suffering from the death of a king, a father . . . but it is suffering first of all and by that very token, *as memory*, from amnesia, from an amnesia that is not natural."[22] His amnesia concerns the exact date of his father's death:

The proof that "the time is out of joint"? One proof at least? Well, no one can agree about the time, about the date of the King's death, and about the time that separates present speech from this event which, in spite of or because of all that destines it to repetition, plays an inaugural, founding, or instituting role in the story. No one can agree about the time of mourning, which is finally the true subject of the play.[23]

The time of mourning is always a disjointed time, dismembered, disarticulated, *deconstructed*. In this sense, one cannot say that it "is."

Perhaps deconstruction would consist, if at least it did consist, in precisely that: deconstructing, dislocating, displacing, disarticulating, disjoining, putting "out of joint" the authority of the "is."[24]

The history of deconstruction or the deconstruction of history perhaps roams around the disjointed pivot of this copula "is," this clause of inclusion "in," or this conjunction "and" by which one seeks at the same time to couple, enclose, or conjoin a subject and a predicate. For example here, "Deconstruction and (in, is, as) America.[25]

The fact that deconstruction cannot refer back to any founding event, the fact that, like mourning, it has no time, is precisely what destines it to roaming or voyaging:

This translativity of deconstruction destines it to erring and voyage, which is to say, to a destination and destinerrance. Now, when I discovered with some surprise the title of this colloquium, the title such as it was chosen not by me but by Tom Bishop and Anselm Haverkamp, I let myself dream about all the readings one could give of it. I read it suddenly as if in a newspaper, a travel diary, or a press release: Hey, deconstruction, on this date finds itself here these days, it is in America, it landed yesterday at JFK and, more or less incognito and for a little while, is passing through the United States, in the American season of its tour. Today, deconstruction is, happens to be, it turns out that it is in America. Where was it yesterday? Where will it be tomorrow? etc. With that slash in the middle (is/in America) which interrupts the reverie and gives us a start by marking clearly with an implacable injunction that we have to choose: either *is* or else *in*.

Here then again the difference of a single letter, *n* or *s*. It marks for us very well, *in the first place*, that if deconstruction *is in America*, "in" can well indicate inclusion as well as provisional passage, the being-in-transit of the visitor (Deconstruction is just visiting—and from visitation one passes quickly to the visor, to the visor and haunting effect in Hamlet—return to Hamlet's father). If, then, *Deconstruction is in America*, that means also, *in the second place*, that it is not America. If D is in A, it is not A; if D is A, it is not in, etc. The slash indeed inscribes or incises a disjunction in the copula "is," in the coupling of the present that interests me here.[26]

Deconstruction wanders in the disjointed time of mourning. As a result, any prognosis concerning its death has little sense:

The diagnoses and the prognoses are here at once more true and (as many signs also attest) less true than ever. This implies that the teleological schema (birth, growth, old age, sickness, end or death) can be applied to everything, and to everything about deconstruction, except, in all certitude and in the mode of a determinant knowledge, to that which in it begins by questioning, displacing, and dislocating the machine of this teleology, and thus this opposition between health and sickness, normality and anomaly, life and death.[27]

Such are the terms Derrida employs, in the mode of the language of Shakespeare colored by his "own" French, in speaking about deconstruction in America. It is by multiplying the languages within language that he replies to the question concerning a possible identification of deconstruction with or in a country or a language. Languages make love to one another among themselves.

1. "The time **is** out of joint."

2. "Deconstruction **is**/in America."

I signed neither the one nor the other [of these statements], that is true, but I have loved both of them. Moreover, one can never love anything other than that: what one cannot sign, he or she in the place of whom one neither can, could, or wants to sign. . . .

What do they have in common, these two beloved sentences? First of all, I have loved them, which at least for me is priceless. This love renders them desirably ineffaceable within me. Next, these two sentences pretend to say what is, what is "is," only in order to end up also by forcing me to relinquish the "is," by dis-locating, discrediting, and suspending the very authority of the "is."[28]

[21]

Saint Monica

The out-of-joint, dismembered, dispersed time of mourning obsesses the son's memory. In Derrida's writing, an insistent and haunting motif of the death of the mother corresponds to the death of the father in *Hamlet*. California thus comes to be inscribed in his texts as the place from which a son cries for his dying mother and revisits through his thinking the geography of her agony. Her bedsores become those volcanoes on the body whose memory evokes images of landscapes or certain cities, articulated in the tightwoven fabric of a confession.

While teaching at Irvine, Derrida stays in Laguna Beach, in the region of Los Angeles and Santa Monica. Monica is also the name of Saint Augustine's mother.

as though Augustine still wanted, by force of love, to bring it about that in *arriving* at God, something should happen to God, and *someone* happen to him who would transform the science of God into a learned ignorance, he says he has to do so in *writing*, precisely, after the death of the mother, over whom he does not deplore the fact of not having wept, not that I dare link what he says about confession with the deaths of our respective mothers, I am not writing about Saint Georgette, the name of my mother, whom her brother sometimes used to call Geo, nor about Saint Esther, her sacred name, the one not to be used, the letters of a name I have used so much so that it might re-

University of California, Irvine, 1995.
(Jacques Derrida Archives)

main, for my mother was not a saint, not a Catholic one in any case, but what these two women had in common is the fact that Santa Monica, the name of the place in California near to which I am writing, also ended her days, as my mother will too, on the other side of the Mediterranean, far from her land, in her case in the cemetery in Nice which was profaned in 1984.[1]

March 31, 1990, in two weeks . . . , I shall return close to Santa Monica, toward the first word of Laguna Beach, privatization of literature, anniversary of the initial periphrasis, end of the revolution I noted when I returned from Moscow two weeks ago, perhaps my mother will still survive the circulation of the trip around the world, in advance I love the triumph of her survival, along with billions of others forever she knows nothing of what I write, never having wanted in all her life to read a single sentence of it.[2]

April 10, 1990, back in Laguna, not far from Santa Monica, one year after the first periphrasis, while for several days now I have been haunted by the word and image of mummification, as though I were proceeding with the interminable embalming of Mother alive, surviving or dying, surrounding her tightly with my 59 prayer bands, and now last night a dream throws me back toward her again, and toward her words, these words for her, who will never read them.[3]

1990, 1989, 1988, different voyages with their disjointed temporalities. Toledo, Madrid, Barcelona, then Nice. Memory entangles the different places.

. . . this December 2, 1989, in Madrid, when it's a year ago, to the day, that I thought my mother was already dead from her fall and that I know her to be alive without knowing what I know in this way, about her who is all over me, whom as regards the eyes and lips I resemble more and more, as I see her for example today at Toledo, this Saturday afternoon, with her ancestors, Saint Augustine as an extra returned at the moment of the burial of the Conde de Orgaz to place his remains in the tomb, and here I am stopped with her, in the corner of the picture, I am the son of the painter, his signature in my pocket . . . and on my return from Barcelona, where I stayed in the *via Augusta*, I reread "The Burial of the Conde de Orgaz" signed by J.-C.[4]

. . . and I saw then the first mourning as the mourning of my mother who could not, then, literally weep for me, me the sole replacement, weep for me as my sons will have to, whereas my sole desire remains that of giving to be read the interruption that will in any case decide the very figure, this writing that resembles the poor chance of a provisional resurrection, like the one that took place in December 1988 when a phone call from my brother-in-law sent me running for the first plane to Nice, tie, dark suit, white *kippa* in my pocket, trying in vain not only to cry but, I don't know, to stop myself crying.[5]

The wounds on his mother's body are like so many accidents or catastrophes occurring on the earth's crust.

I love words too much because I have no language of my own, only false *escarres*, false foci (*eskhara*), those blackish and purulent crusts which form around the wounds on my mother's body, under her heels, then on the sacrum and the hips, numerous, living, crawling with homonymies.[6]

The *escarre* [bedsore], an archipelago of red and blackish volcanoes, enflamed wounds, crusts and craters, signifiers like wells several centimeters deep, opening here, closing there.[7]

She is becoming . . . this volcano I tell myself I'm well out of.[8]

. . . at the bottom of the bedsore open to the sky or on the edge of the crater whose lavas have bloodied my life.[9]

It is his mother who is the origin of his first infantile portmanteau word [*mot-valise*], the word "valise":

Nor will they believe me if I say that the word "valise" for me will always be the piece of something I shouted out at her birth, a child's joke famous in the family: "Put her back in her valise." (At this moment I am saying to myself that "put back" says no less than "valise.") My mother's father had just introduced me into the bedroom after the delivery, they had come up with nothing better: to leave me believing that the valise (in my memory an enormous trunk that doubtless contained all the necessities for delivery at that time; it had been in the room for weeks), that this valise . . . was preparing her birth, perhaps even contained her like a belly. They still recount how my grandfather laughed at it more than anyone else. Doubtless this was the first desired holocaust (as one says a wanted child, a desired girl).[10]

She who wept as much as Monica at each of my departures, from the first, on the *City of Algiers* in the autumn of 1949, seasickness bad enough to make you give up the ghost, and so many times since, I lied to her all the time, as I do to all of you.[11]

[18]

22

The Other Heading

The imminence of the absolute *arrivant,* of the wholly other, calls for a rigorous thinking of the "messianic" or of "messianicity without messianism," and nothing less than that thinking will be able to take account of what comes to pass in the world today. To take a single example, what is currently happening in Europe, the construction of the new political, social, and cultural reality that is the European Union, cannot be thought through *responsibly* unless the concept of national and supra-national identity is made to emerge precisely as possibility of opening to the wholly other. Every identity to self must open to its difference, set its course toward and head for the other. And especially toward the heading of the other. Only such an itinerant [*voyageuse*] identity bodes well for the future.

The Absolute *Arrivant* and the Messianic

The wholly other is a figure without a face [*figure*], with the unpresentable visage of the *arrivant.*

What is the event that most arrives [*l'événement le plus arrivant*]? What is the *arrivant* that makes the event arrive? I was recently taken by this word, *arrivant*, as if its uncanniness had just arrived to me in a language in which it has nonetheless sounded very familiar to me for a long time. The new *arrivant*, this word can, indeed, mean the neutrality of *that which* arrives, but also the singularity of *who* arrives, he or she who comes, coming to be where s/he was not expected, where one was awaiting him or her without waiting for him or her, without expecting it [*s'y attendre*], without knowing what or whom to expect, what or whom I am waiting for—and such is hospitality itself, hospitality toward the event. One does not expect the event of whatever, of whoever comes, arrives, and crosses the threshold—the immigrant, the emigrant, the guest, or the foreigner. But if the new *arrivant* who arrives is new, one must expect—without waiting for him or her, without expecting it—that he does not simply cross a given threshold, whose possibility he thus brings to light before one even knows whether there has been an invitation, a call, a nomination, or a promise (*Verheissung, Heissen,* etc.). What we could here call the *arrivant*, the most *arrivant* among all *arrivants*, the *arrivant* par excellence, is whatever, whoever, in arriving, does not cross a threshold separating two identifiable places, the proper and the foreign, the proper of the one and the proper of the other, as one would say of the citizen of a given identifiable country who crosses the border of another country as a traveler, an émigré or a political exile, a refugee or someone who has been deported, an immigrant worker, a student or researcher, a diplomat or a tourist. Those are all, of course, *arrivants*, but in a country that is already defined and in which the inhabitants know or think they are at home. . . . No, I am talking about the absolute *arrivant*, who is not even a guest. He surprises the host—who is not yet a host or an inviting power—enough to call into question, to the point of annihilating or rendering indeterminate, all the distinctive signs of a prior identity, beginning with the very border that delineated a legitimate home and assured lineage, names and language, nations, families, and genealogies.[1]

The absolute *arrivant* thus has no name and no identity. The imminence of his or her or its coming demands a hospitality without reserve, the opening of the Same to an unassimilable difference. This hospitality is not an anticipation. To wait for or expect the coming of the *arrivant* necessarily comes down to lessening the surprise of such an event. What is required here is a waiting without any horizon of waiting, a singular waiting that Derrida calls the "messianic":

The messianic, or messianicity without messianism. This would be the open-ing to the future or to the coming of the other as the advent of justice, but without horizon of expectation and without prophetic prefiguration. The coming of the other can only emerge as a singular event when no anticipa-tion sees it coming, when the other and death—and radical evil—can come as a surprise at any moment. Possibilities that both open and can always in-terrupt history, or at least the ordinary course of history. But this ordinary course is that of which philosophers, historians and often also the classical theoreticians of revolution speak. Interrupting or tearing history itself apart, doing it by deciding, in a decision that can consist in letting the other come and that can take the apparently passive form of the decision of the other: even there where it appears in itself, in me, the decision is moreover always that of the other, which does not exonerate me of responsibility. The mes-sianic exposes itself to absolute surprise and, even if it always takes the phe-nomenal form of peace or of justice, it must, exposing itself so abstractly, be prepared (waiting without awaiting itself, without expecting) for the best as for the worst, the one never coming without opening the possibility of the other.[2]

"Something Unique Is Afoot in Europe"

The messianic involves welcoming a modality of arrival that is freed from any relation to an end (*telos*) and from any order of derivation. The political reach of this hospitality is clearly brought to light with respect to Europe in *The Other Heading*. The latter text is explicitly written in a con-dition of imminence: something is promised in Europe, something other than everything that has traditionally been thought under the name of Eu-rope: "Something unique is afoot in Europe, in what is still called Europe even if we no longer know very well *what* or *who* goes by this name."[3]

By proposing the title "The Other Heading" for some brief, quasi-improvised reflections, I was thinking at first, while on board a plane, of the language of

Cracow, Katowice, Warsaw, 9–14 December 1997

. . . First visit to Poland. Late in my life, like Greece, will tell you why. The "delay" in certain of my "first" public voyages to this or that country is rarely unconnected to matters political. Often I haven't visited a country until after the beginnings of "democratization." In this regard, I am thinking of all the Eastern European countries that I went to for the first time only after 1990 (except for Budapest in 1973—but Hungary was already an exception, and Prague in 1981—but that was in secret and I ended up in prison). Other "first times" visiting "brand new" democracies: Greece, Spain, Portugal, Uruguay, Argentina, Chile, Brazil, South Africa. I would have liked to undertake the necessary analysis of the cartography and political body of that period. And hence of those "first visits." "Only yesterday there was a dictatorship, the task ahead is difficult—and the memory, even the archive of it, is still to come": that is the sigh common to all those first encounters, I might even dare to say their breath or breathing.

Spoke a lot also about the lie and pardon (today, in politics, but also beyond the political or juridical). Well received. No perceptible bad conscience on their part, just a discourse of the victims—of Nazism, then communism, now of "postmodernism," that word so many intellectuals, here and everywhere else, stuff everything into, and which here they confuse with the symmetrical liberal antithesis of totalitarianism: the market, money, drugs, anything at all. Anything whatsoever, really. It's difficult. I'll have to give up describing all that to you, like the press and television, which, as you know, I consent to more easily abroad. Wrongly, but why? . . .

I went to Auschwitz but won't talk about that here. . . .

Still reading you, glad that you insisted on the child "getting lost." . . .

air or sea navigation. On the sea or in the air, a vessel has a "heading": it "heads off," toward another continent, perhaps, toward a destination that is its own but that it can also change. One says in my language "*faire cap*" but also "*changer de cap*"—to "have a heading" but also to "change headings." The word "*cap*" (*caput, capitis*) refers, as you well know, to the head or the extremity of the extreme, the aim and the end, the ultimate, the last, the final moment or last legs, the *eschaton* in general. It here assigns to navigation the pole, the end, the *telos* of an oriented, calculated, deliberate, voluntary, ordered movement: ordered most often by the *man* in charge. . . . The expres-

sion "The Other Heading" can also suggest that another direction is in the off-
ing, or that it is necessary to change destinations. To change direction can
mean to change goals, to decide on another heading, or else to change cap-
tains, or even—why not?—the age or sex of the captain. Indeed it can mean
to recall that there is another heading, the heading being not only ours [*le
nôtre*] but the other [*l'autre*], not only that which we identify, calculate, and
decide upon, but the *heading of the other*, before which we must respond,
and which we must *remember, of which* we must *remind ourselves*, the
heading of the other being perhaps the first condition of an identity or identification that is not an egocentrism destructive of oneself and the other.

But beyond *our heading*, it is necessary to recall ourselves not only to the
other heading, and especially to the *heading of the other*, but also perhaps to
the *other of the heading*, that is to say, to a relation of identity with the other
that no longer obeys the form, the sign, or the logic of the heading, nor even
of the *anti-heading*—of beheading, of decapitation. The true title of these reflections, even though a title is a heading or headline, would orient us rather
toward the other *of* the heading.[4]

The event that is promised in Europe is thus announced as a change in direction: another heading, the heading of the other, the other of the heading, other than everything symbolized by Europe in the Western tradition,
that is to say, the "capital form, the figure-head [*figure de proue*] of the advanced point, and of capitalizing reserve."[5]

Within that tradition, in fact, Europe has always defined itself as a heading or cape. In the geographic sense first of all, both extreme salience of a
continent into the sea, and center; in the spiritual sense in the second
place, the cape being a place of gathering where self-memory capitalizes on
itself, a privileged place, one that shows its example to the rest of the
world. Europe, structured by the Athens–Rome–Jerusalem–Byzantium
axis,[6] has always thought of itself as the "advanced point of exemplarity,"[7] a
guide for the world, opening the way, departure point and end point for
civilization in general. From Hegel to Valéry, from Husserl to Heidegger,
"this transcendental teleology would have, from the origin of philosophy,
shown the way, indicated the heading." [8]

To open to the other of the heading would be the "secret of a Europe emancipated from both Athens and Rome,"[9] and would presuppose that the totalizing logic of Europe, to which a Europe defined by the Maastricht Treaty is constantly tempted to return, were unable to provide for what is thereby announced.[10] The future of Europe depends on the way in which the European Union is able to affirm its identity while at the same time attesting to its opening to an outside and its capacity to welcome its own difference. It is a question of knowing to what extent Europe can remain itself while at the same time exposing itself to its alterity.

The Ethics of Responsibility

Such a question involves *responsibility*. Now, being *responsible* consists in not providing ready-made *responses* for a problem, not transforming the promise or imminence of the wholly other into a calculable program. Thinking the future of Europe indeed requires that that injunction be responded to; thinking that future is our duty. But it is a matter of a contradictory injunction, one whose "requirement" must not prescribe. The injunction is hardly uttered before it gets declined as a series of unsynthesizable "fission reactions,"[11] something that cannot be gathered into a solution.

It is necessary to make ourselves the guardians of an idea of Europe, of a difference of Europe, *but* of a Europe that consists precisely in not closing itself off in its own identity and in advancing itself in an exemplary way toward what it is not.[12]

This injunction "in effect divides us; it puts us always at fault or in default."[13]

On the one hand, European cultural identity cannot be dispersed (and when I say "cannot," this should also be taken as "must not"—and this double state of affairs is at the heart of the difficulty). It cannot and must not be dispersed into a myriad of provinces, into a multiplicity of self-enclosed idioms or petty little nationalisms, each one jealous and untranslatable. It cannot and must not renounce places of great circulation or heavy traffic, the great avenues or thoroughfares of translation and communication, and thus, of mediatization. But, *on the other hand*, it cannot and must not accept the capital of a centralizing authority that, by means of trans-European cultural mechanisms, by means of publishing, journalistic, and academic concentrations—be they state-run or not—would control and standardize, subjecting artistic discourses and practices to a grid of intelligibility, to philosophical or aesthetic norms, to channels of immediate and efficient communication, to the pursuit of ratings and commercial profitability. . . . Neither monopoly nor dispersion, therefore.[14]

The question of responsibility leads us back in this way to the thinking of hospitality as messianicity without messianism:

Otherwise [deconstruction] rests on the good conscience of having done one's duty, it loses the chance of the future, of the promise or the appeal, of the desire also (that is its "own" possibility), of this desert-like messianism (without content and without identifiable messiah). . . . Otherwise justice risks being reduced once again to juridical-moral rules, norms, or representations, within an inevitable totalizing horizon (movement of adequate restitution, expiation, or reappropriation).[15]

Being responsible involves letting the other come, making their voyage finally possible.

[24]

23

Japan

> . . . on the border of this Pacific that some predict will be the ocean of the 21st century.[1]

Insularity and Imminence

While in Japan, Derrida remarks that insularity is imminence made of earth and water; an island is a place where one can only wait without waiting for what comes, the event arriving necessarily from elsewhere, from another shore, from nowhere.

Insularity has always been a privileged and, by the same token, an ambiguous place, the edge of every hospitality as well as every violence. Insularity, excuse this tautology, outlines a place in which the edges (shores, sides, banks) do not share any terrestrial frontier, either natural or artificial, with the other, such that this habitat, naturally protected on its borders, also sees its body disarmed, open, offered on all its borderlines, given over to everything that, on its shores, can happen [arriver] ("arrive," "happen," in the sense of coming as well as of the event). The body of an insular habitat seems to defend itself and expose itself more than any other. It offers itself to the foreigner whom it welcomes, and this is politeness and hospitality; it opposes the foreigner whom it fears, the warrior, the invader, the colonist, and this is rejection, introverted closure, hostility. Unless through a certain incorporation of the foreigner in itself, it mourns both the other and the opposition.[2]

Insularity is not just anywhere. Especially when it is double, that of an island within an island, in truth in this archipelago that is Japan. A country that is in the form of an archipelago, is this not a singular spacing? It is, hypothetically, the political, cultural, and linguistic unity of a general insularity, as well as a State whose spacing assembles and at the same time disperses in its large body a multiplicity of insular unities.[3]

Future-Architecture

"Faxitexture" is the title of a lecture given on the island of Yu Fuin in June 1991 at a conference ("Anywhere") that brought together architects and urbanists from every continent. As a country and an archipelago, Japan would be a privileged place for conceptualizing architecture and the city in the new millennium. In his lecture, Derrida discusses the possibility of "a certain politics of the earth"[4] on the threshold of the twenty-first century, that is to say at the dawn of an era where humankind is very close to becoming capable of leaving the earth; an era whose "'where' is anywhere."[5] How are we to construct, reconstruct, place, and replace today? Derrida poses this question and deals with it in what is above all its political sense, by addressing in particular his hosts, the architects Izosaki and Asada.[6]

When they distinguish among the sedentary of European architecture, the nomadic mobility of the tent "which temporarily occupies a place," and the nomadic immobility of a certain Japanese architecture for which the "substance" is ephemeral, passing, transitory, but whose "form" is eternal ("e.g., the Shrine of Ise, which is *rebuilt* every twenty years . . . "), Isozaki and Asada do not ask us, if I understand them correctly, to trust in this opposition of substance and form or eternal and transitory. Rather, they would orient us beyond these oppositions toward *the very thing* that these traditional couples are destined to interpret, arrest, master, control, that is, in the *middle-place*, an uncontrollable paradox of replacement, of re-building as replacement—and of *replacement* as the very possibility of place, the originary and non-supervened possibility of all *placement*. Re-placing translates into English both *remplacement* and *re-placement*, and this equivocation seems interesting to me. In this respect it would be easy to demonstrate that between re-building and de-construction there is no opposition, nor even any difference: because deconstruction is affirmation, no doubt, but also because the displacement of the accent, the strategy of emphasis, that comes to privilege sometimes (here) deconstruction and sometimes (there) re-building, will never erase this durable paradoxicality—which . . . links, in re-placing, the fatality of *any* to *where* and *anywhere* to any experience of place. Replacement (more precisely, replaceability) as repetition (or rather as iterability) *gives place or gives rise to place.* As replaceability, this originary iterability produces rather—and earlier—than follows the placement of place. There is no placement without replacement, or at least without re-placeability. And that does not exclude, on the contrary, the finite singularity that always manages to detach itself from that principle as precisely *what happens to or arrives at this replacement,* to this placement as replacement. I insist on keeping for this word "placement" all its virtual meanings, that concerning the phenomenon of place as well as that of military, police, or financial investment, whether of capitals or capital. In other words, whether it corresponds to the so-called monumental and irremovable "substance" of occidental architecture or the so-called eternally replaced "form" . . . of a certain Japanese architecture, the non-replacement is always a singular and finite response to the abyss of originary replaceability, that is to say, without origin and without end.[7]

Tokyo Basements

Derrida also experiences the originary replaceability of place "from anywhere to anywhere" in the basements of Tokyo. No place without re-placement: demonstrating that this motif is inscribed in the center of Joyce's work, Derrida himself embarks upon an *errance* that takes him to Cornell, Tokyo, and Frankfurt, three places where he prepares, then delivers the lectures that compose the French volume *Ulysse Gramophone.* How to say "yes" to the chance of an interminable wandering? The "yes" that is called into question here sets in train, in Tokyo and elsewhere, a series of hilarious adventures or misadventures.

Kyoto, 1983.
(Jacques Derrida Archives)

The throw of the dice to which I said *oui,* deciding in the same gesture to subject *you* to it too: I give it the proper name—Tokyo.

Tokyo: does this city lie on the western circle that leads back to Dublin or to Ithaca?[8]

We were wondering what happens to the *yes* when it is repeated in a "mention" or in a quotation. But what happens when it becomes a trademark, a kind of nontransferable commercial license? And since we are spinning and curdling in the milk here, what happens when *yes* becomes, yes, a brand, or a brandname, of yoghurt? I shall come back to Ohio, this place marked in *Ulysses.* Now in Ohio there exists a type of Dannon yoghurt which is simply called YES. Underneath the YES to be read on the lid, we find the slogan: "Bet You Can't Say No to Yes."[9]

So I am in the process of buying postcards in Tokyo, pictures of lakes, and apprehensive about the intimidating talk to be given before "Joyce scholars" on the subject of *yes* in *Ulysses,* and on the institution of Joyce Studies when, in the shop in which I find myself quite by chance, in the basement of the Hotel Okura, I fall upon—"coincidence of meeting"—a book entitled *16 Ways to Avoid Saying No* by Massaki Imai. It was, I believe, a book of commercial diplomacy. It is said that out of courtesy the Japanese avoid, as far as possible, saying *no,* even when they mean no. How can you make *no* heard, when you mean it without saying it? How can *no* be translated by *yes,* and what does translation mean when dealing with the odd pair yes/no; this is, then, a question that will catch up with us later. Next to this book, on the same shelf and by the same author, there was another book, again in English translation: *Never Take Yes for an Answer.*

Now if it is difficult to say anything at all that is very certain, and with any certainty, metalinguistic, on this odd word, *yes,* which names nothing, describes nothing, whose grammatical and semantic status is among the most enigmatic, it seems at least possible to affirm the following: it must be taken for an answer. It is always in the form of an answer. It occurs after the other, to answer a request or a question, at least implicit, of the other, even if this is the other in me, the representation in me of some other spoken word. *Yes* implies, as Bloom would say, an "implicit believer" in some summons of the other. *Yes* always has the meaning, the function, the mission of an *answer,* even if this answer, as we shall also see, sometimes has the force of an originary and unconditional commitment. Now our Japanese author advises us never to take "yes for an answer." Which may mean two things: *yes* can mean "no," or *yes* is not an answer. Outside the diplomatic-commercial context in which it is situated, such prudence could take us further.

But I am continuing the chronicle of *my experiences.* Just as I was jotting down these titles, an American tourist of the most typical variety leaned over my shoulder and sighed: "So many books! What is the definitive one? Is there any?" It was an extremely small bookshop, a news agency. I almost replied, "Yes, there are two of them, *Ulysses* and *Finnegans Wake,*" but I kept this yes to myself and smiled inanely like someone who does not understand the language.[10]

To a Japanese Friend

Such motifs as the affirmation of imminence, of originary replaceability, and of the plurality of languages within a language, are brought together in the "Letter to a Japanese Friend," addressed to Professor Izutsu, who asks Derrida for clarification concerning the word "deconstruction" in view of a translation into Japanese. If deconstruction is "more than one language," attempting to translate it in some way comes down to translating translation itself. Translation is never a "derived" phenomenon. In this respect, one can only say yes to it. In more than one way and in several idioms.

Chusonji, Sendai, 1983.
(Jacques Derrida Archives)

Dear Professor Izutsu,

. . . At our last meeting I promised you some schematic and preliminary reflections on the word "deconstruction." What we discussed were prolegom-
ena to a possible translation of this word into Japanese. . . . There is already
in "my" language a serious [*sombre*] problem of translation between what
here or there can be envisaged for the word, and the usage itself, the reserves
of the word. And it is already clear that even in French, things change from
one context to another. More so in the German, English, and especially American contexts, where the *same* word is already attached to very different con-
notations, inflections, and emotional or affective values. Their analysis would
be interesting and warrants a study of its own.

When I chose this word, or when it imposed itself upon me—I think it
was in *Of Grammatology*—I little thought it would be credited with such a
central role in the discourse that interested me at the time. Among other
things I wished to translate and adapt to my own ends the Heideggerian

words *Destruktion* or *Abbau*. Each signified in this context an operation bearing on the *structure* or traditional *architecture* of the fundamental concepts of ontology or of Western metaphysics. But in French "destruction" too obviously implied an annihilation or a negative reduction much closer perhaps to Nietzschean "demolition" than to the Heideggerian interpretation or to the type of reading that I proposed. So I ruled that out. I remember having looked to see if the word "deconstruction" (which came to me it seemed quite spontaneously) was indeed French. I found it in the *Littré*. The grammatical, linguistic, or rhetorical senses [*portées*] were found to be bound up with a "mechanical" sense [*portée "machinique"*]. This association appeared very fortunate, and fortunately adapted to what I wanted at least to suggest. Perhaps I could cite some of the entries from the *Littré*. "*Déconstruction*: action of deconstructing. Grammatical term. Disarranging the construction of words in a sentence. 'Of deconstruction, common way of saying construction,' Lemare, *De la manière d'apprendre les langues,* chap. 17, in *Cours de langue latine. Déconstruire*: 1. To disassemble the parts of a whole. To deconstruct a machine to transport it elsewhere. 2. Grammatical term. . . . To deconstruct verse, rendering it, by the suppression of meter, similar to prose. Absolutely. 'In the system of prenotional sentences, one also starts with translation and one of its advantages is never needing to deconstruct,' Lemare, ibid. 3. *Se déconstruire* [to deconstruct it-self]. . . . To lose its construction. 'Modern scholarship has shown us that in a region of the timeless East, a language reaching its own state of perfection is deconstructed [*s'est déconstruite*] and altered from within itself according to the single law of change, natural to the human mind,' Villemain, *Préface du Dictionnaire de l'Académie.*"

Naturally it will be necessary to translate all of this into Japanese but that only postpones the problem. . . . The word "deconstruction," like all other words, acquires its value only from its inscription in a chain of possible substitutions, in what is too blithely called a "context." For me, for what I have tried and still try to write, the word has interest only within a certain context, where it is replaced and lets itself be determined by such other words as *écriture, trace, différance, supplément, hymen, pharmakon, marge, entame, parergon,* etc. By definition, the list can never be closed, and I have cited only nouns, which is inadequate and done only for reasons of economy. In fact I should have cited the sentences and the interlinking of sentences which in their turn determine these names in some of my texts.

What deconstruction is not? everything of course!

What is deconstruction? nothing of course!

I do not think, for all these reasons, that it is a *good word* [*un bon mot*]. It is certainly not elegant [*beau*]. It has definitely been of service in a highly determined situation. In order to know what has imposed it in a chain of possible substitutions, despite its essential imperfection, this "highly determined situation" would need to be analyzed and deconstructed. This is difficult and I am not going to do it here.

One final word. . . . I do not believe that translation is a secondary and (derived) event in relation to an original language or text. And as "deconstruction" is a word, as I have just said, that is essentially replaceable in a chain of substitutions, then that can also be done from one language to another. The chance for "deconstruction" would be that another word (the same word and an other) were *to be found* or *invented* in Japanese to say the same thing (the same and an other), to speak of deconstruction, and to *lead it elsewhere*, to its being written and *transcribed*, in a word which will also be more beautiful.

When I speak of this writing of the other which will be more beautiful, I clearly understand translation as involving the same risk and chance as the poem. How to translate "poem," a "poem"?

. . . With my best wishes.[11]

[8]

24

Island, Promised Land, Desert

(This, perhaps, is what I would have liked to say of a certain Mount Moriah—while going to Capri, last year, close by the Vesuvius of Gradiva. Today, I remember what I had just finished reading in Genet at Chatila, of which so many of the premises deserve to be remembered here, in so many languages, the actors and the victims, and the eves and the consequence, all the landscapes and all the spectres: 'One of the questions I will not avoid is that of religion.' Laguna, 26 April 1995.)[1]

Aporia

Isn't a responsibility without a program, a responsibility that doesn't believe in the response, if by "response" one intends an axiomatic evidence, eminently aporetic? It is indeed the strange logic of the aporia that Derrida invokes in order to question and analyze *viability* or *voyage-worthiness* itself. The voyage should owe its possibility to an originary impossibility, the impossibility of going straight to the end, that is to say also of proceeding or deriving from an origin.

What does "aporia" signify literally?: "a certain *impossibility* as nonviability, as nontrack or barred path. It concerns the impossible or the impracticable. (*Diaporeō* is Aristotle's term here; it means 'I'm stuck [*dans l'embarras*], I cannot get out, I'm helpless.')"[2]

Of the *aporos* or of the *aporia*: the difficult or the impracticable, here the impossible passage, the refused, denied, or prohibited passage, indeed the nonpassage, which can in fact be something else, the event of a coming or of a
future advent [*événement de venue ou d'avenir*], which no longer has the
form of the movement that consists in passing, traversing, or transiting. It
would be the "coming to pass" of an event that would no longer have the
form or the appearance of a *pas*: in sum, a coming without *pas*.[3]

What [is] at stake in this word [is] the "not knowing where to go." It had to be
a matter of [*il devait y aller du*] the nonpassage, or rather from the *experience*
of the nonpassage, the experience of what happens [*se passe*] and is fascinating [*passionne*] in this nonpassage, paralyzing us in this separation in a way
that is not necessarily negative: before a door, a threshold, a border, a line, or
simply the edge or the approach of the other as such. It should be a matter of
[*devrait y aller du*] what, in sum, appears to block our way or to separate us
in the very place where *it would no longer be possible to constitute a problem*, a project, or a projection, that is, at the point where the very project or
the problematic task becomes impossible and where we are exposed absolutely without protection, without problem, and without prosthesis, without
possible substitution, singularly exposed in our absolute and absolutely naked
uniqueness, that is to say, disarmed, delivered to the other, incapable even of
sheltering ourselves behind what could still protect the interiority of a secret.
There, in sum, in this place of aporia, *there is no longer any problem*. Not
that, alas or fortunately, the solutions have been given, but because one could
no longer even find a problem that would constitute itself and that one would
keep in front of oneself, as a presentable object or project, as a protective representative or a prosthetic substitute, as some kind of border still to cross or
behind which to protect oneself.[4]

I will even venture to say that ethics, politics, and responsibility, *if there are
any*, will only ever have begun with the experience and experiment of the
aporia. When the path is clear and given, when a certain knowledge opens
up the way in advance, the decision is already made, it might as well be said
that there is none to make: irresponsibly, and in good conscience, one simply applies or implements a program. Perhaps, and this would be the objec-
tion, one never escapes the program. In that case, one must acknowledge

this and stop talking with authority about moral or political responsibility. The condition of possibility of this thing called responsibility is a certain *experience and experiment of the possibility of the impossible: the testing of the aporia from which one may invent the only possible invention, the impossible invention.*[5]

"There Where Every Other Is Every (Bit) Other"

The aporia is not synonymous with unproductivity or acquiescence; indeed, it involves rather the matter of decision. To decide to take such and such a direction, in and toward the future, cannot by definition obey the certainty of a calculable program. To decide is to know how to let the other decide, the other understood not as *alter ego*, as the same as me (there is no question of another deciding for me in that sense), but as wholly other: on that basis only the future can decide. Yet, this wholly other is inaccessible in its source: the "utterly other . . . is inaccessible in its absolute source. . . . There, where every other is every (bit) other, utterly other [*là où tout autre est tout autre*]."[6]

"There where every other is every (bit) other" can be understood in at least three senses:

1) In the place without place that is the source of every voyage, of every displacement, the other is wholly other. It has no common currency with me, that is to say also, with the other understood usually as another me. It is wholly other than "my" other;

2) At the same time, my *alter ego* is the wholly other by means of a certain trait of itself (through its future, through whatever "of it" has not arrived or occurred) by means of which it is not itself. Every other—no matter what other—is the wholly other to the extent that its presence never exhausts its possibility of being.

3) Finally, the formula "there where every other is every (bit) other" allows us to think the origin, the source (*là où*) as a wholly other origin and a wholly other source. Who or what has not arrived indicates a "duplicity of origin," an originary surplus, the non-place of an origin other than the one

from which everything is derived. In "Faith and Knowledge," Derrida again names this resource of the source the "messianic" and "khōra":

> *Since everything has to be said in two words, let us give two names to the duplicity of these origins. For here origin is duplicity itself, the one and the other. Let us name these two sources, these two wells, or these two tracks that are still invisible in the desert. Let us lend them two names that are still 'historical,' there where a certain concept of history itself becomes inappropriate. To do this, let us refer . . . first to the 'messianic,' and second to the chōra. . . .* [7]

Rational Faith

Without this duplicity of the source, no event is possible. The future reserve of the source opens thinking to the horizon of what Kant calls a "rational faith"[8]: faith in the other, precisely, that must orient every voyage that remains truly *open to the world*. It is in questioning religion that Derrida highlights this horizon of faith that is older than any determinate religion.

Island

The philosopher finds himself on an island (Capri) with a number of friends while devoting himself to this meditation on religion.

> *To play the card of abstraction, and the aporia of the* no-way-out, *perhaps one must first withdraw to a desert, or even isolate oneself on an island. And tell a short story that would not be a myth. Genre: 'Once upon a time,' just once, one day, on an island or in the desert, imagine, in order to 'talk religion,' several men, philosophers, professors, hermeneuticians, hermits, or anchorites, took the time to mimic a small, esoteric and egalitarian, friendly and fraternal community. Perhaps it would be necessary in addition to situate such arguments, limit them in time and space, speak of the place and the setting, the moment past, one day, date the fugitive and the ephemeral, singularize, act as though one were keeping a diary out of which one were going to tear a few pages. Law of the genre: the ephemeris (and already you are speaking inexhaustibly of the day). Date: 28 February 1994. Place: an island,*

the isle of Capri. A hotel, a table around which we speak among friends, al-
most without any order, without agenda [ordre du jour], no watchword [mot
d'ordre] save for a single word, the clearest and most obscure: religion.[9]

Thinking religion today necessarily implies analyzing the phenomenon that goes by the name of "the return of the religious," or "return of religions," a phenomenon that is taking on more and more the catastrophic form of terror, of fanaticism, of "*reaffirmative outbidding* [surenchère réaffirmatrice]."[10] Now, to take account of this raising of the stakes requires first of all that one retire to a certain place—an island—that one remove oneself from what one usually thinks concerning the concept of religion. It is a matter of finding again what religion might offer in the way of surprise, that is to say of *what has not yet arrived.*

We are not far from Rome, but we are no longer in Rome. Here we are liter-
ally isolated for two days, insulated on the heights of Capri, in the difference
between the Roman and the Italic, the latter potentially symbolizing every-
thing that can incline—at a certain remove from, somewhat out of sight of,
the Roman in general.[11]

Always More than One Source

How can a concept—that of religion—be split or separated from itself? Let us recap the reasoning here. The phenomenon of the "return of religions" is very difficult to comprehend and to critique. Derrida notes that the question of the return is never simple. One cannot criticize or condemn the return of the religious without causing religion to return in a certain sense. Not such and such a dogma of such and such a particular religion, but a type of faith, precisely, faith in the other, credit accorded the other, faith that something completely other might come to pass, that atrocities cease being committed, in Algeria or Afghanistan, for example, in the name of religion. It is therefore always in the name of a certain understanding of religion—faith in the other—that one is able to criticize religious fanaticism. It would be naive to think that the return of the religious can be combated solely in the name of reason, as if reason were able to function completely independent of belief, or as if knowledge, that old problem, could be absolutely independent of faith.

This faith in the other, since it doesn't *"depend essentially upon any historical revelation,"* is, to borrow Kant's definition, a *"reflecting [reflektierende] faith."*[12]

How, then, to think—within the limits of reason alone—a religion which, without again becoming 'natural religion,' would today be effectively universal? And which, for that matter, would no longer be restricted to a paradigm that was Christian or even Abrahamic?[13]

Like all the names we are invoking, like all names in general, these designate at once a limit, a negative limit, and a chance. For perhaps responsibility consists in making of the name recalled, of the memory of the name, of the idiomatic limit, a chance, that is, an opening of identity to its very future.[14]

The future of religion or of faith in the other (*"good faith of the utterly other"*)[15] relies therefore on the possible coming of justice (*"opening to the future or to the coming of the other as the advent of justice"*)[16] and of democracy (*"whatever our relation to religion may be . . . , we also share . . . an unreserved taste, if not an unconditional preference, for what, in politics, is called republican democracy as a universalizable model"*).[17] This faith without dogma is necessarily lodged in the heart of *"every act of language and every address to the other."*[18]

Promised Land and Desert

Such faith has its source in a place that leads back to the non-place of *khōra*, more originary than any place, history, or genealogy. In "How to Avoid Speaking," Derrida insists on the "barren [*désertique*], radically non-human, and atheological character of this place."[19] In "Faith and Knowledge," this pure possibility of place, which is itself without any existing localization, pure possibility of space that does not itself occupy any space, this source, "there where every other is every (bit) other," is named "desert" ("desert within the desert"), or again, "Promised Land."

In this desert any trace of the historical founding of the law or of authority is lost. The desert refers to the improbable distance that separates the determinate origin of a given religion from the very possibility of every beginning and every event: "*Testamentary and Koranic revelations are inseparable from a historicity of revelation itself.*"[20] Yet, what the Promised Land promises is precisely the possibility of questioning the "before-the-first" basis for this historicity, so that "*a 'revealability' [Offenbarkeit] be allowed to reveal itself, with a light that would manifest (itself) more originarily than all revelation [Offenbarung].*"[21]

In this same light, and under the same sky, let us this day name three places: the island, the Promised Land, the desert. Three aporetical places: with no way out or any assured path, without itinerary or point of arrival, without an exterior with a predictable map and a calculable programme. These three places shape our horizon, here and now. (But since thinking and speaking are called for here, they will be difficult within the assigned limits, and a certain absence of horizon. Paradoxically, the absence of horizon conditions the future itself. The emergence of the event ought to puncture every horizon of expectation. Whence the apprehension of an abyss in these places, for example a desert in the desert, there where one neither can nor should see coming what ought or could—perhaps—be yet to come. What is still left to come.)[22]

Let us step up the pace in order to finish: in view of a third place that could well have been more than archi-originary, the most anarchic and anarchivable place possible, not the island nor the Promised Land, but a certain desert—and not the desert of revelation but a desert within the desert, that which makes possible, opens, hollows or infinitizes the other. Ecstasy or existence of the most extreme abstraction.[23]

Before the island—and Capri will never be Patmos—there will have been the Promised Land. How to improvise and allow oneself to be surprised in speaking of it? How not to fear and how not to tremble before the unfathomable immensity of this theme? The figure of the Promised Land—is it not also the essential bond between the promise of place and historicity? By historicity, we could understand today more than one thing. First of all, a sharpened specificity of the concept of religion, the history of its history, and of the genealogies intermingled in its languages and in its name. Distinctions are required: faith has not always been and will not always be identifiable with re-

ligion, nor, another point, with theology. All sacredness and holiness are not necessarily, in the strict sense of the term, if there is one, religious.[24]

For, in addition to investigating the ontotheologico-political tradition that links Greek philosophy to the Abrahamic revelations, perhaps we must also submit to the ordeal of that which resists such interrogation, which will have always resisted, from within or as though from an exteriority that works and resists inside. Chora, the 'ordeal of chora', would be, at least according to the interpretation I believed justified in attempting, the name for place, a place name, and a rather singular one at that, for that spacing which, not allowing itself to be dominated by any theological, ontological or anthropological instance, without age, without history and more 'ancient' than all oppositions (for example, that of sensible/intelligible), does not even announce itself as 'beyond being,' in accordance with a path of negation, a via negativa. *As a result,* chora *remains absolutely impassive and heterogeneous to all the processes of historical revelation or of anthropo-theological experience, which at the very least suppose its abstraction. It will never have entered religion and will never permit itself to be sacralized, sanctified, humanized, theologized, cultivated, historicized. Radically heterogeneous to the safe and sound, to the holy and the sacred, it never admits of any* indemnification. *This cannot even be formulated in the present, for* chora *never presents itself as such. It is neither Being, nor the Good, nor God, nor Man, nor History. It will always resist them, will have always been (and no future anterior, even, will have been able to reappropriate, inflect or reflect a* chora *without faith or law) the very* place *of an infinite resistance, of an infinitely impassive persistence [*restance*]: a faceless wholly other.*[25]

This messianicity, stripped of everything, as it should, this faith without dogma which makes its way through the risks of absolute night, cannot be contained in any traditional opposition, for example that between reason and mysticism. It is announced wherever, reflecting without flinching, a purely rational analysis brings the following paradox to light: that the foundation of law—law of the law, institution of the institution, origin of the constitution—is a 'performative' event that cannot belong to the set that it founds, inaugurates or justifies. Such an event is unjustifiable within the logic of what it will have opened. It is the decision of the other in the undecidable. Henceforth reason ought to recognize there what Montaigne and Pascal call an undeniable 'mystical foundation of authority.' The mystical *thus understood allies belief with credit, the fiduciary or the trustworthy, the secret (which here signifies 'mystical'), with foundation, with knowledge, we will later say also, with science as 'doing', as theory, practice and theoretical practice—which is to say, with a faith, with performativity and with technoscientific or tele-technological performance. Wherever this foundation founds in foundering, wherever it steals away under the ground of what it founds, at the very instant when, losing itself thus in the desert, it loses the very trace of itself and the memory of a secret, 'religion' can only begin and begin again: quasi-automatically, mechanically, machine-like,* spontaneously. Spontaneously, *which is to say, as the word indicates, both as the origin of what flows from the source,* sponte sua, *and with the automaticity of the machine. For the best and for the worst, without the slightest assurance or anthropo-theological horizon. Without this desert in the desert, there would be neither act of faith, nor promise, nor future, nor expectancy without expectation of death and of the other, nor relation to the singularity of the other. The chance of this desert in the desert (as of that which* resembles to the point of non-recognition, *but without reducing itself to, that* via negativa *which forges its way from a Graeco–Judaeo–Christian tradition) is that in uprooting the tradition that bears it, in atheologizing it, this abstraction, without denying faith, liberates a universal rationality and the political democracy that cannot be dissociated from it.*[26]

This *condition of possibility* of the event is also its *condition of impossibility*, like this strange concept of messianism without content, of the messianic without messianism, that guides us here like the blind. But it would be just as easy to show that without this experience of the impossible, one might as well give up on both justice and the event.[27]

The Undeniable Possibility

Faith in the absolute *arrivant* is thus born in this strange place where the very concept of birth trembles, where there echoes the dizzying question that cannot but haunt every tradition, every history, every genesis, every linking of facts: what if something else were to take place, something wholly other, something unheard of, something wholly other than what has happened or arrived? This same question is also posed in the direction of the future: and what if something else, the wholly other, another chance, another possibility were capable of coming to pass? One cannot know of this, one can have no certainty concerning it, one can only *believe* in it. Yet one can believe in it because the possibility of this other possibility is *undeniable*.

But it seems impossible to deny the *possibility* in whose name—thanks to which—the (derived) necessity (the authority or determinate belief) would be put on trial or in question, suspended, rejected or criticized, even deconstructed. One can *not* deny it, which means that the most one can do is to deny it.[28]

The other possibility, the other chance, is undeniable. It is on this basis that one can and must give it credence or credit. To be possible means to be undeniable. In this sense, what is possible appears as the pure and simple impossibility of being denied. To remain at the level of the possible, to support the discovery of the world by means of this faith in the wholly other rather than proposing political diagnoses, axiomatic programs, or edifying discourses, to let oneself be guided aporetically by the event that can only come from the "to come" of the future, such is the ethics of travel that Derrida never stops putting into practice. It would perhaps rely on this single injunction: "Come."

"Come" Does Not Derive from Coming

It is in order to speak to you of coming [*la venue*], of what happens or arrives or doesn't that I have called you, only you. I wasn't able to converse about coming before saying *come* [viens], to you. But will I have been able to say, to you, *viens*, without knowing [*sans savoir*], without having [*avoir*], without seeing [*voir*] in advance what "to come" means?

My hypothesis: one cannot (derive) or construct the sense, status, or function, as they say, of *viens*, of the event *viens*, on the basis of what one presumes to know about the verb *venir* and its modifications. *Come* [viens] is not a modification of *to come* [venir]. On the contrary. Of course, this contrary is not simply a contrary, rather a wholly other relation. And as a consequence, my "hypothesis" no longer points to a logical or scientific operation, in the usual sense of these words, to something one would have to verify or disprove. It describes, rather, the unusual inroad [*avance*] made by *come* on *to come*.[29]

"Come," as inroad made on going and coming, comes from the "to come" of the future. As memory of every movement, as undatable call of the open sea, "come," of course, underived, alone speaks of the invention of travel.

[Conclusion]

Athens, 18–21 December 1997

. . . saw all the friends from "Demeure . . . " once again, those you talk about in your chapter on "The Greek Delay." You know them now. Still in the same hotel, on the Lycabette. Didn't sleep last night: the Acropolis, visible from the balcony, illuminated through the mist until sunrise, I loved . . . I also love "through," the word "through" [*à travers*]. What if one were to perform the *shibboleth* of this viaticum? Just about untranslatable, like the subtle difference between *à travers* and *au travers de*, or *de travers* [sideways, crooked], like the nouns *le travers* [foible] and *la traversée* [crossing] (by sea rather than by air or land, except for crossing the desert, and the desert within the desert was referred to on an island, Capri, during the first of two trips there). The crossing is the figure for every voyage: between the trance or transport, and overdoing it, the extravagance [*outrance*] that crosses the frontier. But if one traverses (traveling, crossing, or going through the Latin memory of) this word, one finds in it, besides the idea of a limit being crossed, that of a deviation [*détournement*], the oblique version of a detour. It says, in a word, everything about my *crosstruths*. My little truths, if there are any, are neither "in my life" nor "in my texts," but through what traverses them, in the course of a traverse that, right at the last moment, diverts their encrypted references, their sidelong wave, down a counterpath [*le salut en contre-allée*]. From him or her—to the other. Cross-cut-reference [*référence de traversée*], that's the edge the texts of imminence I was talking to you about last time are written from; en route toward the uninscribable that is *going to come*—or that *has just come* [vient de venir] to me, but always without horizon, without prior announcement. At least without my knowing about it, and neither "in the text," nor "in life," but *between* and *through*. When all is said and done, the work of this crossing is what I have always called the trace: traveling itself. . . . Someone asked me the other day what my "influences" were then, stupid question. Replied quick as a flash: "none, none that might tell you anything," but it is true that I always write "under (the) influence," most often *through* my two sons, toward an encounter with them. They are my sole judges in the long phantasm, as one says "in the long run," that's all there is to it, the sole influence I recognize, oblique but intractable. Two metabolizers of hyperbole; the formula? negotiating more than one superego. To be influenced by one's sons is not a simple narcissistic closed circle as those in a hurry to reach a conclusion might allege, presuming to know what narcissism is. And the Odyssey. There is there, in the infinite detour, really another origin of the world, an insurmountable secret, and death on the way, the other that is the least reducible to the inside (careful, not the other "inside," but the other least reducible to the inside). The one that commands us *through* a transversal, or *transversified* deviation: the poem of the wholly other. For we are indeed talking about a poem, a whole poem, theirs, they know it before me, they know everything before me. You will see what authority Félix holds over you already . . .

25

Portrait of the Traveler as Hedgehog

Let me continue: if the *trait* of the *envoi* is not a being, we must indeed suppose that it is in a certain sense *automobile*: we should discover in its retreat the violence of the machine, of the engine, of a sense of the mechanical that means lurching blindly forward, sweeping aside in a frenzy the presence of the origin. Yet Heidegger never accords the status of vehicle to the vehicular condition. Derrida instead asks what a way [*voie*] is, what makes a way a way; an essence, or a vehicle [*voiture*]: "I am taking your car [*voiture*] (the word is more and more abstract for me, *voiture*, that which makes a *voie* into a *voie*, your *Weglichkeit*(?), etc.)."[1] It is impossible to decide one way or the other. Poetry and thinking travel together, but their voyage is without truth; unguarded, it is totally exposed to the accident, to overturning.

Like a hedgehog crossing the highway.

The Poematic Catastrophe

Hedgehog: that is the poetic response (for "it sees itself, the response, dictated to be poetic, by being poetic")[2] that Derrida proposes in reply to the question "What is poetry?" Precisely because it is dictated and consequently "obliged to address itself to someone,"[3] to be destined abroad, outside, the poem is a "traversal *outside* yourself,"[4] a crossing of no return, a voyage toward the other as if toward "the being lost in anonymity, between city and nature, an imparted secret, at once public and private, *absolutely* one and the other, absolved from within and from without, neither one nor the other, the animal thrown onto the road, absolute, solitary, rolled up in a ball, *next to (it)self*. And for that very reason, it may get itself run over, *just so*, the *hérisson*, *istrice* in Italian, in English, hedgehog."[5]

The "poetic" is the very experience of the *envoyage* ("*experience*, another word for voyage") to the extent that it gives itself, or dictates, like "the aleatory rambling of a trek, the strophe that turns but never leads back to discourse, or back home, at least is never reduced to poetry—written, spoken, even sung."[6] The poem is what one desires to learn from the other, thanks to the other, and as dictation. It therefore always happens in passing. It traverses the other, who learns it by (way of the) heart. But it is precisely in the course of this traverse that it exposes itself and so risks catastrophe.

In rushing toward the other, the poem already betrays the secret that constitutes it, the fact that it wants to be kept by the other, and this fact is what causes it to run to its ruin, for it can always be effaced or forgotten. Like the hedgehog that rolls itself into a ball, thinking that it will thereby protect itself, like the traveler who asks him or her who remains behind not to forget, the poem is entrusted to the heart of the other. But in doing this it exposes itself to the power of an engine of death, for the "by heart," for being an interiorization, is nonetheless a mechanism. The "by heart" is the breaking in of the outside into the inside of the heart. Every traveler is condemned to entrust their life to a machine (in a train, plane, car, is one inside or outside?).

The poem speaks:

Destroy me, or rather render my support invisible to the outside, in this world (this is already the trait of all dissociations, the history of transcendences), in any case, do what must be done so that the provenance of the mark remains from now on unlocatable or unrecognizable. Promise it: let it be disfigured, transfigured or rendered indeterminate in its *port*—and in this word you will hear the shore of the departure as well as the referent toward which a transla-

Jerusalem, Tel Aviv, Ramallah, 11 January 1998

. . . In the question "Am I in Jerusalem?" that you cite, ageless locommotion, infinite but something of a fiction or a projection (I don't think so, I don't believe in it very strongly, thus I can only believe in it), there was indeed a basis for the "I am." In Jerusalem, *am I?* That is the emphasis I gave to the question. What does "I am" mean in the memory of all the words that echoed here, in this inappropriable Jerusalem, to the point of causing to tremble all intelligibility, all the times of an "I am he who . . . ," you know. . . . Put the accent on the time or tense of these words, even before the question of place, with a view to causing it to tremble. . . . I wonder how I manage to allow all these things to cohabit within my body, through a sleepwalking specter: millennia of amnesic love for every stone, every dead person in Jerusalem, *and* my "difficulties" (that's an understatement, and they are not only, and so seriously, so radically political) with so many Israelis, on the basis of my innocent culpability—that is to say perhaps, the last link that remains indestructible in me—that *with* every Jewish community in the world, to the extent that we remain infinitely guilty, and well beyond Israel itself, of the violence inflicted on the Palestinians, *and* my alliance with the Palestinian cause, *and* my affection and limitless compassion for so many Palestinians—and Algerians. . . . Enormous subject for meditation about which I can't tell you anything in a letter. Lecture on forgiveness, again, in Jerusalem, another one, but in the end the same as the one in Poland the day before Auschwitz, then a sort of show organized by them in a large auditorium in Tel Aviv (2,000 people to hear me talk about "The Foreigners That We Are," in English!). Relatively peaceful debate; there were Palestinians there, both in Jerusalem and Tel Aviv. Conversation with Peres the next day (in his office, I'll tell you more) before dancing all night with friends. . . . Next day, very early, set out for Palestine, passing checkpoints toward Ramallah. The Palestinian friend told me with a bitter smile that these checkpoints, these *shibboleths* established by the Israeli police, make entering Jerusalem more difficult than before the "Peace Process." Remarkable discussion at Birzeit University (Institute for Democracy) after the lecture (on hospitality and citizenship), with Palestinian colleagues who suffer and resist on all sides: present Israeli government, Palestinian Authority, Islamic fundamentalists, international conspiracies. Absolute confidence, this time, I can breathe, we don't avoid any subject, starting with the violence of the beginning, expulsions, refugee camps, and all the way to the sinister curse of the arrogant Netanyahu. But also their impatience with the insufficient democratization of the Palestinian authorities. . . . The last day,

tion is portered. Eat, drink, swallow my letter, carry it, transport it in you, like the law of a writing become your body: *writing in (it)self*. The ruse of the injunction may first of all let itself be inspired by the simple possibility of death, by the risk that a vehicle poses to every finite being. You hear the catastrophe coming. From that moment on imprinted directly on the trait, come from the heart, the mortal's desire awakens in you the movement (which is contradictory, you follow me, a double restraint, an aporetic constraint) to guard from oblivion this thing which in the same stroke exposes itself to death and protects itself—in a word, the address, the retreat of the *hérisson*, like an animal on the autoroute rolled up in a ball. One would like to take it in one's hands, undertake to learn it and understand it, to keep it for oneself, near oneself.[7]

Literally, you would like to retain by heart an absolutely unique form, an event whose intangible singularity no longer separates the ideality, the ideal meaning as one says, from the body of the letter. In the desire of this absolute inseparation, the absolute non-absolute, you breathe the origin of the poetic. Whence the infinite resistance to the transfer of the letter which the animal, in its name, nevertheless calls out for. That is the distress of the *hérisson*. What does the distress, *stress* itself, want? *Stricto sensu*, to put on guard. Whence the prophecy: translate me, watch, keep me yet awhile, get going, save yourself, let's get off the autoroute.

Thus the dream of *learning by heart* arises in you. Of letting your heart be traversed by the dictated dictation. In a single trait—and that's the impossible, that's the poematic experience. You did not yet know the heart, you learn it thus. From this experience and from this expression. I call a poem that very thing that teaches the heart, invents the heart, *that which*, finally, the word *heart* seems to mean and which, in my language, I cannot easily discern from the word itself. *Heart*, in the poem "learn by heart" (to be learned by heart), no longer names only pure interiority, independent spontaneity, the freedom to affect oneself actively by reproducing the beloved trace. The memory of "by heart" is confided like a prayer—that's safer—to a certain exteriority of the automaton, to the laws of mnemotechnics, to that liturgy that mimes mechanics on the surface, to the automobile that surprises your passion and bears down on you as if from an outside: *auswendig*, "by heart" in German."[8]

"Two years ago I visited the hut with Heidegger's older son." The latter is holding a wooden star that his father cherished. Todtnauberg. (Jean Greisch)

an interview filmed in Jerusalem for the Yad Vashem archives, the death-camp museum. . . . I wonder whether these experiences are guarantees [*gages*], geopolitical engagements, or alibis, ways of being elsewhere, quite simply (there would have to be a thousand cards on the map [*carte*] of what I flee, there where I feel myself "sent away"; you wouldn't only find there the coastlines and coteries of a certain suffocating Parisian microculture . . .). Both one and the other, no doubt. Ethics of the out-of-joint, distraction, wandering, without certainty or assurance, but also the *punctuality* of the no-show. How can one never miss a meeting (that's me all over) while regularly giving being-there the slip? I suffer from that more than anyone, but I refuse to justify anything, even if it doesn't work. To justify oneself is an obscene gesture finally, that's all that remains of moral certainty for me in the

The Unconscious of the Retreat

Is the hedgehog a metaphor for the poem? Is the poem a metaphor for the hedgehog? Which would be the literal sense and which the tropic derivation of the other? If there is no poetic experience—or voyage—without an experience of the heart, then there is no poetic experience without stupidity [*bêtise*]. In two senses: firstly, nothing is more asinine [*bête*] than learning by heart, parrot-fashion; secondly, nothing is more alive in life than the heart, possessed in common by all animals. There is thus animal in the poem, and poem in the animal; in the neighborhood of poem and hedgehog it is not possible to distinguish which, properly speaking, comes before the other and precedes it in the *envoyage*. Metaphoric origin is stricken with amnesia.

In order to respond in two words: *ellipsis,* for example, or *election, heart, hérisson,* or *istrice,* you will have had to disable memory, disarm culture, know how to forget knowledge, set fire to the library of poetics. The unicity of the poem depends on this condition. You must celebrate, you have to commemorate amnesia, savagery, even the stupidity of the "by heart": the *hérisson.* It blinds itself. Rolled up in a ball, prickly with spines, vulnerable and dangerous, calculating and ill-adapted (because it makes itself into a ball, sensing the danger on the autoroute, it exposes itself to an accident). No poem without accident, no poem that does not open itself like a wound, but no poem that is not also just as wounding. You will call poem a silent incantation, the aphonic wound that, of you, from you, I want to learn by heart.[9]

You will call poem from now on a certain passion of the singular mark, the signature that repeats its dispersion, each time beyond the *logos,* a-human, barely domestic, not reappropriable into the family of the subject: a converted animal, rolled up in a ball, turned toward the other and toward itself, in sum, a thing—modest, discreet, close to the earth, the humility that you nickname, thus transporting yourself in the name beyond the name, a catachrestic *hérisson,* its arrows held at the ready, when this ageless blind thing hears but does not see death coming.[10]

When the hedgehog rolls into a ball, it retreats (or thinks it retreats)

end. Not to say, in the meantime, that I think one has to give in to the unjustifiable. . . .

Fribourg, 26 January 1998

. . . The other Fribourg, wholly other. Meeting in memory of Lévinas, who taught here for twenty-five years. I can't report everything, but I really tried, with all my strength, to see him, *him*, really him, going so far as to halluci- nate, seeing him arrive by train with his wife, each time, walk in the streets, stay in the home of the rich family that founded the Chair of Contemporary Jewish Thought in this bilingual university (something rare, take note). Do- minicans, I'm told, formed the larger part of his audience—they were there, moreover, at the lecture, all in white. Jean Halpérin also, Lévinas's great friend, he was right next to me at the Pantin Cemetery. I think of Lévinas in- tensely, I follow him. He was there, himself, I think I see him. Tried an anal- ogous hallucination last year in Cordoba, next to the statues of Averroes and Maimonides, near the Mosque, a hundred meters apart. (A propos, have I ever told you about the *Guide des Egarés*—for the *Perplexed*—that I opened and touched eight years ago in my grandfather's glass-paneled bookshelves? Look up the words *égarer, s'égarer*, to do with getting lost, therefore, and *garer*. You'll find all you need to talk about travel, and about *my* voyages, all the way to the truths to park [*garer*], keep [*garder*]—or no, to keep one- self from or to steer clear of.) And I think of the other phantom of the other Freiburg, as if E.L. held fast to *his* Fribourg. Two years ago I visited the hut with Heidegger's older son, and about twenty years ago was my first visit to Freiburg-im-Breisgau (I allude to it, I think, in *The Post Card*, "Martin's *Weg*" again . . .). "Every other is every (bit) other," the sentence that you quote, Catherine, fell first, if I dare say so, like a stone in Lévinas's garden. . . .

Tunis, 19–22 February 1998

. . . About this first trip to Tunis, too much to say. Miracles. At home at someone else's place. . . . I am writing this letter-card, which I should have sent you yesterday, in Paris. In the end, I didn't go to Sidi-Bou-Saïd. I didn't dare insist that my hosts take me there. But this name, Sidi-Bou-Saïd, identi- fied one of my first destinations some fifty years ago, a voyage before the voyages. It bears Gide's signature, I must have read and dreamed of it. After decades of separation, I again open what was the Bible of my adolescence, and find again my Jardin d'Essai. *Les Nourritures terrestres* [*Fruits of the*

from the traffic and withdraws from circulation by means of retraction. In this sense, it is susceptible to withdrawal [*retrait*] (to the extent of withdrawing like a metaphor for the poem). However, the senses of the *retrait* are not brought together in it. It doesn't know them, it is in a way the "unconscious . . . of the retreat."[11] It exposes itself to death without knowing:

The poem can roll itself up in a ball, but it is still in order to turn its pointed signs toward the outside. To be sure, it can reflect language or speak poetry, but it never relates back to itself, it never moves by itself like those machines, bringers of death. Its event always interrupts or derails absolute knowledge, autotelic being in proximity to itself. This "demon of the heart" never gathers itself together, rather it loses itself and gets off the track (delirium or mania), it exposes itself to chance, it would rather let itself be torn to pieces by what bears down upon it.[12]

Being exposed to an accident—the fate of every traveler—is not something that can be known as such; it is all the more radical for not having any "as such." That also means that the polysemy of the word *retrait* cannot be brought together in any superior univocity. It does not sublate its dissemination.

Heidegger would doubtless consider the dissemination of meaning in writing, beyond the controlled polysemia that he basically recommends, to be an effect of *Witz*. I am not making a case for *Witz*. But the writing-hedgehog links the essence of the poematic to the aleatory, not only to the aleatory factor of language or nomination, but to that of the mark, and this is what destines it to a "learning-by-heart" whose letter is not thoroughly nominal, discursive, or linguistic. In all this, a great proximity to Heidegger does not exclude some misgiving on the subject of nothing less than poetry and truth (*Dichtung und Warheit*): things are played out between the *Versammlung* (which is to say also, for Heidegger, the *logos*) and dissemination.[13]

The motif of the heart links those of intimacy and the mechanical, but without gathering them, and always in a singular and unique way. This linkage is a "contamination, and this crossroads, this accident here. This turn, the turning around of *this* catastrophe."[14] Hence:

Earth]: "In Tunis, the only garden is the cemetery. In Algiers, in the Botanical Gardens [*Jardin d'Essai*] (palm-trees of every species), I ate fruits that I had never seen before."[21]

A family superstition that I still respect today: when leaving, once the threshold has been crossed, never retrace one's steps back inside. It gives rise to comic situations I don't dare describe. Especially when, before a long voyage, mother or sister or wife has already thrown water at you on the doorstep to mark the moment when, having left, only then must you turn around and say goodbye. One returns alive only on that condition. But the fact that I never retrace my steps when leaving, not at any price, in no way contradicts the irresistible desire: to return to the places of a voyage, come back, turn around, repeat again and again, and to create out of a counterpath a work that reminisces on and commemorates this insistence. . . . Do you know Richard Long's sculptures? He lays down the archive, so to speak, of certain trajectories, often with stones or even with dried mud that draws a circle in a landscape that is literally sculpted by the memory of the artist—and what remains of the work-at-work-in-walking [*oeuvre-en-marche*] is then exhibited, the voyage becomes a work ("A Walk of Ten Days in the High Sierra California 1995," "Asia Circle Stones," "Gobi Desert Circle," "White Mud Circle"). . . . Predestinations and coincidences, encounters (responses to the question "what does to (re)turn (oneself around) mean?"). On the last day we all went to Thuburbo Majus. Aïcha Ben Abed showed us the archeological site that she had worked on for a long time. I admire and observe her as much as what she shows us. The science and magic of living hospitality, a smile that is sweet and a little painful. We follow her through the ruins. When she was living alone at this site for weeks on end (I then think only of sharing her solitude, inhabited by Roman specters whose daily schedule she describes to us), the people living round there warned her, never go to such and such a place within the archeological site at the time of a full moon, the Djinns will transform you into a pillar of salt. She didn't listen to them, she said, confident that she had overcome an infantile and irrational fear ("Obscurantism!" she thinks; didn't dare ask her if she was confident she had escaped that threat, that night, and whether she wanted to). . . . But that very evening, back in the luxurious palace I am living in in the heart of the Medina, I find again on the shelves my great friend-enemy and eternal compatriot (at the same time Algerian and Tunisian, he is very present here, as you know), and, in *The City of God*, an allusion, indeed, to the

[21] [André Gide, *Fruits of the Earth*, 56. (D.W.)]

Our poem does not hold still within names, nor even within words. It is first of all thrown out on the roads and in the fields, thing beyond languages, even if it sometimes happens that it recalls itself in language, when it gathers itself up, rolled up in a ball on itself, more threatened than ever in its retreat: it thinks it is defending itself, and it loses itself.[15]

Accident without Sacrifice

The accident that can befall the hedgehog is not to be conceived of in the sense of a sacrifice. For the sacrifice "is never accidental." Derrida continues: "When there is sacrifice, the ritual victim is not run over by history in an accidental way, as on the highway." Now, in Heidegger, accident is always tied to sacrifice, which is to say, to the truth, it always comes to be invested with "destinal meaning."[16] As Derrida makes clear: "This propensity to magnify the disastrous accident is foreign to what I called the humility of the poematic hedgehog: low, very low, close to the earth, humble (*humilis*)."[17]

To say that the hedgehog has no relation to itself is to say that it doesn't see death coming; in that sense it is blind. It does not walk freely toward death like the *Dasein*. The poematic experience is that of a living creature that is foreign to the logos, exposed to a death without words, a death that Heidegger would call "perishing," precisely in order to distinguish it from "death as such": "the verb 'to perish' retains something of the *per*, of the passage of the limit, of the traversal marked in Latin by the *pereo, perire* (which means exactly: to leave, disappear, pass—on the other side of life, *transire*)."[18] The hedgehog is perishable; that is its humility, the fact of exposing itself to death without expecting it or waiting for it, in the experience of crossing. It is on the road, on the way, unconscious, knowing neither from whence it comes nor whither it goes, not *deriving*, just passing. It keeps itself "very low, close to the earth." It is down to earth; it advances along the ground—a strip of asphalt—which is not a pathway, not a *Bewëgung*, not opening onto any sense. The hedgehog is assured of no *already there* nor any destination; it passively resists that logic, "this logic of destination that permits one to say, everywhere and always, 'I have always already arrived at the destination'."[19]

pillar of salt![22] And then this, also, which I dedicate to you, for around my name, Jacob the sedentary one, Augustine refers in Greek to a certain *aplasticity*. He is not speaking of the ruse of Ulysses the traveler, but of a Jacob who never leaves his house:

> But, lest we should suppose this device of Jacob's to have been a fraudulent deception, and so fail to comprehend the great truth which it symbolizes, the Scripture first says: "Esau was a cunning hunter, a man of the field; and Jacob was a plain man, dwelling in tents" (Gen. 25:27). Some of our translators have rendered "plain" here as "without guile"; but whether the Greek word *aplastos* means "without deceit" or "plain" or—better—"without pretence" (απλαστος), what deceit is there in the obtaining of a blessing by a man "without deceit"? What deceit is there in a plain man? What pretence is there in a man who tells no lies, unless there is here a profound and mysterious truth?[23]

I come back to the pillar of salt. I am (following) it. Since my return to Ris-Orangis, desire to reread Gide, to look for Sidi-Bou-Saïd there. Lo and behold, in the fourth book of *Les Nouvelles Nourritures*, final scene ("Passionately leaning over the vessel's prow, I watch, advancing toward me, the innumerable waves, the islands, the adventures of the unknown land which already . . . "), on the same page, after he evokes a type of kenosis (an "immense void" and a refusal of the "mystical"), I stop short, falling upon the same pillar of salt, three times in one day, without counting the Bible, which I also wanted to reread (Gen. 19:26). Gide:

> I know best of all that one can only go forward by pushing the past behind one. We are told that Lot's wife, because she looked behind her, was changed into a pillar of salt—that is of frozen tears. Turning towards the future, Lot then lies with his daughters. So be it![24]

Do you know what happened to Saint Louis here? . . . And to me, on the point of returning, at the Tunis airport, just about to climb the gangway. For the first time in my life, after a slight malaise (light head, everyday hypoglycemia, no doubt), I said to myself, "Now, I'm ready [*prêt*]." Ready to die, of course, near [*près*] to dying also. I didn't say it to myself, I *heard* myself say it, like

---

[22] "Or that the angels in human form whom Abraham received as guests, and through whom he received God's promise that he was to have offspring, should also have foretold the destruction of Sodom by fire from heaven? Or that Abraham's nephew Lot should have been delivered from Sodom by angels just as the fire was descending, while Lot's wife, who looked backwards as she went and was immediately turned into salt, became a sign warning us that no one who has set foot on the path of redemption should yearn for what he has left behind?" (Augustine, *The City of God against the Pagans*, 401–2.) At that rate, I would have been lost a long time ago; myself, I am nothing but a pillar of salt.

[23] Ibid., 752.

[24] [André Gide, *Fruits of the Earth*, 255. (D.W.)]

Far from the Amazonian forest, not knowing how to turn around like a heliotrope, foreign to the house of being and to properly dying, the hedgehog travels without a sound. Like the interchanges across which it hazards its journey and risks misfortune, it is destined for only one thing, to "remain of little meaning [*rester de peu de sens*]."[20]

[14]

With Nelson Mandela, 11 August 1998.
(Jacques Derrida Archives)

someone else to someone else, like a quotation that, however, couldn't be detached from me. I addressed it to myself without really believing it, in the way one pays attention to something someone is reported to have said—but it was something that I wouldn't previously have even let pass. Even yesterday I wouldn't have allowed it to come into my place. A leftover superstition that will always survive, testifying to an inextinguishability [*l'increvable*] that keeps me and watches me. Stop right there! Just below the plane, I let myself say it, yes, like an anonymous whisper, I let myself pretend, barely, to say it to myself, on someone else's behalf, some invisible third person who still resembles me too closely, without violent protest, without the incredulous cry that would have made me revolt, body and soul, just yesterday. Never, never would I myself have said that to myself with this slight movement of acquiescence, the almost serene acceptation of him who (illegible . . . I scribbled this down in the plane before it took off). I remain quite astonished by it, a little wounded. . . .

Would I therefore be ready to die? I will have spent my life trying to do so, to accept that (the sole source, for me, of what "to accept" could mean): I will indeed have to arrive there one day, doing everything to reach that bank, and my life is used up determining that this "wisdom" won't ever fall to me, that I will never manage it or arrive there. These words ("Now I am ready") surprise me like a foreign language surprises a lost child, they don't come *from* me, this old code has never been mine, they come *upon* me—in the refusal, infinite protest, radical incomprehension of the "one must die." Yet there it was, I was able to say it to myself, between believing and not believing, as if I were another: "I am ready." I hope that soon I won't even have thought it, that everything will become normal again. But I don't think it will be like that at all. Nothing will be "like before" again. Something has happened, I was dying, even if I didn't want to say what I heard being said: "I am ready." A wound has tainted my virginity (did you know that I was a virgin still yesterday, Catherine?), death has touched me, it has dared approach, without even any drama, sickness, accident, trauma, without the least apparent commotion, without identifiable threat, no, under a sky that was so serene, I can't get over it. It had to be under an African sky.

And I wonder, for your sake, Catherine: the fact that that befell me while traveling, at the moment I was about to return (this morning it is raining, but the Tunisian sky had remained "pure" all through these last few days), in an airport, at the foot of the gangway, does that mean—at the end of such a long underground labor, no doubt—something relating to departure and arrival, to arrival at the point of departure? And if I am asking you whether the calm waters of the "I am ready" announce the return, the silence of the motor, the end of life. The approach to the harbor. Or on the contrary, finally, pulling up to leave [*un lever de la partance*]. For I was going to leave, and it all came to pass at the foot of the passageway to a plane whose motors could not have been more deafening. It is true that I was leaving to return. . . .

I will return to Africa this summer, but to South Africa, and for the first time also, God willing, as one used to say back home whenever one spoke in the future. In August, Capetown, where I am to meet Mandela and Tutu, then Stellenbosch, Pietermaritzburg, Potchefstroom, Pretoria, Johannesburg. The discussions and lectures will often turn around the "pardon," and the Truth and Reconciliation Commission. As in Australia the following summer, purposely arranged to overflow your book. . . .

Baltimore (Johns Hopkins), 31 March 1998

. . . Three seminars and two lectures in a week. In spite of all my returns to this place, probably ten or so times, it is always the "first times" that I commemorate, with a childlike enthusiasm, upon arrival (beginning with the silhouettes of the 1966 colloquium: Lacan, Barthes, Hyppolite, Vernant, de Man, and so many others. . . . Hillis Miller was there already, but we be-

Cloverhill Road, "'first' dwelling," alley entrance (*contre-allée*). (Jacques Derrida Archives)

Gilman Hall.
(Jacques Derrida Archives)

came friends only in 1968—we haven't left each other since, from Hopkins to Yale to Irvine, lunching together every Tuesday for thirty years). Memory no longer knows whether what haunts along these alleys faithfully accompanies footsteps or names, places or prayers: Cloverhill Road, the "first" dwelling, "first" American street in 1968, where Jean took his first steps and five-year-old Pierre told us (how well we understand each other in these words): "we have to return now, I'm losing my French"; then Wolman Hall, then the house and magic hospitality of the Mackseys, for more than a quarter of a century the most miraculous and well-tried private library I know of, in the image of its creator; then Poe's room and tomb visited in 66 and so many times since, etc. If you knew everything that has happened to me in this city, Catherine, each time. No one, not even I, will ever be able to reassemble it, cinders there are (this sentence, *il y a là cendre*, was first of all, right here, in 1971, a signature sealed from that time, mine)[25]. . . . Tomorrow morning, at dawn, I am returning alone, thirty years on, in a rental car, to Penn State, four hours away by road, to give a lecture on Celan ("Poetics and Politics of Witnessing"). Come back the next morning (seminar in the afternoon, imagine how rushed) and set off again in two days, from Washington for Los Angeles . . .

25 [Cf. *Cinders* (C.M.)]

Laguna Beach.
(Gil Kofman)

Laguna Beach, 8 May 1998

I didn't have the heart for postcards this time, my stay will have been too sad (death of Jean-François Lyotard, with whom I timeshared the same house at Laguna Beach for years—I have been teaching at Irvine, twenty minutes from here, several weeks a year for twelve years—and still other commotions . . .). A letter just before returning, therefore, instead of cards. I would have liked to tell you of my love for Laguna and for those I call, also in "Circumfession," "my friends the birds" on their white rock. I took some photos of them for your book. Haven't moved this year, the telephone is hell when the news isn't good. One trip only, to Davis, for a conference on, in the main, de Man's concept of "materiality." I talked about (I have to sim-

"'My friends the birds' ("Circumfession") on their white rock. I took some photos of them for your book." (Gil Kofman)

plify) a certain stolen ribbon (Rousseau in the *Confessions*), like a typewriter ribbon, and then about those insects in Normandy that they just discovered in the very place where they were taken, seized, or surprised in amber at the moment they vampirized or made love to one another, 54 million years before the appearance of man on the earth (how's that for scale, says Jacob).[26] On the way back with Hillis, we stopped in the Californian vine-

---

[26] ["*Voilà la bonne échelle, dit Jacob.*" *Échelle* means "scale," but also "ladder." (D.W.)]

yards, somewhere I hadn't been, Napa Valley, and the forest of trees petrified millions of years ago. . . . Normally I go several times to Newport Beach, past Corona del Mar (Fashion Island or South Coast Plaza, for shopping or to buy French newspapers), once or twice to Los Angeles, which is nearby. Sometimes I leave Laguna Beach for two or three days on a trip I wouldn't admit to (Las Vegas, Death Valley, Boulder City, and the Hoover Dam, or the Grand Canyon by night train—the South West Chief, my very own American cinema . . .). Failing always impossible stories—anyway, we won't have the time or place—be content with dreams from Laguna, as promised. In the night of 16–17 April (on the eve of the other commotion—helicopter from the Ile de Groix to Lorient, as you know, I almost died, me the first), I find myself here before a fatal ordeal: I am ordered to pilot an airplane, although I know I am inexperienced; someone, I don't know who, commands me to do various impossible dives. But I accept, terrified, "you have to" I tell myself—and I wake up immediately as if the "you have to" meant to me "you have to wake up." The law. Feeling of duty, someone in me (but who?) enjoins me to accept the provocation of the event. I easily recognize these situations where there are all the reasons in the world telling me to hold back, to flee, "not to go," and where something, however, neither courage nor masochism but another law, that no longer belongs to the world, dictates to me the compelling need *to go*, precisely, on the contrary, and to *countergo*, to accept the wager ("here I am, I'm coming"). So I unfailingly obey some other—"what" or "whom" I couldn't say. Could make a list of these passive and typical quasi-decisions that have magnetized or dis-oriented my life, but I think that the whole process of what I write, *such as* I write it, is marked by that, legibly, signed in that way. Moreover, every decision arrives on the given *date* of this singular "passivity." That's also what I nickname my counterpath.

May 2nd, another dream, "we"(?) are received by Blanchot. He makes us wait, something secret is going on in his apartment. I find him looking well and, a little irritated by the wait he has imposed, I eagerly inspect the premises. Have I ever dreamed of Blanchot before? Fear of premonition, of the gods' signal. I am superstitious, ten times more so when traveling. . . .

May 6th, "someone" (a certain Clifford Duffy) thinks it clever, and desirable, to post on the web from Canada (site dedicated to *Glas*) the news of my death. After a serious car accident in California, he says. At the moment that Peter Krapp, who controls the site, is giving a lecture at Irvine on "*Glas* as Hypertext." Flurry of phone calls (from Geoff in England, who had just read the news on his computer early in the morning, to Marguerite, then Marguerite to me, who reassures her, at one in the morning at Laguna

Beach, then from me to Geoff, who disclaims the news on the internet, etc.).
I pinch myself . . . what if it were true? The following night I dream[27] that
while traveling I learn of my father's death (you know he has been dead
since 1970 and that *Glas* is not unrelated to that bereavement). I can't bring
myself to believe it—or to doubt it. I try to force myself to take this news seriously, right into my body, to cry, to suffer there where, in suffering, I can
also accuse myself of not suffering, in order to suffer from not suffering
enough, and especially for not daring to phone my sister and brother (argument: what else remains to say to each other, without pretending, on the
telephone? Acute feeling, in my dream the words really aren't there any
more. Not a single available word left. Except those that wait for me and
that I don't yet know. Nothing is viable between us any more. We are therefore going to have to separate, all of us, I and mine, without a word) . . .

[27] I think I spoke to you of the *Book of Stops* [*Kitāb al-Mawāqif*] by the great 'Abd al-Kader (who now has
his equestrian statue in Algiers, replacing that of Marshal Bugeaud). This book has very little to do with
travel in explicit terms. But it contains a gloss on the *isthmus* of the Koran (55, 19–20). In a very classical
way, no doubt. All the mediations of philosophy. The isthmus (*barzakh*) begins between two seas, then becomes the general figure of the middle, of the threshold or the between. Its third category is the dream, precisely between sleep and waking, life and death. Man can see himself "elsewhere" there, he can inhabit
two places at once, all the while remaining at home—and do the *impossible there* (*Mawāqif*, 235).

A Trio of Ways [*A trois voies*]

Voi(c)e 1: Have we arrived?

Voi(c)e 2: What are you asking? Whether the journey is over? whether we can now conclude? Or whether we, these pathways, or the pathway in general, means arrival? Whether it can be confused with the very movement of arriving?

V. 1: Both. All that at the same time.

Voi(c)e 3: Another question. We are three, at least three; we have been forged in the work itself, following three directions that, although separable, remain no less particular and irreducible one to the other. I am not sure, however, whether our separateness or our parting resists arrival. Haven't we ended up being confused one with the other?

V.2: Both. All that at the same time.

V.3: Explain yourself.

V.2: We are separate *and* we are confused. But that is to be understood in two senses which seem themselves to be irremediably separate one from the other.

V.1: First sense first.

V.2: We are separate *and* we are confused: that means, in the first place, that the space of separation [*l'écart*] is our common lot. We are confused at least to the extent that we always proceed from that space—from the originary *trait* or breach/broaching [*entame*]—whatever voyages we make possible and which, in return, render us possible. We manage to, or arrive from, not deriving. Of course that provokes catastrophe—reversal, upset, peril, destruction, or chance, in a word, imminence—all over the map, in the whole deck, in every tracing, on all the landmarks of a metaphysical geography. And all over the earth. Henceforth, the voyage *signifies* the separation between drift and arrival.

V.3: A separation that makes room without itself taking place, isn't that so? But if that is the case, how does one know, how can one ever know if it arrives, whether, when, and how it arrives? Whether catastrophe doesn't reduce, after all, to being a destination like any other?

V.1: "What is it, a destination?

V.2: There where it arrives.

V.1: So then everywhere that it arrives there was destination?

V.2: Yes.

V.1: But not before?

V.2: No.

V.3: That's convenient, since if it arrives there, it is because it was destined to arrive there. But then one can only say so after the fact?

V.1: When it has arrived, it is indeed the proof that it had to arrive, and arrive there, at its destination.

V.3: But before arriving, it is not destined, for example it neither desires nor demands any address? There is everything that arrives where it had to arrive, but no destination before the arrival?

V.2: Yes, but I meant to say something else.

V.3: Of course, that's what I was saying.

V.1: There you are."[1]

V.2: As you know, the pathway does not predate the voyage. Pathway, traveler, and voyage arrive and reach each other's shore together. For better or for worse.

V.1: I admit to not having completely understood how a pathway, you or I, can destine in this way, go *envoyaging*, within an improbable but same time, out of step but still one and the same, subject, vehicle, and place.

V.2: If you prefer, "I interrupt a moment . . . everything I told you about the step [*pas*], the way [*voie*], viability, our viaticum, the car and *Weglichkeit*, etc.," in order to ask you a riddle: "I came upon it yesterday evening: ' . . . we have being and movement, because we are travelers. And it is thanks to the way that the traveller receives the being and the name of the traveller. Consequently, when a traveller turns into or sets out along an infinite way and one asks him where he is, he replies that he is on the way; and if one asks him where he has come from, he replies that he has come from the way; and if one asks him where he is going, he replies that he is going from the way to the way. . . . But be careful about this [oh yes, because one could easily be careless, the temptation is great, and it is mine, it consists in not being careful, taking care of nothing, being careful of nothing (*prendre garde, garde de rien, garde à rien*), especially not the truth which is the guarding itself, as its name suggests]: this way which is at the same time life, is also truth.' Guess [*devine*], you the soothsayer [*devine*], who wrote that, which is neither the *tô* (path and discourse) nor Martin's *Weg*; guess what I have missed out. It is called *Where is the King of the Jews?*"[2]

V.1: Wait, I think I know. It's a text by Nicolas de Cues. Let me fill in the part you omitted: "Now Paul said that in God . . . "[3] It begins like that. Then:

And it is thus said that the infinite way is the place of the traveler, and that this way is God. Consequently, this way, outside of which no traveler could be found, is this very being, without princeps or end, to which the traveler owes his being a traveler, and his having everything that makes him a traveler. But the fact that the traveler begins being a traveler on the way adds nothing to the infinite way, nor does it produce any change in the perpetual and immobile pathway.

Also be mindful of the way in which God's Word declares that it is the way [John 14:16]; you can understand that a really living intellect is a traveler on the pathway (that is to say, in the Word) of life, the pathway thanks to which he is said to be a traveler and along which he moves. For if movement is life, the way of movement is life, and it is the living way of the living traveler; it is to the living pathway that the living traveler owes his being a living traveler, and he moves on this pathway and starts out from it, along this pathway and in the direction of it. It is thus justly that the Son of God calls himself the way and the life.[4]

If I understand the sense of the riddle, you mean that giving back the traveler to the path and the path to separation or to the forging of the path implies leaving out God?

V.2: No, not if by God one means the real leap of chance or the throw of the dice. Yes, if by God one means an origin excepted from the way that it still manages to open up, a non-vehicular or non-conveyed instance, still alive to the extent that it never exposes itself to the possibility of accident, to catastrophe in general. The traveler moves along the pathway, he comes from the pathway, he goes from pathway to pathway. . . . If one leaves out the origin of this *viability*, "the princeps to which the traveler owes his being a traveler," then the voyage no longer derives from anything and the origin becomes transportable and is, as a result, always missing in its place. The way is neither infinite nor immobile. For that reason every event arrives or happens as a catastrophe.

V.3: And we are confused there, all the pathways, in the place of this finite mobilization. And we part ways there also, each of us having to trace their own history without being able to take care of the others. The pathways cannot be gathered together, or be kept in truth. The three courses that we have marked out, reversal, traversal, and version, do not form a whole: that is their paradoxical unity.

They still come back to the same thing in a way. All three state that no voyage flows from a source. And it is also for that reason that they detach themselves one from the other.

V.1: Well then, what is the second sense, the other sense of "we are separate *and* we are confused"?

V.2: The second sense points toward a type of contradiction. It could be a question of an aporia, a paradox, an opposition. A problem in any case.

V.3: I think I can see that already. According to the logic of this second sense, and contrary to everything that has just been said, we are confused in that we are separated precisely from what we think we are: underived separations, partings, or forgings.

V.1: You can't mean that we will always be lacking with respect to the very thing that we claim to divert, namely derivation?

V.2: Yes, exactly that. By the end of our three tours it seems in fact difficult, even impossible, to avoid it; at bottom, one cannot do without it, it always arrives by coming back, "succeeds in returning."[5] Look at it rebounding, rising out of the texts, circumscribe it with a line, it remains there, everywhere, vigilant. Repulsed, repressed, exorcised, it is there, in spite of everything, throughout everything. Be very careful: one day we would need to demonstrate systematically how derivation, or drifting, haunts Derrida's texts. It seems to impose itself in the same way, for example, that the supplement does in Rousseau. The catastrophe is in the fact that arrival cannot really say adieu to derivation.

V.1: But he never said otherwise. Declaring, concerning *dérive*, that he has "abused the word," doesn't amount to ostracizing it. Besides, you know what promises not to abuse something are worth. *Dérive* would be THE *pharmakon*, something one can in fact only abuse as long as there is the *envoi*. Deconstructing the derivative schema does not imply an attempt to replace it with a different one. For Derrida, it is not a matter of playing arrival off *against* derivational drift, but of showing that the latter is in no way essential; that as far as thinking is concerned it is merely an unavoidable derivative.

V.3: In this sense, there is no problem with the fact that a text is haunted—obsessively so—by the derivational drift that it has set itself the task of deconstructing.

V.1: If you like. "There is no contradiction here, but rather a displacement of concepts."[6]

V.2: All the same, something still bothers me. Look again, for example, at this extract from "Faith and Knowledge": "But it seems impossible to deny the *possibility* in whose name—thanks to which—the (derived) *necessity* (the authority or determinate belief) would be put in question, suspended, rejected, or criticized, even deconstructed."[7] It is strange. Why speak here of the " (derived) necessity?" What is its necessity? How would history, a sequence of events, everything that takes place in general, be derived? If the original *envoi* is subject to chance, even if it gets dated and authorized as a founding event, if it is always after the event that one can say that what has arrived had to arrive, then why speak of derived necessity? From what could it, in fact, be derived? Isn't speaking in this way tantamount to maintaining the fact of there being derivational drift as something certain? Doesn't it still amount to having faith in it?

V.1: I am not very convinced.

V.3: I don't see where you are heading.

V.2: Let me take another example. When he seems "tempted to consider mourning and ghosting [*revenance*], spectrality or living-on, surviving, as non-derivable categories or as non-reducible derivations,"[8] or, again, speaks of "replacement as the very possibility of place, the originary and non-supervened [*non survenue*] possibility of all placement,"[9] how can one be sure that the originary-derived couple does not continue to play its traditional role? Why affirm that the supplement (mourning, specter, replacement, substitute, remainder, etc.) cannot be derived, or irreducibly derived, or indeed has not occurred [*non survenu*]? Doesn't that amount to negatively conferring a sort of certificate of authenticity on it, the bonus of an origin [*prime d'origine*]? What is meant in the final analysis by "non-derived"? Doesn't such a formula always refer back to an order of arrival? The use of the word *dérive* and its derivatives is not accidental. One must "*never treat as an accident the force of the name in what happens* [arrive]."[10]

V.3: You mean that derivational drift, even if *reversed*, even if *traversed*, even if fallen into catastrophe, even if seen according to another *version* of the facts, does not appear to travel as far as one might think in Derrida's thinking?

V.2: Let's say that there would perhaps be an irreducible indigenousness to derivation in the country of arrival.

V.1: In other words, how not to derive?

V.2: Or how not to see that *dérive* and disavowal cover the same question?

V.3: Showing that would mean a whole other voyage.

V.2: That's what I was saying. There you are.

APPENDICES

Stops

El Biar, Jacques
Derrida racing
(*left*), 1945.
(Jacques Derrida
Archives)

Curriculum: the word pertains more to the route taken by a race than to the pursuit of a ca-
reer. A race that will be described here practically without commentary. *Dis-cursion*
without discourse, geographic figuration of a life, telegraphic *aide-mémoire* also,
cursory, scribbled down in a rush by a runner quite out of breath and not even stop-
ping to do it carefully. This *curriculum peregrinationis* risks neglecting everything that
moves along with it, including the emotion. By simply naming a series of stops, it will
immobilize, as in a tableau, the stages, destinations, place-names, perhaps even the
rhythm of a mode of travel that, at least since 1968, has been almost incessant.

As cartography—not even a travel journal—this dreary list of places and dates
that, to save time, I have to limit to a minimal form of notation, also appears, by
means of another convention, as an *annual*: year after year, the proper names of
cities that recall algebraic metonymies or toponyms. This nomenclature finally lists
nothing more than localities [*lieux-dits*], understood in the sense of simulacra, each
of them the ciphered diminutive for experiences whose narrative keeps on going.
(The calendar remains incomplete in more than one respect: unable to trust either my

Ski slopes, near the Plateau d'Assy,
1955. (Jacques Derrida Archives)

On the Elba, near Prague, 1960.
(Jacques Derrida Archives)

memory or some "archive" that I in fact never recorded, on top of that I set myself the rule of listing here only those trips that, for one reason or another, were not purely private.)

The sadly comic effect of all this (in my computer I have given it the filename "travel agency") doesn't escape me. If I am to be given credit for that, then one will no doubt be sensitive to a sort of misery that is expressed here. Indeed, all of these travels represent for me a jubilant commotion for which I berate myself and which is a source of suffering. For, believe me, there is someone in me who never would travel, who insists on not doing it at all, who insists that he never in fact did. If only I were never to travel, at least never far from home, which is somewhere that I already feel as it were *moved* enough, more than necessary, by what comes and happens to me. And by what doesn't come or happen, to me, to one or another.

Thus it is that since 1930, the year of my birth, until 1949, apart from the odd excursion in Kabylie with my father, I never left El Biar or Algiers; never more than from five to seventy kilometers away, as far as the beaches of Bab-el-Oued, Saint-Eugène, Deux-Moulins, Madrague, or to Guyotville, Sidi-Ferruch, Zéralda, Cherchell, or Tipasa.

1949 first departure, boat and train to the *Métropole*: Marseilles and Paris.

1950 Easter Holidays, first trip within France, to Aix-les-Bains with a friend. Until 1954, no more traveling either in France or abroad, some Paris–Algiers roundtrips, often semi-clandestinely, in any case not according to regulations, on board small cargo planes that didn't look very reassuring (a less expensive way to travel, but which could be rather frightening when they hit air pockets with altogether more vertiginous results given that one was seated on a bench in the middle of cases full of vegetables). Regular Parisian addresses: boarding hostels at the Lycée Louis-le-Grand (rue Saint-

Jacques) and the Ecole normale supérieure (rue d'Ulm), and for more than a year (1951–52) in a minuscule maid's room without running water at 17, rue Lagrange, near the Place Maubert.

1954 first "border crossing," first "foreign country." While studying at the Ecole normale supérieure (1952–56), I made a brief field trip to Leuven to consult the Husserl Archives.

1956 within France I had visited only some ski resorts in the Alps (1953), Loire Valley châteaux (1955), and Normandy (Honfleur, 1956) by the time that, following the *Agrégation* exams, I left by boat with Marguerite Aucouturier for the United States (New York, Cambridge, Harvard University, Boston—where we got married—then by car as far as Cape Hatteras, South Carolina). Return by the same boat (Le Liberté) in June 1957.

1957–59: military service in Algeria. At my request I did not wear a uniform and was assigned to teach in a school for the children of servicemen at Koléa, thirty kilometers from Algiers. Some trips during the summer, to Paris and in the Charente *département*; in 1959, to my first Cerisy-la-Salle colloquium.

1959 Le Mans Lycée.

1960 return to Paris, assistantship at the Sorbonne. First trip to Prague, in a tiny Citroën *deux chevaux*.

1962 return to Algiers with my parents to help them organize their "exodus" from the country. Since then, vacations in France have always been either in the Charente (a village near Angoulême) or near Nice. Second trip to Prague in the Citroën.

1965 first trip to Italy (Venice, a month on the Lido).

1966 first lectures abroad. Parma, on Artaud; Bressanone (conference on tragedy). First return to the United States, Baltimore, for the famous Johns Hopkins conference. Following that event the travels never stopped multiplying and accelerating. Most of them involved, at least as a pretext, some academic invitation. I haven't retained any reliable memory of the subjects or titles. Besides the fact that recalling them all here would not be particularly helpful, most of them have been recorded as the publications that such seminars and lectures gave rise to. In the interests of brevity and clarity, I will therefore classify the *occasions* for these trips under *three* headings, and will indicate in italics for the record—what counts, by definition, here—the names of *places*, cities, or countries:

Yale, in front of Bingham Hall.
(Jacques Derrida Archives)

1. Regular teaching obligations (from one to five weeks) at the following universities: Johns Hopkins, *Baltimore*, 68, 71, 74, 96, 97, 98; *Algiers*, 71; *Oxford*, 71–72; *Zurich*, 72; *Berlin* (West), 73–74; Yale, *New Haven*, fall or spring each year from 1975 to 1986; UC *Berkeley*, 78; *Geneva*, 78; Minnesota, *Minneapolis*, 79; *Toronto*, 79, 84, 87; *San Sebastian*, 82; Cornell, *Ithaca* (Andrew D. White Professor-at-Large), 82–88; CUNY, *New York*, every fall from 86–91; Dartmouth College, *Hanover*, 87; UC *Irvine*, every spring from 87 to the present; *Siegen*, 88; New York University, New School for Social Research, Cardozo Law School, *New York*, every fall from 92 to the present.

2. Lectures (sometimes on the occasion of a conference): the universities or institutes (where these lectures almost always took place) will be identified by their proper name where the italicized name of the city does not already indicate the same.

1967   Saint-Louis, *Brussels*.

1968   Penn State, *University Park*; State College, *Buffalo*; Northwestern, *Evanston*; Yale, *New Haven*; *Long Island*; NYU and Columbia, *New York*; Berlin (West); *Zurich*; *London*.

Following the time of these trips, and until 1973, I was prevented from traveling by plane by an unsurmountable fear. Whether it could be explained or not, it vanished in 1973. Between 1969 and 1973 I did all my traveling by car, train, or boat, even the longest trips, for example to and from, and within, the United States, in 1971.

1969   *Zurich*.

1970   *London*; *Oxford*; *Turin*; *Milan*; *Naples*; *Florence*; *Bologna*; *Rome*; *Brussels*; *Gent*; *Lille*; *Strasbourg*.

1971   *Algiers*; *Nice*; *Montreal*; *Strasbourg*; Johns Hopkins, *Baltimore*; Northwestern, *Evanston*; Yale, *New Haven*; *New York*.

1972   *Amsterdam*; *Leiden*; *Utrecht*; *Zurich*; *Cerisy-la-Salle*.

1973   *Budapest*; *London*; *Berlin* (West); *Århus*; *Leuven*.

1974   Saint-Louis, *Brussels*; SUNY *Buffalo*; Brown, *Providence*.

1975   *Venice*; Cornell, *Ithaca*; Iowa, *Iowa City*; *Cerisy-la-Salle*.

1976   *Princeton*; *Venice*; Virginia, *Charlottesville*; SUNY *Stony Brook*.

1977   Columbia, *New York*.

1978   UC *San Diego*; UC *Irvine*; Columbia, *New York*; Cornell, *Ithaca*; *Geneva*.

1979   Saint-Louis, *Brussels*; *Freiburg-im-Breisgau*; Cornell, *Ithaca*; SUNY *Buffalo*; McGill, *Montreal*; *Notre Dame*; *New York*; *Oxford*; *London*; *Edinburgh*; *Strasbourg*; *Chicago*; *Cotonou*.

1980   UC *Irvine*; UC *Santa Cruz*; UC *San Diego*; *Rabat*; *Cerisy-la-Salle*; Columbia, *New York*; *Strasbourg*; SUNY *Binghamton*.

1981   *Copenhagen*; *Odense*; *Århus*; *Rabat*; *Berlin* (West); Cornell, *Ithaca*; *Grenoble*; *Prague* (clandestine seminar).

1982   *Cambridge*; Florida, *Gainesville*; Emory, *Atlanta*; *Berlin*; *Leuven*; Cornell, *Ithaca*; *Mexico City*; *Bethesda* (*Maryland*); Johns Hopkins, *Baltimore*; *Cerisy-la-Salle*; *Florence*; *Barcelona*; *Madrid*.

1983   *Liège*; Columbia, New School, *New York*; *Jerusalem*; *Frankfurt*; *Geneva*; *Tokyo*; *Fukuoka*; *Kyoto*; *Sendai*; *Venice*.

1984   Brown, *Providence*; UC *Irvine*; UC *Berkeley*; SUNY *Buffalo*; Williams College, *Williamstown*; Miami, *Oxford*; *Tokyo*; *Frankfurt*; *Urbino*; Washington, *Seattle*; *Lisbon*.

1985   Loyola, *Chicago*; Brown, *Providence*; Johns Hopkins, *Baltimore*; *Vienna*; Florida,

Gainesville; Emory, *Atlanta*; *Montevideo*; *Buenos Aires*; Saint-Louis, *Brussels*; *London*; *Stockholm*; *Trento*; *Villeneuve-lès-Avignon*; *Vienna*.

1986   *Vienna*; Harvard, *Cambridge*; Columbia, *New York*; Minnesota, *Minneapolis*; *Jerusalem*; Strathclyde, *Glasgow*; *Perugia*.

1987   UC *Irvine*; UC *Los Angeles*; UC *San Diego*; *Valencia*; Essex, *Colchester*; *Perugia*; Rutgers, *New Brunswick*; Vanderbilt, *Nashville*; *Memphis*; Alabama, *Tuscaloosa*; *San Francisco*.

1988   UC *Irvine*; UC *Los Angeles*; *Pittsburgh*; Cornell, *Ithaca*; *Jerusalem*; *Bochum*; *Siegen*; *Washington (D.C.)*.

1989   UC *Irvine*; UC *Berkeley*; UC *Los Angeles*; Williams College, *Williamstown*; *Chicago*; *Turin*; *Leuven*; *Louvain-la-Neuve*; *Kassel*; *New York*; *Rabat*; *Fès*.

1990   Essex, *Colchester*; *Moscow*; *Prague*; *Murcia*; Nebraska, *Lincoln*; UC *Los Angeles*; *Florence*.

1991   Johns Hopkins, *Baltimore*; UC *Los Angeles*; Getty Center, *Los Angeles*; UC *Riverside*; Columbia School of Architecture, *New York*; *Venice*; *Prague*; *Chicago*; *Naples*; UC *Riverside*; Théâtre de La métaphore, *Lille*; *Le Mans*; Stadtforum, *Berlin*; *Royaumont*; *Brest*.

1992   *Oxford*; *Prague*; *Naples*; *Vienna*; LSU, *Baton Rouge*; *Kyoto*; *Yu Fuin*; *Budapest*; *Cambridge*; *Strasbourg*; *Belgrade*; *Cerisy-la-Salle*.

1993   *Kassel*; *Lyon*; *Oslo*; *Warwick*; UC *Santa Barbara*; UC *Riverside*; *Pécs*; *Budapest*; *Reykyavik*.

1994   *Grenoble*; *Naples*; *Amsterdam*; *Capri*; *New York*; *Lisbon*; SUNY *Buffalo*; *Strasbourg*; *Turin*; *Berlin*; Villanova, *Philadelphia*; George Mason, *Fairfax*; *Chicago*; *London*; *Oslo*; *Moscow*; *St Petersburg*; *Murcia*; *Madrid*.

1995   *Bordeaux*; *Athens*; *London*; *Madrid*; *Cosenza*; *Turin*; *Vienna*; *Trento*; *London*; *Luton*; *Louvain-la-Neuve*; *New York*; Alabama, *Tuscaloosa*; *Milan*; *Kingston*; *Frieburg-im-Breisgau*; *Buenos Aires*; *São Paolo*; *Santiago*.

1996   *Milan*; *Turin*; *Bucarest*; *Craiova*; *London*; *Rome*; *Toulouse*; *Rabat*; *Frankfurt/Oder*;

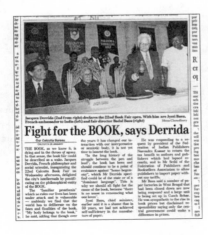

Indian newspaper article inaugurating Calcutta Book Fair, 29 January 1997. (Jacques Derrida Archives)

Athens; Munich; Naples; Capri; Cornell, *Ithaca; Oxford; Bordeaux; London; Berlin;* MOMA, *New York;* Northwestern, *Evanston.*

1997   *Bombay; New Delhi; Calcutta; Dublin; Montreal; Madrid; Istanbul; Tilburg; Cerisy-la-Salle; Meina; Dagniente;* Minguettes, *Lyons;* Cooper Union, *New York;* Villanova, *Philadelphia; Turin; Pisa; London;* Sussex, *Brighton; Porto; Kraków; Katowice; Warsaw; Athens.*

1998   *Jerusalem; Tel Aviv;* Birzeit, *Ramallah; Tunis; Fribourg;* Théâtre de La métaphore, *Lille; Aix-en-Provence;* UC *Davis; Cerisy-la-Salle;* Western Cape, Capetown, *Capetown; Stellenbosch;* Natal, *Pietermaritzburg; Potchefstroom;* Witwatersrand, *Johannesburg; Pretoria; Turin; Brussels; Arles; Madrid; Valencia.*

1999   *Frankfurt; Saint-Paul; Lyon; Oslo; Stanford; Istanbul; Bordeaux; Reading; London; Sydney;* Monash, *Melbourne; Auckland;* SUNY *Albany.*

2000   *Mainz; Cairo; Bordeaux; London; Puerto Rico; Helsinki; Uppsala; Frankfurt; Pécs;* SUNY *Albany; Chicago.*

2001   *Liège; Brussels; Murcia; Saint-Paul;* Florida, *Gainesville; Copenhagen;* Syddansk, *Odense; Heidelberg; Beijing; Nanjing; Shanghai; Hong Kong; Frankfurt* (Adorno Prize); Vanderbilt, *Nashville; Loughborough, Sofia.*

2002   *Lyon; Barcelona; Saint-Paul,* Stanford; *York; Cerisy-la-Salle; Nice;* SUNY *Stony Brook; Toronto; London.*

3. Honorary Doctorates: United States: Columbia, *New York,* 1980; Williams College, *Williamstown,* 1989; New School for Social Research, *New York,* 1989. United Kingdom: Essex, *Colchester,* 1987; *Cambridge,* 1992. Italy: *Palermo* (Nietzsche Prize), 1988; *Turin,* 1998. Belgium: *Leuven,* 1989. Hungary: *Pécs,* 1993. Canada: Queens, *Kingston,* 1995. Rumania: *Craiova,* 1996. Poland: *Katowice,* 1997. South Africa: Western Cape, *Capetown,* 1998. Greece: *Athens,* 1999. Bulgaria: *Sofia,* 2000. China: *Beijing, Nanjing, Shanghai,* 2001.

J.D.

**Sunday morning,
courtyard of Lycée
Louis-le-Grand, 1950.**
(Jacques Derrida
Archives)

Works Cited

WORKS BY JACQUES DERRIDA

Adieu to Emmanuel Lévinas. Translated by Pascale-Anne Brault and Michael Naas. Stanford, CA: Stanford University Press, 1999.

"Aletheia." In *Nous avons voué notre vie à des signes,* by Anonymous. Bordeaux: William Blake & Co., 1996.

"Aphorism Countertime." Translated by Nicholas Royle. In *Acts of Literature,* edited by Derek Attridge. New York: Routledge, 1992.

Aporias. Translated by Thomas Dutoit. Stanford, CA: Stanford University Press, 1993.

"Back from Moscow, in the USSR." Translated by Mary Quaintaire. In *Politics, Theory, and Contemporary Culture,* edited by Mark Poster. New York: Columbia University Press, 1993.

"But, beyond . . . (Open Letter to Anne McClintock and Rob Nixon)." Translated by Peggy Kamuf. *Critical Inquiry* 13 (1986).

Cinders. Translated by Ned Lukacher. Lincoln: University of Nebraska Press, 1991.

"Circumfession." In *Jacques Derrida,* by Geoffrey Bennington and Jacques Derrida, translated by Geoffrey Bennington. Chicago: University of Chicago Press, 1993.

"'Dead Man Running': Salut, Salut." In *Negotiations,* edited by Elizabeth Rottenberg. Stanford, CA: Stanford University Press, 2002.

"Demeure, Athènes (Nous nous devons à la mort)." In *Athènes à l'ombre de l'Acropole,* by Jean-François Bonhomme. Athens: Olkos, 1996.

Dissemination. Translated by Barbara Johnson. Chicago: University of Chicago Press, 1981.

Du droit à la philosophie. Paris: Galilée, 1990.

The Ear of the Other. Edited by Christie McDonald; translated by Peggy Kamuf. New York: Schocken Books, 1985.

"Faith and Knowledge: The Two Sources of 'Religion' at the Limits of Reason Alone." Translated by Samuel Weber. In *Religion*, edited by Jacques Derrida and Gianni Vattimo. Stanford, CA: Stanford University Press, 1998.

"Faxitexture." Translated by Laura Bourland. In *Anywhere*, edited by Cynthia Davidson. New York: Rizzoli, 1992.

"Force of Law: The 'Mystical Foundation of Authority.'" Translated by Mary Quaintance. In *Deconstruction and the Possibility of Justice*, edited by Drucilla Cornell, Michel Rosenfeld, and David Gray Carlson. New York: Routledge, 1992.

"Generations of a City: Memory, Prophecy, Responsibility." Translated by Rebecca Comay. In *Open City* (*Alphabet City* 6), edited by John Knechtel. Toronto: Alphabet City, 1998.

"Geopsychoanalysis: 'and the rest of the world.'" Translated by Donald Nicholson-Smith. In *The Psychoanalysis of Race*, edited by Christopher Lane. New York: Columbia University Press, 1998.

"Geschlecht: Sexual Difference, Ontological Difference." Translated by Ruben Berezdivin. In *A Derrida Reader: Between the Blinds*, edited by Peggy Kamuf. New York: Columbia University Press, 1991.

The Gift of Death. Translated by David Wills. Chicago: University of Chicago Press, 1995.

Given Time. 1. Counterfeit Money. Translated by Peggy Kamuf. Chicago: University of Chicago Press, 1992.

"How to Avoid Speaking: Denials." Translated by Ken Frieden. In *Languages of the Unsayable*, edited by Sanford Budick and Wolfgang Iser. New York: Columbia University Press, 1989.

"Joue—le prénom." *Les Inrockuptibles* 115 (20 August–2 September 1997).

"Khōra." In *On the Name*, edited by Thomas Dutoit; translated by David Wood, John P. Leavey Jr., and Ian McLeod. Stanford, CA: Stanford University Press, 1993.

"La Langue de l'autre." *Les Inrockuptibles* 115 (20 August–2 September 1997).

"Letter to a Japanese Friend." Translated by David Wood and Andrew Benjamin. In *Derrida and Différance*, edited by David Wood and Robert Bernasconi. Evanston, IL: Northwestern University Press, 1988.

"Living On: Border Lines." Translated by James Hulbert. In *Deconstruction and Criticism*, edited by Harold Bloom et al. New York: Seabury Press, 1979.

Margins of Philosophy. Translated by Alan Bass. Chicago: University of Chicago Press, 1984.

Memoires: for Paul de Man. Translated by Cecile Lindsay, Jonathan Culler, Eduardo Cadava, and Peggy Kamuf. New York: Columbia University Press, 1989.

Monolingualism of the Other or the Prosthesis of Origin. Translated by Patrick Mensah. Stanford, CA: Stanford University Press, 1998.

"My Chances/*Mes Chances*: A Rendezvous with Some Epicurean Stereophonies." Translated by Irene Harvey and Avital Ronell. In *Taking Chances*, edited by Joseph Smith and William Kerrigan. Baltimore: Johns Hopkins University Press, 1984.

"No Apocalypse, Not Now (full speed ahead, seven missiles, seven missives)." Translated by Catherine Porter and Philip Lewis. *Diacritics* 14, no. 2 (1984).

Of Grammatology. Translated by Gayatri Chakravorty Spivak. Baltimore: Johns Hopkins University Press, 1976.

"Of a Newly Arisen Apocalyptic Tone in Philosophy." Translated by John P. Leavey Jr. In *Raising the Tone of Philosophy: Late Essays by Immanuel Kant, Transformative Critique by Jacques Derrida*, edited by Peter Fenves. Baltimore: Johns Hopkins University Press, 1993.

Of Spirit: Heidegger and the Question. Translated by Geoffrey Bennington and Rachel Bowlby. Chicago: University of Chicago Press, 1989.

"On Cosmopolitanism." Translated by Mark Dooley. In *On Cosmopolitanism and Forgiveness.* New York: Routledge, 2001.

The Other Heading: Reflections on Today's Europe. Translated by Pascale-Anne Brault and Michael B. Naas. Bloomington: Indiana University Press, 1992.

Parages. Paris: Galilée, 1986.

Points . . . Interviews, 1974–1994. Edited by Elisabeth Weber. Stanford, CA: Stanford University Press, 1995.

The Post Card: From Socrates to Freud and Beyond. Translated by Alan Bass. Chicago: University of Chicago Press, 1987.

"The Principle of Reason: The University in the Eyes of Its Pupils." *Diacritics* 13, no. 3 (1983).

Psyché: Inventions de l'autre. Paris: Galilée, 1987.

"Les Pupilles de l'Université: Le Principe de raison et l'idée de l'Université." In *Du droit à la philosophie.* Paris: Galilée, 1982.

"The *Retrait* of Metaphor." *Enclitic* 2, no. 2 (1978).

"Sending: On Representation." Translated by Peter and Mary Ann Caws. *Social Research* (Summer 1982).

"Shibboleth: For Paul Celan." Translated by Joshua Wilner. In *Word Traces: Readings of Paul Celan*, edited by Aris Fioretos. Baltimore: Johns Hopkins University Press, 1994 (shorter version in *Acts of Literature*).

"A Silkworm of One's Own (Points of View Stitched on the Other Veil)." In *Veils*, edited by Hélène Cixous and Jacques Derrida; translated by Geoffrey Bennington. Stanford, CA: Stanford University Press, 2001.

"Some Statements and Truisms about Neologisms, Newisms, Postisms, Parasitisms, and Other Small Seismisms." Translated by Anne Tomiche. In *The States of "Theory": History, Art, and Critical Discourse*, edited by David Carroll. Stanford, CA: Stanford University Press, 1994.

Specters of Marx: The State of the Debt, the Work of Mourning, and the New International. Translated by Peggy Kamuf. New York: Routledge, 1994.

Spurs: Nietzsche's Styles. Translated by Barbara Harlow. Chicago: University of Chicago Press, 1979.

"Telepathy." Translated by Nicholas Royle. *Oxford Literary Review* 10, nos. 1–2 (1998).

"The Time Is Out of Joint." Translated by Peggy Kamuf. In *Deconstruction is/in America*, edited by Anselm Haverkamp. New York: New York University Press, 1995.

"Titres (pour le Collège international de philosophie)." In *Du droit à la philosophie*. Paris: Galilée, 1982.

Ulysse Gramophone: Deux Mots pour Joyce. Paris: Galilée, 1987.

"Ulysses Gramophone." In *Acts of Literature*, edited by Derek Attridge. New York: Routledge, 1992.

"Violence and Metaphysics." In *Writing and Difference*, translated by Alan Bass. Chicago: University of Chicago Press, 1978.

Who's Afraid of Philosophy? Right to Philosophy 1. Translated by Jan Plug. Stanford, CA: Stanford University Press, 2002.

OTHER WORKS

Augustine. *The City of God against the Pagans.* Edited and translated by R. W. Dyson. Cambridge: Cambridge University Press, 1998.

Bennington, Geoffrey. "Derridabase." In *Jacques Derrida*, edited by Geoffrey Bennington and Jacques Derrida; translated by Geoffrey Bennington. Chicago: University of Chicago Press, 1993.

De Cues, Nicolas. "Où est le roi des Juifs?" Translated by Maurice de Gandillac. *Le Nouveau Commerce* 10 (1967).

Genet, Jean. *Genet à Chatila*. Paris: Solin, 1992.

Gide, André. *Fruits of the Earth*. Translated by Dorothy Bussy. London: Secker & Warburg, 1949.

Hegel, G. W. F. *The Philosophy of History*. Translated by J. Sibree. New York: Dover Publications, 1956.

Heidegger, Martin. *Acheminement vers la parole*. Translated by Jean Beaufret, Wolfgang Brokmeier, and François Fédier. Paris: Gallimard, 1976.

———. *Aufenthalte*, in *Gesamtausgabe*. Vol. 75. Frankfurt: Klostermann, 2000.

———. *Being and Time*. Translated by John Macquarrie and Edward Robinson. New York: Harper & Row, 1962.

———. *On the Way to Language*. Translated by Peter D. Hertz. New York: Harper & Row, 1982.

———. *The Principle of Reason*. Translated by Reginald Lilly. Bloomington: Indiana University Press, 1991.

Kafka, Franz. *Fragments from Notebooks and Loose Pages*. In *Dearest Father: Stories*

South Street Seaport, New York, September 1998.
(Jacques Derrida Archives)

and Other Writings, translated by Ernst Kaiser and Eithne Wilkins. New York: Schocken Books, 1954.

Kant, Immanuel. "What Is Orientation in Thinking." In *Kant: Political Writings*, translated by H. B. Nisbet. Cambridge: Cambridge University Press, 1991.

Lévi-Strauss, Claude. *Tristes Tropiques.* Translated by John Weightman and Doreen Weightman. London: Jonathan Cape, 1973.

Malabou, Catherine. *L'Avenir de Hegel: Plasticité, Temporalité, Dialectique.* Paris: Vrin, 1996.

Montaigne, Michel de. *The Complete Works of Montaigne.* Translated by Donald Frame. Stanford, CA: Stanford University Press, 1958.

Plato: The Collected Dialogues. Edited by Edith Hamilton and Huntington Cairns. Princeton, NJ: Princeton University Press, 1999.

Sartre, Jean-Paul. "Writing for One's Age." In *"What Is Literature?" and Other Essays*, translated by Bernard Frechtman. Cambridge, MA: Harvard University Press, 1988.

Thom, René. *Prédire n'est pas expliquer.* Paris: Champs-Flammarion, 1991.

Index of Place Names

(Photograph page references are in italics.)

CORRESPONDENCE: LETTERS AND POSTCARDS (EXTRACTS)

Contents (Logical order)

Appendices

Text Credits

Notes

Translations from the cited English versions of Derrida's work have at times been modified, often to emphasize the sense of the French original developed in Malabou's discussion. All translations from French texts for which no published English version is cited are mine. (D.W.)

PREFACE

1. *Given Time*, 7.
2. "Don't lose the thread, that's the injunction that Penelope was pretending to follow . . . " "A Silkworm of One's Own (Points of View Stitched on the Other Veil)," in *Veils*, 22.
3. "Back from Moscow," in *Politics, Theory, and Contemporary Culture*, 225, 226.
4. "To Speculate—on 'Freud'," in *The Post Card*, 261. The double bind or double constraint is a structure that combines two contradictory injunctions. It is impossible to obey the one without at the same time disobeying the other. Derrida also names this effect a "stricture," from the word "striction," meaning "tightening," "constriction," "partial decrease of a fluid in flux." Here and elsewhere, emphasis on "drift," "deriving," and derivatives is mine.
5. *Specters of Marx*, 65.
6. *Memoires: for Paul de Man*, 17. Speaking of deconstruction Derrida declares: "one cannot and should not attempt to survey or totalize the meaning of an ongoing process, especially when its structure is one of transference."
7. "Avant-propos," in *Psyché*, 9.
8. "Differance," in *Margins of Philosophy*, 15.
9. René Thom, *Prédire n'est pas expliquer*, 28, 29. For Thom, there are seven fundamental types of catastrophe: the fold, the gather, the dovetail, the butterfly, and the three umbilici (24ff.).
10. "Circumfession," in *Jacques Derrida*, 199.
11. "Otobiographies: The Teaching of Nietzsche and the Politics of the Proper Name," in *The Ear of the Other*, 5–6.

12. "Envois," in *The Post Card*, 224.

13. "Ulysses Gramophone: Hear Say Yes in Joyce," in *Acts of Literature*, 268.

14. "Faxitexture," in *Anywhere*, 29.

15. "Faith and Knowledge," in *Religion*, 2.

16. "Faxitexture," in *Anywhere*, 29.

17. Ibid., 21.

18. Ibid.

19. "Ulysses Gramophone: Hear Say Yes in Joyce," in *Acts of Literature*, 269.

20. "Envois," in *The Post Card*, 108.

21. "Back from Moscow," in *Politics, Theory, and Contemporary Culture*, 202.

22. Cf. "I will ask myself what to turn around [*tourner autour*] has signified from my birth on or thereabouts" (*The Post Card*, 256). The end of "Envois" thereby announces "Circumfession" ten years before the event.

23. "Envois," in *The Post Card*, 8.

24. "Circumfession" in *Jacques Derrida*, 256–57.

25. Derrida, quoting Jean-Paul Sartre, "Writing for One's Age," in *"What Is Literature?" and Other Essays*, 245.

26. "'Dead Man Running': Salut, Salut," in *Negotiations*, 267–68.

27. In the plane taking him to South America Derrida writes "without knowing if I [will] come back alive" ("A Silkworm of One's Own," in *Veils*, 51).

28. Derrida distinguishes in "Envois" between a "story [*histoire*] of voyages" and travel narrative [*récit de voyage*]" (*The Post Card*, 153).

29. "Back from Moscow," in *Politics, Theory, and Contemporary Culture*, 218.

30. Ibid., 197, 198.

31. Ibid., 215. In *Specters of Marx*, Derrida comments: "There is a French tradition, a kind of "French specialty" of peremptory diagnoses upon returning from a quick trip to a faraway land whose language one does not even speak and about which one knows next to nothing" (70–71).

32. "Back from Moscow," in *Politics, Theory, and Contemporary Culture*, 226.

33. Ibid., 199.

34. "A Silkworm of One's Own," in *Veils*, 23.

35. Ibid., 25.

36. Ibid., 22.

37. *Adieu to Emmanuel Lévinas*, 20.

38. "Violence and Metaphysics," in *Writing and Difference*, 95.

39. *Parages*, 15.

40. See the Note to the Reader (D.W.).

41. *Dérive* is the translation Jacques Lacan proposes for the Freudian concept *Trieb, pulsion* in French, "drive" in English.

CHAPTER 1

1. *Dissemination*, 5–6.
2. *Of Grammatology*, 56.
3. "Envois," in *The Post Card*, 19.
4. Ibid., 46.
5. "White Mythology," in *Margins of Philosophy*, 220. *Physis* means "nature"; *tekhne*, "artifice" or "fabrication"; *nomos*, "law."
6. See, especially, *Of Grammatology*, 97–98, and *Aporias*, 67. Derrida's use of the adjective *dérivé* (Ger. *abgeleitet*) situates it most often at the intersection of three traditions: the Kantian, which differentiates the *intuitus originarius* (originary or divine understanding) from the *intuitus derivativus* (derivative or finite understanding, assimilated to discursivity in general); the phenomenological (Husserl), where *dérivé* signifies modified or phenomenologically reduced, constituted and not constituting˘20; and the Heideggerian, for which all discourse that proceeds from the question of being without posing that question in a radical manner becomes derivative. Thus, for example, traditional ontology is derivative vis-à-vis Heidegger's existential analytic.

CHAPTER 2

1. *Aporias*, 14–15.
2. *Monolingualism*, 58.
3. Ibid., 47–48.
4. Ibid., 53.
5. "Some Statements and Truisms," in *The States of "Theory*," 67–68.
6. *Monolingualism*, 42.
7. Ibid., 52.
8. "The Time Is Out of Joint," in *Deconstruction is/in America*, 27.
9. *Monolingualism*, 70.
10. Ibid., 7.
11. Ibid., 1, 5.
12. Ibid., 67.
13. Ibid., 61.
14. *Memoires: For Paul de Man*, 15.
15. *Monolingualism*, 59.
16. Ibid., 63.
17. Ibid., 64.
18. "Circumfession," in *Jacques Derrida*, 169–70.

CHAPTER 3

1. "Faith and Knowledge," in *Religion*, 58–59.
2. "No Apocalypse, Not Now," 21. [Last two sentences not in English version; see *Psyché*, 365. (D.W.)]
3. "A Silkworm of One's Own," in *Veils*, 21.
4. "My Chances / *Mes Chances*," in *Taking Chances*, 61.
5. *Specters of Marx*, 78.
6. *The Other Heading*, 15.
7. Derrida borrows this formula from Freud. See "Demeure, Athènes," in *Athènes à l'ombre de l'Acropole*, 63.
8. "No Apocalypse, Not Now," 27.
9. "Khōra," in *On the Name*, 93.
10. *Specters of Marx*, 65.
11. *The Other Heading*, 15.

CHAPTER 4

1. *Of Grammatology*, 113.
2. Lévi-Strauss, *Tristes Tropiques*, 296–97.
3. Ibid., 299.
4. Ibid., 300.
5. *Of Grammatology*, 119.
6. Ibid., 116.
7. Ibid., 120, 121.
8. Ibid., 126–27.
9. Ibid., 123–24.
10. Ibid., 106.
11. Lévi-Strauss, *Tristes Tropiques*, 278–79.
12. *Of Grammatology*, 110.
13. Ibid., 109.
14. Ibid., 108–9.
15. Ibid., 15.
16. Ibid., 107–8.

CHAPTER 5

1. "Unsealing ('the old new language')," in *Points*, 119–20.
2. "Circumfession," in *Jacques Derrida*, 306, 308.
3. Ibid., 119–20.
4. *Monolingualism*, 44.
5. "Circumfession," in *Jacques Derrida*, 129–30.

6. Ibid., 247.

7. Ibid., 278.

8. "Envois," in *The Post Card*, 34.

9. "Unsealing ('the old new language')," in *Points*, 120.

10. *Monolingualism*, 43.

11. Ibid., 13.

12. Ibid., 55.

13. Ibid.

14. Ibid., 14.

15. Ibid., 30–31.

16. Ibid., 32.

17. Ibid., 38.

18. Ibid.

19. Ibid., 54–55.

20. Ibid., 52.

21. Ibid., 54. For another account of this Jewish "acculturation," see "Circumfession," in *Jacques Derrida*, 72–73.

22. "Circumfession," in *Jacques Derrida*, 83, 84. The story of the white taleth is in fact told in "A Silkworm of One's Own."

23. "Circumfession," in *Jacques Derrida*, 288, 289.

24. "Envois," in *The Post Card*, 73.

25. *Monolingualism*, 41–42.

26. Ibid., 50–51.

27. "Unsealing ('the old new language')," in *Points*, 120–21. See also "Envois," in *The Post Card*, 87–88.

28. "Circumfession," in *Jacques Derrida*, 58.

29. *Monolingualism*, 15–17.

30. Ibid., 34.

31. Ibid., 60–61.

32. "Demeure Athènes," in *Athènes à l'ombre de l'Acropole*, 45.

33. *Monolingualism*, 56.

34. Ibid., 2.

35. Ibid., 46.

36. Ibid., 45–46.

37. Ibid., 48.

38. "The Crisis in the Teaching of Philosophy," in *Who's Afraid of Philosophy?* 104–5.

39. *Monolingualism*, 30.

40. Ibid., 42–43.

41. "Envois," in *The Post Card*, 102.

42. *Monolingualism*, 31.

43. Ibid., 79.

44. *Aporias*, 74.

45. "Circumfession," in *Jacques Derrida*, 170–71. The letters "SA" are Saint Augustine's initials. In *Glas*, they stand for absolute knowledge [*savoir absolu*].

46. *Aporias*, 77.

47. Ibid., 81.

48. "The Crisis in the Teaching of Philosophy," in *Who's Afraid of Philosophy?* 103.

49. "Geopsychoanalysis: 'and the rest of the world'," in *The Psychoanalysis of Race*, 69.

50. *The Other Heading*, 82–83.

51. Ibid., 7.

CHAPTER 6

1. *Specters of Marx*, 78.

2. As one French translation has it, as Derrida notes, "Time is off its hinges" [*Le temps est hors de ses gonds*]. See *Specters of Marx*, 19.

3. Ibid., 18–19.

4. Ibid., 50.

5. Ibid.

6. "Back from Moscow," in *Politics, Theory, and Contemporary Culture*, 203. Derrida reinforces, however, the irreducible singularity of the name "USSR": "the only name of a state in the world that contains in itself no reference to a locality or a nationality, the only proper name of a state that, in sum, contains no given proper name, in the current sense of the term: the USSR is the name of an etatic individual, an individual and singular state that has given itself or claimed to give itself its own proper name without reference to any singular place or to any national past. At its foundation, a state has given itself a purely artificial, technical, conceptual, general, conventional, and constitutional name, a common name in sum, a "communist" name: in short a purely political name" (198).

7. Derrida's trip took place precisely from 26 February to 6 March 1990, in response to an invitation from the Institute of Philosophy of the USSR Academy of Sciences. The country was then in the midst of *perestroika*. Derrida's interlocutors brought to his attention that "in their eyes the best translation, the translation they were using among themselves for *perestroika*, was "deconstruction" ("Back from Moscow," 222).

8. "Back from Moscow," 223–24.

9. *Specters of Marx*, 37.
10. Ibid., 85.
11. Ibid., 81–84.
12. Ibid., 65.
13. Ibid., 85–86.

CHAPTER 7

1. "Demeure, Athènes," in *Athènes à l'ombre de l'Acropole*, 46–47.
2. Ibid., 44.
3. Ibid., 48.
4. Ibid., 61.
5. Ibid., 141–42.

CHAPTER 8

1. "Generations of a City: Memory, Prophecy, Responsibilities," in *Open City*, 16. Derrida bases his analysis on a reading of Kafka's comments devoted to the "*time of a city under construction*" (ibid., 14) in the latter's *Fragments from Notebooks and Loose Pages*, a text written "shortly after the War, at the just recent and fragile birth of Czechoslovakia" (ibid., 13). Cf. Franz Kafka, *Fragments from Notebooks and Loose Pages*, in his *Dearest Father: Stories and Other Writings*, 237.
2. "Generations of a City," in *Open City*, 27.
3. "On Cosmopolitanism," in *On Cosmopolitanism and Forgiveness*, 16–17.
4. "Generations of a City," in *Open City*, 17–18. On this question, see also *The Other Heading*, 36ff.
5. "On Cosmopolitanism," in *On Cosmopolitanism and Forgiveness*, 4–5.
6. Ibid., 17, 18, 18–19.
7. Ibid., 18.
8. "Sending: On Representation," 296–97.
9. "Generations of a City," in *Open City*, 17.
10. Ibid., 18–19.
11. Ibid., 23–24.
12. "Faxitexture," in *Anywhere*, 28. This lecture was given in Japan, at the opening of a conference entitled "Anywhere," on architecture and urbanism. The question of having to "rebuild" Los Angeles was raised after the devastating violence (riots and repression) that took place following the Rodney King trial in 1991. Further reference to the architectural taxonomy mentioned here can be found in chapter 23. On the subject of *Khōra*, see chapter 11.
13. "Envois," in *The Post Card*, 138–39.

14. Ibid., 50.

15. Ibid., 183.

16. "Tympan," in *Margins of Philosophy*, xviii. The passage sketches out a *map* of the city of Amsterdam.

17. "Demeure, Athènes," in *Athènes à l'ombre de l'Acropole*, 42.

18. "Envois," in *The Post Card*, 164.

19. Ibid., 166.

20. Ibid., 167.

21. "Circumfession," in *Jacques Derrida*, 201–2.

22. *Specters of Marx*, 58. See also "Back from Moscow," where, in his reading of Benjamin, Derrida stages a curious "ellipse with two focal points, Moscow and Jerusalem" (in *Politics, Theory, and Contemporary Culture*, 200).

23. *Gift of Death*, 69–70.

24. "How to Avoid Speaking," in *Languages of the Unsayable*, 13–14.

CHAPTER 9

1. Heidegger, *Aufenthalte*, in *Gesamtausgabe*, vol. 75, 215–16, 218.

2. "The *Retrait* of Metaphor," 12.

3. "Envois," in *The Post Card*, 153.

4. "The *Retrait* of Metaphor," 23.

5. Ibid.

6. "Envois," in *The Post Card*, 65.

7. "Demeure, Athènes," in *Athènes à l'ombre de l'Acropole*, 44; cf. Heidegger, *Gesamtausgabe*, vol. 75, 237.

8. Heidegger, *The Principle of Reason*, 48.

9. "The *Retrait* of Metaphor," 20.

10. "Envois," in *The Post Card*, 20.

11. *Spurs*, 37.

12. "The *Retrait* of Metaphor," 22.

13. Ibid., 19.

14. Heidegger, *The Principle of Reason*, 65.

15. "Envois," in *The Post Card*, 63.

16. Heidegger, *On the Way to Language*, 92 [second sentence from footnote referring to extract missing from English, my translation (D.W.)]. The translators of the French edition (*Acheminement vers la parole*, trans. Jean Beaufret, Wolfgang Brokmeier, and François Fédier [Paris: Gallimard, 1976]) note: "We recognize, thanks to this graphic intervention, the coining of the word *Bewëgung*, 'movement.' *Be-* should be understood as in *Be-dingung, Be-stimmung*, signifying the

fact of endowing or providing. As for *Wëgung*, it lets the path (*Weg*) show through immediately. 'Setting out on the path [*mise en chemin*]' should be understood intransitively; the paths are given the status of being paths" (182n). Also: "All the words mentioned here are Germanic derivatives of the root *uegh*, which gave *vehere* ("to transport") and *via* ("way") in Latin. *Chemin* is a Celtic word" (183n).

17. Ibid.

18. Heidegger, *The Principle of Reason*, 48. The French translation quoted by Derrida in *Margins* has "*la conception déterminante de la 'métaphore' tombe d'elle-même* [collapses by itself]" (cf. *Margins*, 226n29) (D.W.).

19. In "The *Retrait* of Metaphor," Derrida notes: "Two families . . . of words, nouns, verbs . . . cross each other in this contact of the trait in the German language . . . : on the one hand the 'family' of *Ziehen* (*zug, Bezug, Gezüge, durchziehen, entziehen*), and on the other . . . *Reissen* (*Riss, Aufriss, Umriss, Grundriss*, etc.)" (27).

20. Heidegger, *On the Way to Language*, 90. Earlier, Heidegger states that "the neighborhood in question pervades everywhere our stay on this earth and our journey in it" (84).

21. "The *Retrait* of Metaphor," 21.

22. Ibid., 10.

23. Ibid., 20.

24. "18 May 1978. Already the third trip to Geneva. This continual envoyage is exhausting and yet . . . " ("Envois," in *The Post Card*, 140).

25. "Sending: On Representation," 324. I do not have the space to discuss here the extraordinary analysis of Heidegger's reading of Trakl in *Of Spirit: Heidegger, and the Question*, notably chapters 9 and 10, or the commentary on the commentary on "Something Strange Is the Soul on the Earth" (*"Es ist die Seele ein Fremdes auf Erden"*), where the soul is said to be "solitary and voyaging" (*Of Spirit*, 105; cf. Heidegger, *On the Way to Language*, 161–63). Those readings should be heard as silently accompanying our journey.

CHAPTER 10

1. "And we will not get around Freiburg, let it be said in passing" [*Et on ne contournera Fribourg, soit dit au passage*] ("Envois," in *The Post Card*, 63).

2. A minimal outline of the stages in the textual journey is developed in chapter 9.

3. "The *Retrait* of Metaphor," 21–22, 23–26, 28–30.

CHAPTER II

1. *Khōra* emerges in a straight line from the discourse on the origin of the universe. The "matrix" of all forms, of every becoming, it is "the receptacle, and in a manner the nurse, of all generation" (*Timaeus*, in *Plato: The Collected Dialogues*, 1176).

2. "No Apocalypse, Not Now," in *Psyché*, 382 (lines missing in English translation [D.W.]).

3. "Faxitexture," in *Anywhere*, 24.

4. "Khōra," in *On the Name*, 106.

5. Ibid., 99.

6. Ibid., 90–91.

7. "Faith and Knowledge," in *Religion*, 21.

8. "Khōra," in *On the Name*, 92–93.

9. Ibid., 93–94.

10. Ibid., 124–25.

11. Ibid., 100.

12. "Faith and Knowledge," in *Religion*, 19.

13. "No Apocalypse, Not Now," in *Psyché*, 27.

14. Ibid., 20.

15. Ibid., 23.

16. Ibid.

17. Ibid., 24.

18. Ibid., 28.

19. Ibid., 21.

20. Ibid., 28 (cf. *Psyché*, 380; words missing from English version [D.W.]).

21. *Specters of Marx*, 27, 28.

22. Ibid., 28–29.

23. Ibid., 31.

CHAPTER 12

1. *The Post Card*, 27, 54.

2. Ibid., 159.

3. Ibid., 64, 65. One should compare Derrida's "plan" to write a preface with his intention to write a "history of the posts" (ibid., 13, 66): "Want to write and first to reassemble an enormous library on the *courrier*, the postal institutions, the techniques and mores of telecommunication, the networks and epochs of telecommunication throughout history—but the "library" and the "history" themselves are precisely but "posts," sites of passage or relay among others, stases, moments or ef-

fects of *restance*, and also particular representations, narrower and narrower, shorter and shorter sequences, proportionally, of the Great Telematic Network, the *worldwide connection*" (ibid., 27).

4. Ibid., 29.

5. "Sending: On Representation," 324–25.

6. Ibid., 323.

7. *Of Spirit*, 52.

8. "Sending: On Representation," 322.

9. See Derrida's reading of Heidegger's Rectorship Address and analysis of the values of *Führung*, "mission," "conduction," "guide," and "order given," in *Of Spirit*, 31–34.

10. "Sending: On Representation," 322.

11. *Of Spirit*, 90.

12. "Sending: On Representation," 322.

13. "Envois," in *The Post Card*, 65–66.

14. Ibid., 192.

15. Ibid., 66–67.

16. "Envoi," in *Psyché*, 137 (cf. "Sending: On Representation," 323, not in English translation [D.W.]).

17. "Envois," in *The Post Card*, 20–21. Derrida adds in a note: "I must note it right here, on the morning of 22 August 1979, 10 A.M., while typing this page for the present publication, the telephone rings. The American operator asks me if I will accept a "collect call" from Martin (she says Martine or martini) Heidegger. I heard, as one often does in these situations which are very familiar to me, often having to call "collect" myself, voices that I thought I recognized on the other end of the intercontinental line, listening to me and watching for my reaction. What will he do with the ghost or Geist of Martin? I cannot summarize here all the chemistry of the reaction that very quickly made me refuse ("It's a joke, I do not accept") (ibid., 21).

CHAPTER 13

1. "Envois," in *The Post Card*, 43.

2. Ibid., 82.

3. "Aphorism Countertime," in *Acts of Literature*, 420–421.

CHAPTER 14

1. *Parages*, 15.

2. *Dissemination*, 35–36.

3. *Of Grammatology*, 24.

4. Ibid., 162.

5. Ibid.

6. Ibid., 101–2.

7. "Envois," in *The Post Card*, 261.

8. *Dissemination*, 25.

9. *Aporias*, 11. The porousness of borders requires one to rethink the problem of *limitrophy*, in particular within the disciplinary fields of knowledge. On this point, see "Titres (pour le Collège international de philosophie)," in *Du droit à la philosophie*, where Derrida questions especially the limits of philosophy.

10. "Faxitexture," in *Anywhere*, 20.

11. *Parages*, 12.

12. "Shibboleth: For Paul Celan," in *Word Traces: Readings of Paul Celan*, 28 (cf. *Acts of Literature*, 404): "*Shibboleth*, this word I have called Hebrew, is found, as you know, in a whole family of languages: Phoenician, Judaeo-Aramaic, Syriac. It is traversed by a multiplicity of meanings: river, stream, ear of grain, olive-twig. But beyond those meanings, it acquired the value of a password. It was used during or after war, at the crossing of a border under watch. The word mattered less for its meaning than for the way in which it was pronounced. The relation to the meaning or to the thing was suspended, neutralized, bracketed: the opposite, one could say, of a phenomenological *epochē* which preserves, first of all, the meaning. The Ephraimites had been defeated by the army of Jephthah; in order to keep the soldiers from escaping across the river (*shibboleth* also means river, of course, but that is not necessarily the reason it was chosen), each person was required to say *shibboleth*. Now the Ephraimites were known for their inability to pronounce correctly the *shi* of *shibboleth*, which consequently became for them, an *unpronounceable name*; they said *sibboleth* and, at that invisible border between *shi* and *si*, betrayed themselves to the sentinel at the risk of death. They betrayed their difference in rendering themselves indifferent to the diacritical difference between *shi* and *si*; they marked themselves as unable to re-mark a mark thus coded" (ibid., 24–25; *Acts of Literature*, 399–400).

13. *Parages*, 96.

14. *Aporias*, 9.

15. Ibid., 9–10.

16. *Parages*, 106.

17. Ibid., 31.

18. *Spurs*, 39.

19. Ibid., 39, 41.

20. *Parages*, 17.

21. Ibid., 15.
22. "Tympan," in *Margins of Philosophy*, xv.
23. Ibid., xi.
24. Ibid., xxiii–xxv.

1. Cf. "Envois," in *The Post Card*: "This is Europe, *centrale*, the center of Europe, the *carte* between Vienna and Prague, my own in sum, with an extension of the track or of the Orient-Express near Athens or Reading, between Oxford and London" (35).
2. "Circumfession," in *Jacques Derrida*, 300.
3. "Unsealing ('the old new language')," in *Points*, 128–29. On this point, see also "Rhetoric of Drugs," in *Points*, 253.
4. "Back from Moscow," in *Politics, Theory, and Contemporary Culture*, 203.
5. "Circumfession," in *Jacques Derrida*, 292–94.

1. "Envois," in *The Post Card*, 43.
2. Ibid., 109–10.
3. Ibid., 55–56.
4. Ibid., 8.
5. Ibid., 11.
6. Ibid., 14.
7. Ibid., 27.
8. Ibid., 35.
9. Ibid., 8.
10. Ibid., 10–11.
11. Ibid., 30–31.
12. Ibid., 39.
13. "Faxitexture," in *Anywhere*, 21.
14. Ibid., 25.
15. "Telepathy," 13–14.
16. Ibid., 16.

1. "Envois," in *The Post Card*, 10.
2. Ibid., 20.
3. Ibid., 83.

4. Ibid., 15.
5. Ibid., 16–17.
6. Ibid., 9–10.
7. Ibid., 12.
8. Ibid., 150.
9. Ibid., 13.
10. Ibid., 28.
11. Ibid., 24.
12. Ibid., 22.
13. Ibid., 159.
14. Ibid.
15. Ibid., 47.
16. Ibid., 225.
17. Ibid., 123–24.
18. Ibid., 115.
19. Ibid., 81.
20. Ibid., 111–12.
21. Ibid., 33–34.
22. "Telepathy," 6.
23. "Envois," in *The Post Card*, 23.
24. Ibid., 32–33.
25. Ibid., 28–29.
26. Ibid., 107–8.
27. Ibid., 126–27.
28. "Circumfession," in *Jacques Derrida*, 123–24.
29. "Envois," in *The Post Card*, 21.

CHAPTER 18

1. *The Other Heading*, 69.
2. Ibid., 19.
3. Ibid., 5.
4. Ibid., 5–6.
5. *Crito*, in *Plato: The Collected Dialogues*, 28–29, quoted in "Demeure, Athènes," in *Athènes à l'ombre de l'Acropole*, 59.
6. *Phaedo*, in *Plato: The Collected Dialogues*, 41, quoted in "Demeure, Athènes," in *Athènes à l'ombre de l'Acropole*, 51.
7. "Demeure, Athènes," in *Athènes à l'ombre de l'Acropole*, 51.
8. "Awaiting (at) the Arrival" is the title of the last section of *Aporias* (43–81).

The formula "arrive at the departure" is from "Demeure, Athènes" (in *Athènes à l'ombre de l'Acropole*, 61): "The woman does not predict a departure for Socrates but an arrival. More precisely, since one has to part and separate, because one has to abandon, by quoting the *Iliad* she orients this departure from the point of view of the endpoint or *arrival* of the voyage" (59).

9. "Demeure, Athènes," in *Athènes à l'ombre de l'Acropole*, 41–42.

10. "A Silkworm of One's Own," in *Veils*, 24. Text written "Toward Buenos Aires, November 24–29, 1995."

11. Ibid., 37–38.

12. Geoffrey Bennington, "Derridabase," in *Jacques Derrida*, 5.

13. "Circumfession," in *Jacques Derrida*, 39.

14. "Envois," in *The Post Card*, 163.

15. "Ulysses Gramophone: Hear Say Yes in Joyce," in *Acts of Literature*, 309 (last words of text).

16. "A Silkworm of One's Own," in *Veils*, 31.

17. "Envois," in *The Post Card*, 163.

18. Ibid., 77.

19. "Circumfession," in *Jacques Derrida* (last words of text), 314–15.

20. "A Silkworm of One's Own," in *Veils*, 28.

CHAPTER 19

1. "Envois," in *The Post Card*, 64.

2. "Faxitexture," in *Anywhere*, 20.

3. "The *Retrait* of Metaphor," 6.

4. Ibid., 7–8.

5. "White Mythology," in *Margins of Philosophy*, 215.

6. Cited in ibid., 234.

7. "The *Retrait* of Metaphor," 23.

8. "White Mythology," in *Margins of Philosophy*, 241.

9. Cited in ibid., 253.

10. "The *Retrait* of Metaphor," 19.

11. "White Mythology," in *Margins of Philosophy*, 215–16. On the double sense of *usure*, see ibid., 209n2.

12. "Living On: Border Lines," in *Deconstruction and Criticism*, 76.

13. "White Mythology," in *Margins of Philosophy*, 211.

14. Ibid., 225–26.

15. Ibid., 251.

16. Ibid., 253.

17. Ibid., 254.

18. For Hegel, for example, the history of spirit is confused with the course of the sun. See his *Philosophy of History*, 103.

19. "White Mythology," in *Margins of Philosophy*, 251.

20. Ibid., 270.

21. "Envois," in *The Post Card*, 178.

22. "Of a Newly Arisen Apocalyptic Tone in Philosophy," in *Raising the Tone of Philosophy*, 168.

23. "White Mythology," in *Margins of Philosophy*, 258.

24. "To Speculate—on 'Freud,'" in *The Post Card*, 284.

25. Ibid.

26. "Violence and Metaphysics," in *Writing and Difference*, 112–13. On the question of the originary spatiality of language, see also "Geschlecht: Sexual Difference, Ontological Difference," in *A Derrida Reader*: "Every language is first of all determined by spatial significations" (395).

27. "White Mythology," in *Margins of Philosophy*, 270.

28. "The Rhetoric of Drugs," in *Points*, 472–73.

29. "Envois," in *The Post Card*, 177.

CHAPTER 20

1. "The Time Is Out of Joint," in *Deconstruction is/in America*, 17 (cf. "Some Statements and Truisms," in *The States of "Theory*," 85).

2. Ibid., 27 (cf. *Memoires: for Paul de Man*, 15).

3. *Monolingualism*, 51.

4. *Memoires: for Paul de Man*, 14.

5. Ibid., 14–15.

6. Cf. the title of a book published in 1983, *The Yale Critics: Deconstruction in America* (Minneapolis: University of Minnesota Press): "It was in 1984; in America, at the University of California, Irvine, where I had not yet begun to teach regularly. At that time, and for some time yet to come, I remained more of an East-coast American since I was teaching every year for several weeks at Yale after having done the same thing at Johns Hopkins. In 1984, then, I had been invited to give the Wellek Lectures at Irvine. David Carroll and Suzanne Gearhart had suggested that I speak—this was ten years ago—on what already for some time had been called 'Deconstruction in America'" ("The Time Is Out of Joint," in *Deconstruction is/in America*, 26).

7. Published in *Writing and Difference*. Derrida speaks of his first trip to the United States, in 1956, in his discussion with the jazz musician Ornette Coleman,

insisting on the racial segregation that held harsh sway over the country at that time: "The first time I went to the United States, in 1956, there were "Whites Only" signs everywhere, and I remember being struck by the brutality of it" ("La Langue de l'autre," *Les Inrockuptibles* 11, 20 August–2 September 1997, 40).

8. "The Principle of Reason: The University in the Eyes of Its Pupils," 6–7. Derrida makes clear in a note to the French edition that "the construction of the lecture retains an essential relation with the architecture and site of Cornell: the top of a hill, the bridge and barriers over a certain abyss ("gorge" in English), commonplace for many anxious reflections on the history and rates of suicides ("gorging out" in the local idiom) on the part of students and faculty. What should be done to stop people from throwing themselves into the gorge? Is the university responsible for these suicides? Should barriers be erected?" ("Les Pupilles de l'Université: Le Principe de raison et l'idée de l'Université," in *Du droit à la philosophie*, 469–70. Cf. "The Principle of Reason, 5–6: "Beneath the bridges linking the university to its surroundings, connecting its inside to its outside, lies the abyss" [6]).

9. "The Time Is Out of Joint," in *Deconstruction is/in America*, 15.

10. *Memoires: for Paul de Man*, 14, 17–18.

11. "Some Statements and Truisms," in *The States of Theory*, 71.

12. Ibid., 64–65.

13. Cf. ibid., 74–76.

14. Ibid., 82.

15. Ibid., 84.

16. Ibid., 65.

17. Ibid., 68.

18. Ibid., 84, 85.

19. Ibid., 88.

20. "The Time Is Out of Joint," in *Deconstruction is/in America*, 17.

21. Ibid., 16.

22. Ibid., 17.

23. Ibid., 18.

24. Ibid., 25.

25. Ibid., 26–27.

26. Ibid., 28–29.

27. Ibid., 30–31.

28. Ibid., 25.

CHAPTER 21

1. "Circumfession," in *Jacques Derrida*, 18–19.

2. Ibid., 232–33.

3. Ibid., 260.

4. Ibid., 148, 150.

5. Ibid., 52–53.

6. Ibid., 92–93.

7. Ibid., 82.

8. Ibid., 80.

9. Ibid., 76.

10. "Envois," in *The Post Card*, 253–54.

11. "Circumfession," in *Jacques Derrida*, 177.

CHAPTER 22

1. *Aporias*, 33–34.

2. "Faith and Knowledge," in *Religion*, 17–18. *Specters of Marx* already characterizes the messianic as a "desert-like messianism (without content and without identifiable messiah)," opening to "the coming of the other, the absolute and unpredictable singularity of *the arrivant as justice*" (28).

3. *The Other Heading*, 5.

4. Ibid., 13–16.

5. Ibid., 27.

6. *The Gift of Death* brings to light the paradigmatic value of this axis through the motif of "secrets of European responsibility" (1–34). See also "Faith and Knowledge" ('*Difficult to say "Europe" without connoting Athens–Jerusalem–Rome–Byzantium*' [in *Religion*, 4]), and "Back from Moscow" (in *Politics, Theory, and Contemporary Culture*, 199).

7. *The Other Heading*, 24.

8. Ibid., 33.

9. *The Gift of Death*, 29.

10. In *Specters of Marx*, Derrida asks concerning Denmark: "Ought one to have recalled here that in the West, near the end of the European peninsula, Denmark almost became, precisely along with England, the last State of resistance to a certain Europe, that of Maastricht?" (178). Elsewhere, in *The Other Heading*, he notes that today still, as in Hegel's time, "European discourse coincide[s] with spirit's return to itself in Absolute Knowledge, at this 'end-of-history' that today can give rise to the prating eloquence of a White House advisor (this was, let me recall, before what is known as the Gulf War . . .) when he announces with great media fanfare 'the end-of-history.' This, if one were to believe him, because the essentially European model of the market economy, of liberal, parliamentary, and capitalist

democracies, would be about to become a universally recognized model, all the nation states of the planet preparing themselves to join us at the head of the pack, right at the forefront [*cap*], at the capital point [*pointe*] of advanced democracies, there where capital is on the cutting edge of progress [*à la pointe du progrès*]" (32–33).

11. *The Other Heading*, 75.

12. Ibid., 29.

13. Ibid.

14. Ibid., 38–39, 41.

15. *Specters of Marx*, 28.

CHAPTER 23

1. "Faxitexture," in *Anywhere*, 25.

2. Ibid., 23. The question of Japan's relation to imminence is brought to light again by Derrida in "Aletheia," a text dedicated to the photography of Kishin Shinoyama.

3. Ibid.

4. Ibid., 21.

5. Ibid., 23.

6. The taxonomy of the different forms of architecture proposed by these architects is as follows:

ARCHITECTURAL SPACE. Traditionally there have been several types of architectural space, including:

> *Sedentary.* European architecture as "the House of Being" (Heidegger).
>
> *Nomad.* Mobile tent of the nomad, which temporarily occupies a space.
>
> *Nomad-Immobile.* A Japanese architecture in which the substance is ephemeral but the form is eternal (e.g., the Shrine of Ise, which is rebuilt every twenty years).

How should we reconsider these types of space given the conditions of contemporary society? Are they relevant to contemporary architecture? Should new types of architectural space be invented for the next millenium?

ARCHITECTURE IN URBAN SPACE. Today we are confronted with several types of urban space such as:

> *Real.* Cities that have preserved their historical contexts.
>
> *Surreal.* Metropolitan cities like Tokyo where all kinds of elements (old and new, West and East, etc.) are put into play without regard for context.

Hyperreal/Simulated. Theme-park cities like Disney World which are devoid of any context and based on fiction and artifice.

How should today's architects cope with these different environments? Traditionally the notions of *genius loci* (in the Occident) and *fen sui* (in the Orient) have served as mediators between architecture and its environment. Are these notions relevant today? If not, what is functioning in their place? How can we invent new forms of mediation or even non-mediation for architecture and the city?

Architecture in universal space. Today space is dichotomous: open and closed, outer and inner, public and private, homogeneous and heterogeneous, general and particular, etc. On the one hand, we are coming to live Anywhere, floating on the global network of air transportation and electronic real-time communication; on the other hand, we are confined in Anywhere—in an arbitrary cell of a city as a theater of memory in ruin. How can we slip out of those dualities and find a new axis connecting hermetic/cryptic–cryptographic/grotesque space and postal/telegraphic-telephonic-televisual space? In other words, how can we conceive the singular-universal axis apart from the particular-general axis (given the importance of "virtual space")? In that direction, how can an architect cut-up and fold-in (ply/*plier*) the space? How is the deconstruction of the past heritage and the urbanization of the real-time possible? (*Anywhere,* 16–17)

7. "Faxitexture," in *Anywhere,* 24.

8. "Ulysses Gramophone: Hear Say Yes in Joyce," in *Acts of Literature,* 258.

9. Ibid., 259.

10. Ibid., 264–65.

11. "Letter to a Japanese friend," in *Derrida and Différance,* 1–2, 4–5.

CHAPTER 24

1. "Faith and Knowledge," in *Religion,* 66. The final quotation is from Genet, *Genet à Chatila,* 103.

2. Aporias, 13.

3. Ibid., 8.

4. Ibid, 12.

5. *The Other Heading,* 41.

6. "Faith and Knowledge," in *Religion,* 33.

7. Ibid., 17.

8. Kant, "What Is Orientation in Thinking," in *Kant: Political Writings,* 244 ["rational belief" in English (D.W.)].

9. Ibid., 2–3.

10. Ibid., 2.

11. Ibid., 4.

12. Ibid., 10.

13. Ibid., 14.

14. *The Other Heading*, 35.

15. "Faith and Knowledge," in *Religion*, 36.

16. Ibid., 17.

17. Ibid., 7–8.

18. Ibid., 18.

19. "How to Avoid Speaking," in *Languages of the Unsayable*, 39.

20. "Faith and Knowledge," in *Religion*, 9.

21. Ibid., 15.

22. Ibid., 7.

23. Ibid., 16 (words missing in English translation [D.W.]).

24. Ibid., 8–9.

25. Ibid., 20–21.

26. Ibid., 18–19. See also *Specters of Marx*, 166–69, and the whole first section of "Force of Law: The 'Mystical Foundation of Authority,'" in *Deconstruction and the Possibility of Justice*, 3–29.

27. *Specters of Marx*, 65.

28. "Faith and Knowledge," in *Religion*, 59.

29. *Parages*, 25.

CHAPTER 25

1. "Envois," in *The Post Card*, 174.

2. "*Che cos'è la poesia*," in *Points*, 289.

3. Ibid.

4. Ibid., 291.

5. Ibid., 289.

6. Ibid., 291.

7. Ibid., 293.

8. Ibid., 293, 295.

9. Ibid., 295, 297.

10. Ibid., 297.

11. Ibid., 291.

12. Ibid., 299.

13. "*Istrice 2: Ich bünn all hier*," in *Points*, 305. In *On the Road to Language*, Heidegger declares that the "multiple ambiguousness of the poetic saying does not scatter in vague equivocations," and further on: "The peerless rigor of Trakl's essentially ambiguous language is in a higher sense so unequivocal that it remains in-

finitely superior even to all the technical precision of concepts that are merely scientifically univocal" (192).

14. "*Che cos'è la poesia,*" in *Points,* 297.

15. Ibid., 293.

16. "*Istrice 2: Ich bünn all hier,*" in *Points,* 308.

17. Ibid., 309.

18. *Aporias,* 31. Heidegger distinguishes between "to die [*sterben*]" and "to perish [*verenden*]." Only the *Dasein* properly dies; the animal perishes.

19. "*Istrice 2: Ich bünn all hier,*" in *Points,* 304.

20. Ibid., 311.

CONCLUSION

1. "Envois," in *The Post Card,* 244–45.

2. "Telepathy," 14.

3. Acts 17:28.

4. De Cues, "Où est le roi des Juifs?" 89–90.

5. "Faith and Knowledge," in *Religion,* 39.

6. "Violence and Metaphysics," in *Writing and Difference,* 88.

7. "Faith and Knowledge," in *Religion,* 59.

8. *Aporias,* 61.

9. "Faxitexture," in *Anywhere,* 24.

10. "Faith and Knowledge," in *Religion,* 6.

Andreas Huyssen, *Present Pasts: Urban Palimpsests and the Politics of Memory*

Talal Asad, *Formations of the Secular: Christianity, Islam, Modernity*

Dorothea von Mücke, *The Rise of the Fantastic Tale*

Marc Redfield, *The Politics of Aesthetics: Nationalism, Gender, Romanticism*

Emmanuel Levinas, *On Escape*

Dan Zahavi, *Husserl's Phenomenology*

Rodolphe Gasché, *The Idea of Form: Rethinking Kant's Aesthetics*

Michael Naas, *Taking on the Tradition: Jacques Derrida and the Legacies of Deconstruction*

Herlinde Pauer-Studer, ed., *Constructions of Practical Reason: Interviews on Moral and Political Philosophy*

Jean-Luc Marion, *Being Given: Toward a Phenomenology of Givenness*

Theodor W. Adorno and Max Horkheimer, *Dialectic of Enlightenment*

Ian Balfour, *The Rhetoric of Romantic Prophecy*

Martin Stokhof, *World and Life as One: Ethics and Ontology in Wittgenstein's Early Thought*

Gianni Vattimo, *Nietzsche: An Introduction*

Jacques Derrida, *Negotiations: Interventions and Interviews, 1971–1998*, ed. Elizabeth Rottenberg

Brett Levinson, *The Ends of Literature: Post-transition and Neoliberalism in the Wake of the "Boom"*

Timothy J. Reiss, *Against Autonomy: Global Dialectics of Cultural Exchange*

Hent de Vries and Samuel Weber, eds., *Religion and Media*

Niklas Luhmann, *Theories of Distinction: Redescribing the Descriptions of Modernity*, ed. and introd. William Rasch

Johannes Fabian, *Anthropology with an Attitude: Critical Essays*

Michel Henry, *I Am the Truth: Toward a Philosophy of Christianity*

Gil Anidjar, *"Our Place in Al-Andalus": Kabbalah, Philosophy, Literature in Arab-Jewish Letters*

Hélène Cixous and Jacques Derrida, *Veils*

F. R. Ankersmit, *Historical Representation*

F. R. Ankersmit, *Political Representation*

Elissa Marder, *Dead Time: Temporal Disorders in the Wake of Modernity (Baudelaire and Flaubert)*

Reinhart Koselleck, *The Practice of Conceptual History: Timing History, Spacing Concepts*

Niklas Luhmann, *The Reality of the Mass Media*

Hubert Damisch, *A Childhood Memory by Piero della Francesca*

Hubert Damisch, *A Theory of /Cloud/: Toward a History of Painting*

Jean-Luc Nancy, *The Speculative Remark (One of Hegel's Bons Mots)*

Jean-François Lyotard, *Soundproof Room: Malraux's Anti-Aesthetics*

Jan Patočka, *Plato and Europe*

Hubert Damisch, *Skyline: The Narcissistic City*

Isabel Hoving, *In Praise of New Travelers: Reading Caribbean Migrant Women Writers*

Richard Rand, ed., *Futures: Of Derrida*

William Rasch, *Niklas Luhmann's Modernity: The Paradox of System Differentiation*

Jacques Derrida and Anne Dufourmantelle, *Of Hospitality*

Jean-François Lyotard, *The Confession of Augustine*

Kaja Silverman, *World Spectators*

Samuel Weber, *Institution and Interpretation: Expanded Edition*

Jeffrey S. Librett, *The Rhetoric of Cultural Dialogue: Jews and Germans in the Epoch of Emancipation*

Ulrich Baer, *Remnants of Song: Trauma and the Experience of Modernity in Charles Baudelaire and Paul Celan*

Samuel C. Wheeler III, *Deconstruction as Analytic Philosophy*

David S. Ferris, *Silent Urns: Romanticism, Hellenism, Modernity*

Rodolphe Gasché, *Of Minimal Things: Studies on the Notion of Relation*

Sarah Winter, *Freud and the Institution of Psychoanalytic Knowledge*

Samuel Weber, *The Legend of Freud: Expanded Edition*

Aris Fioretos, ed., *The Solid Letter: Readings of Friedrich Hölderlin*

J. Hillis Miller / Manuel Asensi, *Black Holes / J. Hillis Miller; or, Boustrophedonic Reading*

Miryam Sas, *Fault Lines: Cultural Memory and Japanese Surrealism*

Peter Schwenger, *Fantasm and Fiction: On Textual Envisioning*

Didier Maleuvre, *Museum Memories: History, Technology, Art*

Jacques Derrida, *Monolingualism of the Other; or, The Prosthesis of Origin*

Andrew Baruch Wachtel, *Making a Nation, Breaking a Nation: Literature and Cultural Politics in Yugoslavia*

Niklas Luhmann, *Love as Passion: The Codification of Intimacy*

Mieke Bal, ed., *The Practice of Cultural Analysis: Exposing Interdisciplinary Interpretation*

Jacques Derrida and Gianni Vattimo, eds., *Religion*